'Harrison Hill's *The Oracle's Daughter* is a staggering achievement, synthesizing rigorous reportage, incisive cultural analysis, and a deeply compassionate gaze into a propulsive and unforgettable narrative'

Leslie Jamison, author of *Splinters: Another Kind of Love Story*

'*The Oracle's Daughter* does far more than delineate in vivid detail the alarming story of the Aggressive Christianity Mission Training Corps, surely one of the most frightening cults in modern religious history ... Anyone trying to understand religious cults should consider *The Oracle's Daughter* required reading – it's that comprehensive and excellently written besides'

Jeff Guinn, author of *Manson*, *The Road to Jonestown* and *Waco*

'Troubling, uplifting, heartbreaking, unforgettable – tapping into seminal issues of our increasingly divided nation – Harrison Hill has written a masterwork of narrative nonfiction. A must-read'

Ron Suskind, author of *A Hope in the Unseen*

'With dogged research and rare access to victims and their stories, Harrison Hill has created a riveting portrait of one of the strangest American cults in recent memory ... offers compelling insights into the makings of religious cults and why their allure is increasing in our hyper-polarized, grievance-infused age'

Joby Warrick, author of *Black Flags: The Rise of ISIS*

'*The Oracle's Daughter* is both an intimate portrait of one insular group and a revealing exploration of the broader cult history woven through America. Harrison Hill has written a gripping and deeply-researched account of belief, belonging, and betrayal. If you've ever wondered how a person could fall prey to a high-control group, or what it takes to get out, this book is essential reading'

Rachel Monroe, author of *Savage Appetites*

'A moving, true and complex family story that sheds light on individual struggles for freedom. Anyone seeking to understand how extremism and coercion can touch all of our lives would do well to read it. I couldn't put it down. Intimate and expansive, it is both disturbing and hopeful'

Suzanne Joinson, author of *The Museum of Lost and Fragile Things*

'*The Oracle's Daughter* is a propulsive reckoning with a mother, her daughter, and the extremism woven through the story of American religion. Beautifully told, unputdownable, and urgently necessary, Hill offers a novelesque account of a cult that pushes beyond familiar narratives, asking us to consider just how far we truly are from the most radical edges of American life'

Heather Radke, author of *Butts: A Backstory*

'Hill is unsparing in his reportage. But more, he offers thoughtful notes on how cults work ... A compelling study of the meeting of religious zealotry with the cult of personality'

Kirkus Reviews

The Oracle's Daughter

HARRISON HILL

The Bridge Street Press

THE BRIDGE STREET PRESS

First published in the United States by Scribner in 2026
First published in Great Britain in 2026 by The Bridge Street Press

1 3 5 7 9 10 8 6 4 2

Copyright © 2026 by Harrison Hill

This is a work of non-fiction. Some names have been changed. Select elements of this book were previously published in *New York* magazine's *The Cut* in 2021.

The moral right of the author has been asserted.

All rights reserved.
No part of this publication may be reproduced, stored in a retrieval system, or transmitted, in any form, or by any means, without the prior permission in writing of the publisher, nor be otherwise circulated in any form of binding or cover other than that in which it is published and without a similar condition including this condition being imposed on the subsequent purchaser.

A CIP catalogue record for this book
is available from the British Library.

Hardback ISBN 978-0-349-13685-1
Trade paperback ISBN 978-0-349-13684-4

Interior design by Jaime Putorti
Printed and bound in Great Britain by Clays Ltd, Elcograf S.p.A.

Papers used by The Bridge Street Press are from well-managed forests
and other responsible sources.

The Bridge Street Press
An imprint of
Little, Brown Book Group
Carmelite House
50 Victoria Embankment
London EC4Y 0DZ

The authorised representative
in the EEA is
Hachette Ireland
8 Castlecourt Centre,
Dublin 15, D15 XTP3, Ireland
(email: info@hbgi.ie)

An Hachette UK Company
www.hachette.co.uk

www.littlebrown.co.uk

AUTHOR'S NOTE

The Oracle's Daughter is a work of nonfiction. I have used pseudonyms for five individuals, either for legal and privacy reasons (Trinity, Ruth), or when real names are unknown (Omondi, Gabriel, Wally). Nothing further has been invented or altered. All dialogue comes verbatim from legal records or from sources who participated in the relevant exchange. In reporting this book I conducted approximately two hundred interviews between 2019 and 2025; reviewed tens of thousands of pages of court documents, trial transcripts, and police records; consulted letters, emails, evangelizing tracts, sermons, and unpublished memoirs; and traveled throughout California and New Mexico.

*for my parents, Kemp and Tommy Hill,
and my godmother, Joanne Bartlett*

> The sanest and best of us are of one clay
> with lunatics and prison inmates.
>
> WILLIAM JAMES,
> *THE VARIETIES OF RELIGIOUS EXPERIENCE*

CONTENTS

Prologue	*1*
Part One: Signs and Wonders	*5*
Part Two: The Blessing	*99*
Part Three: Born Again	*163*
Part Four: Deliverance	*223*
Epilogue	*267*
Acknowledgments	*279*
A Note on Sources	*285*
Notes	*287*
Index	*321*

# The
Oracle's
Daughter

PROLOGUE

Sarah is already awake when the alarm clock goes off. She silences it and pulls herself out of her sleeping bag. It is midnight. Around her, on the floor, lie her husband and three young children. No doubt the alarm has roused them, too, but they'll fall asleep again before long. They always do.

Sarah pulls on a T-shirt and a long dark skirt. She is twenty-six years old, with swishy nutmeg hair, blue-green eyes, and a bracing, falcon-like beauty. She steps over and around the warm little bodies at her feet. In the darkness she watches their chests rise and fall, rise and fall. And then, silently, she says good-bye.

In western New Mexico, a single sky can contain a multitude of weather systems—rain in one area, sun in another, haze in a third. But on this particular night in September 1999, the sky screams with a uniform, navy clarity. The moon casts a chalky paleness over the scrub trees and the wildflower patches Sarah rushes past—quickly, quietly—on her way to the wood stack, maybe forty feet from the house.

Already her heart is racing with terror, with excitement, with guilt. What if she's caught? What if someone walks into the kitchen and notices she isn't there, baking banana bread, as she has so many thousands of midnights before this one? What if the dogs catch a whiff of her scent in the cool, loamy air? She can hear them even now, whining and trotting along the bluffs out back.

At the wood stack Sarah digs out a backpack she has hidden in preparation for her escape. It contains everything of value Sarah owns, plus supplies for the journey ahead: a water bottle, a passport, some granola bars, about $200 cash. She has also packed a flat metal cheese grater that belongs—*belonged*—to her mother, who bought it at a sidewalk sale many years earlier. The grater is a reminder, to Sarah, of who her mother once was. Before she changed. Before she realized she was God's holy chosen oracle.

Nervous sweat trickles down Sarah's back as she turns and takes in the compound before her. It's a jumble of rusty vehicles, wooden shacks, and thick, teeming orchards. An old school bus sits parked near a massive metal warehouse. About thirty men, women, and children live here under the leadership of Sarah's parents, self-proclaimed Generals of the Aggressive Christianity Missions Training Corps. "True Spirit-led Christianity is war," the couple preaches. "Civilian Christians" have gone "whoring from God," transforming his temple into an "orgy parlor." The Generals' idiom always veers toward the extreme, often with a distinctly sexual emphasis. The mainstream church is a "harlot," they say, an "abomination," a "spiritual brothel." It is a "monster" covered in "cankered, oozing sores"; a "repugnant," "putrefying mess"; a "morgue."

The group, by contrast, is actually serious about its faith. "WE ARE A WAR MACHINE," Sarah's parents insist. "God is absolute and He is a dictator."

Since its earliest days in Sacramento, California, in the eighties, the Aggressive Christianity Missions Training Corps has warded off prying investigators, angry families, conniving journalists—even a million-dollar lawsuit. As a result of these persecutions the group has been forced to flee here, to the land of jackrabbits and mule deer, along the western flank of the Continental Divide, where only the coyotes can find them.

There is a self-evident extremism to the Aggressive Christianity Missions Training Corps. But the group has also long embodied more mainstream trends in American religious life—trends evident not just since the late 1960s, when Sarah's parents were hippies, but from the very founding of the country. What appears radical about the group is, in fact, a product of the same forces that have given the United States its particular spiritual character; and in this way, Sarah's parents have illuminated how hazy, indeed, are the lines between faith and fanaticism, between devotion and destruction.

It is a haziness evident in ACMTC members themselves, most of them otherwise ordinary men and women who have, through years of inurement, come to accept the brutality of their lives as ordinary. They are a self-contained unit, this group, almost entirely off the grid. They wake early, at around four o'clock in the morning, and submit to violent "deliverance" ceremonies where demons of lust and laziness and a thousand other vices are purged from their bodies. They eat little and fast often; children are forced to go weeks at a time living only on broth. They take biblical names like Joab, Obadiah, and Philemon. They have no contact with friends and family on the outside.

Sarah wants more than this. She wants a proper education. She wants to wear regular clothes, not military uniforms. She wants to eat junk food, to be touched by a man other than her husband, whose mere presence repels her. Five years earlier, following the birth of her first child, she'd felt as if she had something to live for. But Sarah's love of being a mother has been counterbalanced by an oppressive sense, equally strong, that if she doesn't leave now, she will remain chained here forever.

Sarah gazes through the darkness for the young man who has agreed to come with her. Anthony is a recent recruit, a handsome drifter type from New Zealand who has only ever planned to stay at ACMTC for a short time, until his visa expires. He and Sarah have grown close in the months since his arrival—too close. They've taken walks on the trail behind the compound. They've held hands. They've kissed.

Sarah was the one to propose leaving together. What if they headed north, to Seattle, where Sarah could enroll in midwifery school and Anthony could catch a ride up to Canada? Then, after getting a job and a place to live, she would return to New Mexico for her kids. By this point she'd accepted the impossibility of bringing them with her. She could never get away with three young children in tow, to say nothing of the journey ahead. This, in any case, is what she has told herself. It has been an agonizing decision, and one that lays bare the most fundamental, conflicting loyalties of Sarah's life—to herself on the one hand, and to her children on the other. To her own survival, and to theirs.

Sarah has been crouched at the wood stack no more than a minute or two when she stands up and starts walking toward the front of the compound. She avoids the driveway, where the crunch of the gravel may give her away, passing instead through the orchard, where the soil is soft, moist, muffling.

Near the entryway Anthony materializes out of the darkness. She says nothing to him, nor he to her. Is he as nervous as she is? Does he worry that, by leaving the group, he is damning himself to hell? Sarah can't tell. She's more concerned with the practicalities of escape than with God's judgment, but she still has her misgivings.

Together they arrive at the front of the driveway—and there it is. The road.

They walk slowly at first, taking care not to make a sound. And then, when the compound is decisively behind them, when their fear has rearranged itself into a kind of anxious euphoria—then, at last, they run.

PART ONE

SIGNS AND WONDERS

CHAPTER 1

In the year she'd worked at the Sacramento Medical Center, Maura Aluzas had encountered plenty of interesting patients. But no one had ever arrived chained to a gurney.

It was nearing the end of an otherwise forgettable afternoon shift in 1969. Maura had only just stepped into the hallway when she noticed him—a solemn young man, reclined and shackled at the ankle. At his side stood a security guard.

Intrigued, Maura continued down the hallway. She was twenty-one years old, a lowly nurse's aide without any business reading patients' charts. But she was fascinated by people, by the strange and circuitous turns of their lives. So when no one was looking, Maura ducked into the nurses' station and pulled out the young man's file. What she found there only deepened her curiosity. The patient's name was Carlo. He'd robbed a burger joint. He was suffering from lung cancer that had spread to his liver. And now he was going to die.

Maura returned the chart and slipped back into the hallway. She was a quietly attractive young woman with a warm, open face and a tall forehead she hid with bangs. In her white dress, white oxfords, and white stockings she blended in easily with the other nurse's aides. But Maura had a reputation around the floor for being especially competent and dependable. She was often assigned the most difficult and demanding patients.

Not that Carlo struck her as especially challenging when she entered his room, a private en suite where he lay shackled to a hand-cranked hospital bed. Carlo remained silent as Maura introduced herself and took his vitals. When she tried to start a conversation, he said almost nothing in response. At one point he even turned his head away from her, as if to shield himself from the attempted exchange.

Rather than diminishing Maura's curiosity, however, Carlo's intransigence only intensified it. There was something so mysterious, almost disturbing, about him. It certainly helped that he was handsome, with fair hair, blue eyes, and the slightly feral, hunched look of a boxer. But Maura's interest was existential rather than romantic. Here was an otherwise unremarkable man, only a year younger than Maura, and already he was nearing death.

What did it feel like to face such a fate? Carlo knew. Perhaps by being close to him, Maura could know, too.

It was precisely this kind of curiosity that had brought Maura to nursing in the first place. Even as a young girl growing up around Sacramento, she'd shown an interest in the bigger questions of life. On holiday drives to San Francisco, she would gaze at the cow-speckled hills, daydreaming of a life in the back-to-the-land hippie communes she read about in her mother's old magazines. To be in nature, within a close-knit community, with a clear sense of purpose: This, for Maura, was the dream.

After high school she spent a few semesters at junior college before dropping out and getting a job at a local bank. If during the day she looked relatively "straight"—nice shoes, nylon stockings—at night she assumed the persona of a full-bore hippie. She wore patchouli oil and tried LSD. She fantasized about leaving society and living on what she thought of, vaguely, as "the edge."

There was only one problem: She was pregnant. Reluctant to give up her freedom and unprepared for motherhood, Maura decided to give up the baby for adoption. By this point she was twenty years old. Sometimes she rubbed her belly and apologized to the child inside her. *I'm sorry*, she said. *I love you, I just don't think I'd be a very good mom right now.*

But then she gave birth. Pressing her new daughter to her chest, Maura felt an ecstatic wave of clarity. *This little baby comes out of you, and it's a person*: The blunt simplicity of this fact hardly made it less revelatory.

Maura named the girl Iantha, Greek for "violet flower." She would raise the child herself.

Doing so, however, required making some lifestyle changes. Maura left her apartment in Sacramento and moved to her parents' place outside the city. Inspired by her experience giving birth, she decided to pursue a degree in nursing. Her ultimate goal was to become a labor and delivery nurse, but until then she would work as a nurse's aide—a fine intermediary step, as far as she was concerned. She loved being in what she thought of as the trenches of life, those places where everything superficial drops away and life's most basic questions are laid bare. What truly matters? What is life's ultimate purpose?

Why, in the end, are we here at all?

The weeks following Carlo's arrival at the medical center continued much as they always did on the ward where Maura worked. The ankle cuff was removed and the guard soon departed, but Carlo remained as morose and unsmiling as ever.

Maura was surprised by how few visitors he received. Virtually the only people to see him were his sister and his sister's boyfriend, hippyish figures in their early twenties who often arrived bearing food from McDonald's. The woman's name was Lila. The boyfriend's name was John.

Maura exchanged only a few words with the couple, but as with Carlo, she felt curiously drawn to the sister. Lila was about Maura's age, with a tanned, olive complexion, sharp cheekbones, and a striking gap between her two front teeth. More than any particular physical trait, however, the young woman was marked by an almost preternatural aura of insight—as if behind her quicksilver green eyes there lay a strange and powerful secret just out of reach for everyone else.

Weeks passed and Carlo's condition continued to deteriorate. He lost weight. Soon he was unable to walk. After several months on Maura's floor, he was transferred to another wing of the medical center. Maura's interaction with him—and his sister—ceased entirely.

Maura had been a nurse's aide for about a year now and was beginning to grow ambivalent about the job. She liked her work but couldn't imagine living with her parents the whole time it would take to earn a degree. This was to say nothing of the 4:00 a.m. wake-ups, the days when she didn't get home until dinner. Becoming a mother had forced Maura to make a pivot toward respectability. And yet on some level she remained the same adventurous young woman who'd stared out the window of her parents' Ford, dreaming of something different.

Early one evening on her day off, she decided to go shopping at a local thrift store. She'd only just pulled into the parking lot, however, when an idea occurred to her.

What if she visited Carlo?

More than a month had passed since he'd left her floor. But Maura still felt a kind of loyalty to him, or at least an ongoing curiosity about his proximity to death.

There was his sister, too—his alluring, imperiously beautiful sister. Who *was* she?

Maura backed out of the parking lot and headed to the medical center.

Many of life's most important decisions don't feel especially significant in the moment of their choosing. Some don't even register as decisions. A young woman opts not to go shopping: What could appear less consequential than that? And yet on such a hinge a life often swings, as did Maura's—as did Lila's—in ways neither woman would appreciate for decades to come.

Maura arrived at Carlo's room nervous about how he would receive her; it wasn't as if they'd ever been remotely close. When she arrived, however, his face lit up.

"What are you doing here?" he asked, not unkindly.

"I was just in the neighborhood," Maura lied. "I thought I'd come by to see how you're doing."

If once Carlo had rejected Maura's conversational advances, now he welcomed them. It was a startling shift.

They were still talking when Lila and John appeared in the doorway. Maura exchanged a few words with them. The slender young woman was just as compelling as Maura remembered. Her nose flared when she spoke. Her eyes were green, but they were more than green. They were regal, deep, assured. They flashed with a confidence that bordered on arrogance.

From then on, Maura visited Carlo often, about three times a week, usually after work. Her interest in him remained platonic. But she also started doing things a girlfriend might have done, like rubbing his back and massaging his feet. She gave him ice cream, mixing in wheat germ to help keep him strong. Sometimes she brought along Iantha, now a bubbly one-and-a-half-year-old, much to the confusion of the nurses, who seemed to think Carlo was the child's father.

Lila and John visited often, too, and before long they'd all become friends. Maura was grateful for the company—her world had shrunk dramatically since becoming a mother. When Lila arrived at the medical center one day with a ring that had belonged to her and Carlo's grandmother, she told Carlo to give it to Maura as a token of their friendship. Maura happily accepted the simple gold band and slipped it onto her left ring finger. She said she would wear it forever.

It wasn't long before Maura was spending several evenings a week at John and Lila's house, a funky spot off a back alleyway in West Sacramento. Maura had given up marijuana when she'd gotten pregnant with Iantha, but she started smoking again now, luxuriating in long, heady conversations with the couple late into the night. Lila said she wanted to be an explorer in life; Maura said she did, too.

But it wasn't just the future they discussed. Sometimes Lila also brought up the past.

She had almost nothing good to say about her upbringing. Her father was an alcoholic. Her parents divorced when she was young. Her mother worked at an almond-processing facility—hard, tedious labor that had barely afforded the family a subsistence-level existence in West Sacramento. Lila and her three siblings had lived in a small gray house on Sutter Avenue, a dirt road that dead-ended into a ditch. The yard had barely any grass. Ill-tempered geese nipped at unwelcome visitors.

Even in a neighborhood marked by economic struggle, the Carters' poverty was striking. They used an outhouse where they wiped themselves with the pages of an old Sears catalog. To bathe, they heated water on the stove and poured it into a corrugated metal tub they dragged into the kitchen.

For fun the Carter kids picked clovers in an alfalfa field across the street from the house. They caught frogs, put on plays with the neighbors, and sipped water from old gourds they cut in half to use as "bowls." They bought soda and candy bars from a Chinese grocery at the far end of Sutter Avenue, and when they'd saved up a little money, they visited the nearby Commodore Motel, a shabby flophouse where the begrudging proprietor let them use the pool for a small fee.

Among this band of friends and siblings, Lila was the quiet one, the soft-spoken one, the one who always played along, but never as the leader. Her older sister, Bonnie, was the family flirt. Her younger brothers, Carlo and Calvin, were tough, wild characters. Carlo smoked often and slapped his friends on the bus. He called their mothers whores.

Still, Lila remained devoted to him. She had to be. With her mother off at work and her older sister out with her friends, she became responsible for much of the housework. From her early teens she cooked and cared for her younger brothers, helped little if at all by her grandparents, who lived in a dark, unpainted shack behind the outhouse. Her largely absent father claimed to be Native American, so her relatives on her mother's side would beat her up and called her a dirty squaw.

That she meanwhile cultivated a stellar academic record indicated the tremendous intelligence and grit that lay hidden behind her reserved exterior. Lila was at the top of her class at James Marshall High School, where she served, variously, as Class Treasurer, Commissioner of Publicity, and Girls' Vice President. She rarely met up with classmates after school. But she was still a mainstay, a pretty girl in makeup and glasses whose intelligence and competence were known to all. She never seemed to have a boyfriend, though at one point she was elected "class kitten," a feminine riff on the wildcat, the school mascot. Her classmates were surprised to see her jumping and cheering in costume in front of a crowd.

But you never knew what was inside a person, did you?

Still, Lila was more than a straight-A student, more than a Pep Club stalwart and a capable housekeeper. She was also a deeply sensitive young woman who felt things with an intensity matched by few of her peers. In 1960, when she was thirteen, her best friend and neighbor, Kathie, brought home the new Elvis single, "It's Now or Never." Excitedly the girls and their siblings gathered on the floor around the family record player.

"It's now or never," came the singer's trademark baritone.

Come hold me tight
Kiss me, my darling
Be mine tonight.

When the song was over, Lila was crying.

After graduating from high school, Lila enrolled in Sacramento State College. Was there ever a headier time to be seventeen years old than in the fall of 1964? Not if you were Lila Mae Carter, who quickly fell into the counterculture then burgeoning on campus. Sac State was just a twenty-minute drive from Sutter Avenue, but it might as well have been a whole world away, so radically different—so radical, full stop—were its fashions and mores.

Today the sixties aesthetic is so drenched in sentiment, so overlaid with association, that it can be easy to forget how rainbow-blazingly *fresh* it all seemed at the moment of its first appearance. To smoke a joint after having sex with a stranger, a Grateful Dead record playing in the background: For Lila and hundreds of thousands of young people like her, this was not yet a cliché. It was their altogether unprecedented new way of life.

They came from all over the country, these so-called hippies. They were mostly white and middle-class, expats from the suburbs who hurled themselves into a psychedelic scramble of drugs, protests, and free love. They longed to cede themselves to the group, to let their egos die: to feel, as when they took LSD, constituent to the world in all its wideness. But they could also be aggressively individualistic, insistent on forging their own path. It was a central paradox of the counterculture, if not human nature itself. Hippies claimed the right to be themselves in all their unique specificity. But they also often longed to be part of a group, to feel connected to others just like them.

"Is God Dead?" asked the iconic 1966 *Time* magazine cover, and for many of these young men and women, disillusioned by what they saw at the spiritual and emotional bankruptcy of the era, the answer was a resounding *yes*. This was not, however, cause for despair, but rather a call to fill the void anew. American religious history is marked by three great movements: the First, Second, and Third Great Awakenings, religious uprisings of the eighteenth and nineteenth centuries that decisively and permanently shaped the character of the United States. The spiritual upheaval of the 1960s and early seventies is known to some scholars as the Fourth Great Awakening: a reformation in tie-dye.

How much did Lila participate in the clamorous energy of the era? Enough that within a few short years she was smoking a pipe, wearing a beret, and driving a green Karmann Ghia. The quiet book lover of Sutter Avenue had turned into a rainbow-clad feminist, her transformation a product of broader social dynamics and her own desperation to leave behind the poverty, alcoholism, and turmoil of her early life.

She got a job at a movie theater where she ate popcorn to save money on food. She left college after three years, possibly for medical reasons—a major change for a young woman who'd been among the smartest and most academically driven students of her high school class. But in an era defined by the mantra "turn on, tune in, drop out," perhaps it wasn't so shocking after all. Lila had been through so much, had worked so hard. Maybe she was sick of the struggle. Maybe she just wanted to get high and listen to Bob Dylan records.

Her hair, once a prim bob, grew all the way down to her breasts. She met a guy—John—and moved in with him. She applied for a job as an airline stewardess but was rejected because of her witchy good looks. She was attractive, the interviewers told her, but in a way that might cause trouble.

No matter. She would stay the course, living in Sacramento, going wherever the counterculture took her.

And then her brother got sick.

* * *

Carlo grew weaker and skinnier as the summer progressed. Almost a year had passed since Maura had first spotted him in the hallway. Eventually he was transferred to Camellia Cottage, an adobe-like hospice center with a view of palm trees tilting contentedly in the breeze. The idyllic setting covered a grim new reality. Twenty-one-year-old Carlo was about to die.

Lila, John, and Maura tried to make his final weeks as comfortable as possible. They played him music, changed his bandages, and treated his bedsores. When a chaplain came to visit, Lila shooed the man away. Neither she nor Carlo had any faith background to speak of.

Then, on the morning of September 16, 1970, Maura stopped by Camellia Cottage before work, same as usual.

"Carlo," she whispered. "I'm here to give you a back rub."

Carlo didn't respond. Then Maura noticed his breathing had grown irregular; for seconds at a time he stopped breathing altogether. Maura had been around enough dying patients to know what this meant.

She called Lila and John. The couple hurried to the medical center and tried to rouse Carlo, to no avail. For two hours they waited.

When the moment finally arrived, when they realized Carlo was gone, they hugged each other and cried.

A nurse came by. Still thinking Maura and Carlo had been married, the nurse hugged Maura and said, "You're the bravest."

Maura tried to parry the compliment to Lila. "No, *you* were the bravest one," she said.

But Lila didn't seem bothered by the mistake. The experience of Carlo's death—and the months preceding it—had forged a deep and powerful intimacy between the two young women. They knew each other's frustrations and philosophies, their histories and aspirations. They'd faced mortality together. If there had been any ambiguity before, now there was none. Maura and Lila were friends. *Best* friends.

CHAPTER 2

Would Lila's life have turned out differently if her brother had survived? In another era, a less experimental era, would her grief have resolved into something manageable? Perhaps, perhaps not. Either way, Carlo's death was to be a foundational event in Lila's life—arguably *the* foundational event.

In the weeks after Carlo died, Maura continued to hang out with Lila and John at their apartment. But something had changed. Whatever bitterness and anger Lila had carried over from childhood now blazed into something wild, something uncontrollable. Her beloved brother: gone. For someone of Lila's sensitivity, a young woman who could cry at an Elvis song, it was a cataclysm beyond all measure. Her family held a funeral, but Lila refused to attend. She started talking about leaving Sacramento—anything to get away from the horrors of home.

Near the end of the year she heard about a group of young people who'd established a commune in the forest outside the city in the Sierra Nevada foothills. The Bear Tribe, it was called. The group had been founded by Sun Bear, a Chippewa medicine chief who believed the world was approaching an era of breakdown and purification. Soon the air would be choked with smog, the skies filled with vultures. A new multiracial tribe could provide an escape from this breakdown and a model for a more sustainable alternative.

Like her father before her, Lila described herself as Native American (though the evidence to support Lila's claim to that effect is mixed). Before Carlo's death, Lila had barely mentioned her alleged Sioux heritage. Now she brought it up frequently. Around Christmastime, three months after the funeral, she announced her decision to join the Bear Tribe. She would "go to the mountains and learn a new way of life," she later wrote. John agreed to come with her.

Maura, too, thought seriously about joining, and not just because of her ongoing devotion to Lila. Part of her still longed to move to the woods, to experience life within a small community of like-minded young people. The Bear Tribe seemed like the perfect opportunity to turn that dream into a reality. It would be an adjustment for both her and Iantha, who'd just turned two. Maura would have to abandon her nursing ambitions. But by now she was ready to trade in her constraining white uniform for jeans and a denim shirt.

It wasn't a hard decision in the end. Maura and Iantha would leave their old lives—would strike out in search of something better and new. Something true.

The Bear Tribe had set up camp about an hour northwest of Sacramento, along Shoo Fly Ridge, on an old mining claim that Sun Bear rechristened Medicine Rock. Deer prints dotted the forest floor. Spider webs hung lazily across the footpaths. There was an open area in front of an old cabin and another down by the creek, but the property was otherwise thick with greenery—manzanita, yerba santa, and other plants hearty enough to make a go of the tough mountain soil. Up to twenty people at a time lived in tents and lean-tos. Most were white. Some were Native. All were searching.

Maura and Iantha arrived at the property in the bed of an open truck, a single stuffed duffel bag at their side. It was February 1971. Lila and John had been in the woods for several weeks by now, and Maura was excited to see them. But from the moment Lila emerged from the trees, Maura knew something was off.

There was Lila's name for one thing—now she went by Full Night. Lila had ditched her hippie digs, too, and wore fringed buckskins, moccasins, and a loincloth. A number of other tribe members had also assumed pseudo-Native personas, but in Lila the change felt more significant, as if it corresponded with some deeper shift. In the way she spoke, in the way she reacted to others, in the way she *moved*, there was an uncomfortable new abrasiveness about her.

Was this a temporary development or something more permanent? Maura would have to wait and see.

At Medicine Rock, Maura's days were formless, evolving, subject not to the clock but to the rise and fall of the sun. Tribe members spent their days walking in the woods, hunting, and participating in sweat lodge ceremonies. They tried to grow vegetables but had better luck dumpster diving in what Sun Bear referred to as the Safeway Recycling Program. Mostly the expired produce and sweet rolls were fine to eat, but sometimes it was best to heed one of the group's guiding mantras: *If the salad moves, don't touch it.* At night everyone gathered around the campfire, singing and dancing to the sound of the guitar, flute, and drum. Maura struck up a romance with a man named Grey Wolf, and when it came time to sleep, he, Maura, and Iantha would retreat into a domed structure made from bent saplings and a sheet of clear plastic. Burrowed into their sleeping bags they would gaze up through the tree branches—and, beyond them, at the faint glimmer of stars.

However singular the Bear Tribe might have felt to its members, the group was one of likely "tens of thousands" of communes to operate in the hippie era, according to scholar Timothy Miller. Similar groups have always existed in American history, products of the same separatist, utopian impulse that brought the first European colonists across the Atlantic. In 1776, Thomas Paine wrote of this abiding compulsion, "We have it in our power to begin the world over again. A situation, similar to the present, hath not happened since the days of Noah until now." Almost two hundred years had passed since Paine had written these words, and they still felt apt. *We have it in our power to begin the world over again*: Sun Bear couldn't have said it any better himself.

A commune founded before the 1960s would have been one among hundreds. The Bear Tribe was one of thousands. The movement exploded in 1965 with a Colorado commune called Drop City. Miller writes, "Drop City brought together most of the themes that had been developing in other recent communities—anarchy, pacifism, sexual freedom, rural isolation, interest in drugs, art—and wrapped them flamboyantly into a commune not quite like any that had gone before." Members lived in geodesic domes made from old car roofs. They took new names. They shared their belongings and made sculptures out of floor lamps.

Other communes would follow: Sunrise Hill in Massachusetts, Morning Star Ranch in Sonoma, the Hog Farm in Tujunga, California. All gave radical expression to a widespread dissatisfaction with the isolation and materialism of modern life. What good was a physically comfortable existence if it unfolded in a boxed-off housing development? Better to follow the most basic, even biological of human impulses; better to accept the ecstatic embrace of the collective.

Though American communes were "overwhelmingly white" (per Miller), they often took inspiration from Indigenous customs and rituals. The counterculture more broadly, too, was saturated with Native imagery, dress, and spiritualism. Hippies wore beads and moccasins. They spoke lovingly of the "Earth Mother." In 1967, the legendary "Human Be-In" event in San Francisco was advertised as a "Pow-Wow" and a "Gathering of the Tribes." If there was, for actual Native Americans, a political usefulness to this allyship, the phenomenon still trafficked in stereotypes about the admirably "primitive" ways of Indigenous life. To some Native people, it all smacked of imperialism. It wasn't enough for America to engage in a centuries-long genocide. Now white people wanted to pillage Indigenous culture, too.

"The way of the hippie is completely at variance to that of the Indian," wrote Rupert Costo, a prominent figure in the San Francisco Native American community. "It is disgusting. It is demeaning. It is the Way of the Bum."

Sun Bear took a more accommodating position. In 1967, when asked about hippies who adopted elements of Native life, he said, "More power to them." Sun Bear's vision of the Bear Tribe as a group for Native and non-Native peoples alike sprang from this same conviction. Not everyone approved. "Sun Bear hasn't started a new tribe," Native American leader and advocate Rick Williams later said. "Nobody can just up and start a new tribe. What he's done is start a cult."

Either way, Maura found it deeply strange to see her mostly white, middle-class contemporaries painting their faces, taking peyote, and howling at the moon. Like the others, she had taken an "Indian name," and now went by Evening Light. But this was largely where her commitment to Native customs ended.

ABlila, however, only grew more devoted to her new identity as the weeks went by. She took peyote and told people's fortunes. She pronounced herself a medicine woman. She spoke with the herbs of the forest and engaged in what she described as sorcery.

She also started sleeping with tribe members other than John. Lila had always projected a powerful sexuality—once, back in Sacramento, Maura had watched as Lila massaged John's penis through his pants with her foot. At Medicine Rock she grew more uninhibited than ever. She spent the night in other people's tepees and wandered around topless after sweat lodge ceremonies.

It was all part of an escalating alienation Maura felt not just from Lila but from the tribe more broadly. Maura wasn't interested in pretending to be Native American. She simply wanted to live in a small, off-the-grid community.

Still, she also enjoyed a certain amount of status thanks to her association with Grey Wolf, one of the group's leaders. As spring approached, Maura sensed that Lila was becoming resentful of her status in the group—Maura, a white woman without any Native blood in her veins!

At the campfire one evening, Lila appeared from behind Maura, eyes flashing. In a voice twisted with resentment, she complained about her own lack of power and influence in the group. Maura listened uneasily as the flames cast a flickery glow on the surrounding forest.

What had happened to the mysterious young woman who had entranced Maura at Carlo's bedside? Lila's natural intensity, formerly so intriguing, had gone sour, had curdled into a kind of angry zeal that held little appeal, at least to Maura.

Weeks passed and Maura saw less and less of Lila. Soon the two young women barely spoke at all.

Then Jim Green arrived. He was twenty-five years old, a handsome, wooly-bearded former Army Reservist who went by Buffalo Sun. He wore feathers and a loincloth and moved around the camp with a wild-eyed hostility, a barely subdued hint of violence. He was white, and in full command of the English language, but he often spoke in a kind of monosyllabic TV-Indian pidgin: "Me hunt." "You go." Like other tribe members, he wore a large hunting knife on his hip. But on Jim, the knife didn't look like a tool. It looked like a weapon.

Lila took an immediate dislike to Jim, as if his fervency were a challenge to her own. He was a wild man, Lila said, a threat to the tribe. One day he organized what he called a "Sun Dance" ceremony where participants hooked skewers into their nipples and strung the skewers to the top of a kind of maypole, circling the pole in a peyote haze until they fell to the ground, skewers ripping painfully from their chests.

Several weeks passed. Soon it was early spring, the hills flecked with tomcat clovers and yellow star tulips. Food was often scarce around Medicine Rock, so one day Lila sneaked into Jim's tepee to steal a handful of dried fruit and nuts. On discovering the theft, Jim beat up his one-armed tentmate; feeling guilty, Lila confessed, cooling some of the hostility between them.

Jim subsequently became ill, likely with hepatitis—often a problem in rural communes, where food safety was minimal to nonexistent. Lila stayed with him through the sickness and nursed him back to health. In those delirious, sweaty days, something fateful happened between them. Lila later said that "God told her to go to [Jim's] tent," strip naked, and present herself to him. His flesh became her flesh; her flesh became his.

From then on, they were a couple.

In early April, Jim proposed a "blood oath" ceremony where tribe members would cut themselves and offer their blood to the moon. Ritual cutting felt good, Jim said. It brought reconciliation and release.

On the appointed evening, the group's most devoted members assembled around the campfire. "A knife was placed into the glowing coals" and then "passed around the circle," Jim later wrote. Soon the air was filled with "the stench of burning flesh," "the devilish howls of souls in pain."

Maura and John listened to the ruckus from the cabin. In hushed, bewildered tones they discussed everything that had happened over the past few months. How Lila had changed. How her friendship with Maura had shattered. How she'd cast John aside, swapping him out for a madman.

For months the neighbors along Shoo Fly Ridge had been complaining about the Bear Tribe, and on the night of the blood oath ceremony, they decided they'd had enough. Exasperated by the noise, several neighbors called the sheriff, who drove to Medicine Rock with a handful of deputies. At around 3:00 a.m. they put a stop to the noisy, blood-drenched proceedings. The fire died and the hills grew quiet.

Sun Bear had been absent from the camp at the time of the ceremony, and was distressed to learn what had happened. Further investigation revealed that Jim had been organizing his own splinter faction, perhaps even planning a coup to take over the group. Sun Bear believed in giving people chances, but Jim seemed unstable. On Sun Bear's return to Medicine Rock, he escorted Jim off the property. Lila soon followed after him.

The entire community fell apart shortly thereafter. Sun Bear had become frustrated that people "wanted to play Indian, rather than to learn to live in harmony," he later wrote. The Bureau of Land Management, which controlled the property, may also have ordered the tribe to leave. Whatever the case, everyone had abruptly departed by April 15, 1971, when the *Mountain Democrat and Placerville Times* reported the Bear Tribe was gone. "Tom-toms were still heard Monday night, but by Tuesday they had vanished."

Maura wasn't sorry to go. The season she'd spent at Medicine Rock had been a letdown—a bizarre version of the woodsy paradise she'd dreamed of as a girl. She liked being out in nature, among the trees, the foxes, and the mountain quail. But she'd never felt comfortable among the people.

Living in a community, it turned out, didn't necessarily satisfy a person's *longing* for community.

Maura and Iantha moved with several others to a dairy farm south of Sacramento, where they milked cows and picked fruit for the summer in exchange for a place to stay. Away from Lila, Jim, and the group's more radical adherents, Maura was much happier. And yet there was also something profoundly sad about her relief at saying good-bye to a woman she'd recently considered her best friend. The Bear Tribe had transformed Lila into a harder, more zealous version of the woman Maura had met back in Sacramento.

But there was another possibility. What if the Bear Tribe had simply exposed Lila's true nature? What if it had surfaced a dark, brutal part of her character that had been waiting to roar, claw, scream its way into view?

What if this was who she'd been all along?

CHAPTER 3

Spirituality was knitted into the very fabric of the Bear Tribe, as it was in the counterculture writ large. To be a hippie was to participate in a loose and shaggy faith structure, to pursue truth and transcendence with the same intensity as members of the world's oldest, most established religions. There was no agreed-upon Bible of the counterculture, no explicitly defined catechism. But there *was* a certain reverence mixed up with all the music, drugs, and free love. These were mystical rites of a kind, holy pursuits that brought people closer, if not to God, then to something like him. In this way the counterculture didn't just incorporate elements of religion. In some ways it *was* a religion.

Spiritual expression was everywhere, from the anti-war protesters who "performed a mock-exorcism to levitate the Pentagon and cast out its demons," per one scholar, to the songs of George Harrison and the other Beatles, whose use of the sitar helped bring elements of Hinduism to a broad American audience. Psychedelics pioneer Timothy Leary created a League for Spiritual Discovery for which "LSD" wasn't just an acronym but a central guiding sacrament.

In 1965, the Immigration and Nationality Act ended the quota system of immigration in the United States. The years that followed saw the arrival of spiritual teachers from across Asia: gurus who expanded awareness of Buddhism, Sikhism, Taoism, Sufism, and other faiths. For many young people, Eastern religion presented an alluring counterpoint to the comparatively rigid, doctrine-oriented forms of Protestantism they'd grown up practicing. This was "the dawning of the Age of Aquarius," the hippies of the musical *Hair* announced on Broadway in 1968. A new era in human history required new modes of spiritual inquiry, new ways of accessing "Golden living dreams of visions / Mystic crystal revelation / And the mind's true liberation." Young people meditated and practiced yoga. They consulted divination texts and made meals from the *Zen Macrobiotic* cookbook.

American Christianity wasn't immune to the radicalizing forces of the era. The late 1960s saw the arrival of what became known as the Jesus Movement, a grassroots uprising that began on the streets of Los Angeles and in Orange County, California, in coffeehouses, storefronts, and, in one case, in an ad hoc space outfitted with old movie theater seats. Hippie evangelists spoke of a savior who wore robes and sandals; who threatened the established political order; who proclaimed a message of radical love and acceptance. A savior just like them, in other words. Theirs was a church not of "brick and pews but an invisible community of oneness," as a Christian newspaper in Hollywood put it in 1971.

These, the "Jesus People," or "Jesus freaks" (hippies more generally were often called freaks), were hardly wrong in their characterization of Christ. Jesus *had* been a homeless radical, a pacifist who'd ignited a social justice movement that had changed the course of history. Secular hippies might enjoy more sex and do more drugs than their Christian counterparts, but both groups shared a version of the same freewheeling, tunic-and-tie-dye ethos.

Sometimes the intermingling of Christianity and the counterculture produced comical results, as when hippie believers claimed to be "high on the Lord," or cited Genesis ("Let the earth bring forth grass") as a defense of marijuana. A Jesus Movement bumper sticker put a godly twist on a popular anti-war slogan: "HELL? NO! WE WON'T GO." In New York City, a baby was reportedly baptized "in the name of the Father, the Holy Ghost, and Jesus Christ Superstar," a reference to the enormously popular 1971 Broadway musical.

For all its surface-level silliness, however, the Jesus Movement brought real energy and vitality to American Protestantism. Calvary Christian, a prominent church in the movement, conducted mass baptisms of up to a thousand people at a time along the stony bluffs at Corona del Mar

State Beach in Southern California. It was an ecstatic scene, over-the-top, perhaps, but also striking in its vibrancy.

In June 1971, *Time* magazine ran a cover story titled "The Jesus Revolution," in which a twenty-six-year-old Christian surfer told the magazine, "It's so beautiful when you are with the Lord and catch a good ride. When you are piling out for the next one you just say 'Thank you Lord for being so good to us and for the good waves and the good vibes.'" His was a rhapsodic, groovy reverence—easy to dismiss, perhaps, even to mock. But there was also something profound, almost moving, in the young man's ability to locate the divine in the everyday.

And then there were the cults.

For millennia, cults have proliferated in periods of social unrest or transition: after the fall of the Roman Empire, during the French and Industrial Revolutions, following the fall of the Soviet Union. The late 1960s and seventies was an era of similar upheaval, and triggered a corresponding "meteoric rise" in cults, per scholar Ronald M. Enroth. So much of society was up for grabs, falling apart, or being considered from new and different perspectives. Amid this mayhem, this frenzy of freedom, cults offered something different. They offered clarity, security, order. They offered a home.

"Cult" is a famously slippery term, one that evades simple definition. The word hasn't always had a pejorative topspin: The original Latin, *cultus*, refers to standard elements of religious practice like ritual and worship. Of course, this definitional overlap gestures at the difficulty, even the impossibility, of distinguishing between a cult and a religion. As the old religious studies saying goes, "cult plus time equals religion." What might have once appeared nutty or dangerous becomes familiar, even respected, as the centuries fly by.

"It is all but impossible to define cults in a way that does not describe a large share of American religious bodies," writes scholar Philip Jenkins, "including some of the most respectable." Cults typically operate out of highly regulated, exclusionary communal spaces—but so do Catholic monks and nuns. Cult members wear similar clothes, eat similar foods, and sing the same songs—but so do many Hasidic Jews and fundamentalist Muslims. Cults impose a totalizing way of life centered around a charismatic guru—but so do many ashrams, healing centers, and artist colonies. The beliefs held by cult members are typically seen as extreme and shocking. But what could be more shocking than the Christian Eucharist, where people claim to eat and drink the *actual flesh and blood* of a prophet who died two thousand years ago?

Still, there are several criteria that can help identify a cult as such. A cult is not a casual coming together of friends. It is not a group united by a shared hobby: knitting, horses, archery. Cults proclaim novel or radical belief systems. They are led by charismatic leaders who claim to have a singular connection to God. They disallow contact between members and people outside the group, and prohibit independent thought and action. Cults thrive on "persecution": If the world hates them, they must be doing something right. Cults also subject people to severe exploitation—physical, spiritual, sexual. They *use* people; they use people *up*.

But perhaps the most significant distinguishing factor of a cult is in how it relates to the mainstream. Cults have a self-evident marginality; they are startling, even disturbing, to the average observer in a way that more fully developed religions generally aren't. Perception, in other words, matters as much as belief. Even if early Christianity displayed elements of cultishness—the self-proclaimed messiah, the followers who gave up everything to follow him—the label clearly no longer fit by AD 380, when Roman emperor Theodosius I declared Christianity the official religion of the Roman Empire. Christianity was now too established, too large, too *powerful*, to be anything but a religion.

Hundreds or perhaps even thousands of cults operated in the late 1960s and seventies, fully a third of them in "Cultifornia." Unlike many eastern states, California had no post-statehood history of establishment religion, and thus offered more of a blank slate for self-made messiahs. California also attracted seekers of every stripe, from nineteenth-century gold rushers to Dust Bowl refugees to would-be movie stars and hippies. Experimentation itself was floating in the gold-flecked water.

Cults of the 1960s and the 1970s trafficked in a wide range of kookery. Many groups practiced strung-out versions of Eastern mysticism, seeking enlightenment in yoga, massage, crystals, and meditation. Members of the Hare Krishna movement wore saffron robes and sat chanting on street corners. They took new names, lived in communes, and avoided worldly entanglements. Group leaders "were willing to do anything to keep me out of contact with my parents," recalled a former member. At various points she wore a wig or a fake pregnancy belly to hide her identity from outsiders.

Members of the Divine Light Mission worshiped at the feet of a teenage guru with a taste for ice cream and Rolls-Royces. In the Holy Spirit Association for the Unification of World Christianity, better known as the "Moonies," members used "holy salt" to sanctify food and drive out evil spirits. The group's Korean leader, the Reverend Sun Myung Moon, "had a certain magnificence about him," said one female member. "You felt that if someone were to shoot him, the bullet would swerve." A visit from Moon required extensive preparation. "If you washed a banana, you had to use Q-tips."

Notorious cult leader Charles Manson preyed sexually on his female followers and directed several of them to commit a series of murders in Los Angeles in 1969—an act of extravagant violence that brought cults to the attention of many Americans for the first time. The Peoples Temple of the Disciples of Christ, founded by minister Jim Jones, conducted admirable social justice work in its early years. But Jones's humanitarian spirit had evidently faded by 1978, when he orchestrated the murder-suicide of more than nine hundred souls in the forests of Guyana. It was unthinkable: parents and children consuming cyanide-spiked Flavor Aid, their corpses rotting swiftly in the humid jungle heat. And yet it had happened.

On and on it went like this, cults of the sixties and seventies that demonstrated the extraordinary plasticity of the human mind: its capacity for delusion, whimsy, and violence. The tumult of the counterculture had given rise to this explosion, unleashing a kind of social chaos that, for some, prompted a retreat into spiritual and emotional authoritarianism. But if cults represented the counterculture at its most extreme, they also stood as a reaction *against* the counterculture. Hippies placed a premium on freedom, on the right to improvise their lives as they saw fit. And yet the 1960s and seventies also revealed the limits of freedom—how an endless array of options could be confusing, overwhelming, even debilitating. Sometimes it simply feels better being told what to do.

CHAPTER 4

When Jim Green was five years old, a diamondback rattlesnake bit him twice on the left forearm. At the local doctor's office Jim screamed, scratched, and writhed until a doctor pinned him to the floor and cut a pair of small incisions around each of the snakebites. The doctor then applied a kind of suction device to the wounds—a highly ineffective mode of treatment that, Jim later claimed, nonetheless saved his life.

Jim went on to make a full recovery, but the episode was to stay with him for decades to come. Eventually it took on a metaphorical meaning. Just as the doctor had sucked out the snake venom, so, too, did God suck out people's sins—and Jim's early adulthood was nothing if not full of sin.

He grew up in Kentucky in a family where he was beaten regularly with belts, brooms, and tree limbs. His parents weren't churchy types, but they read the Bible and expected their children to do the same. He got saved at a local church when he was sixteen. There was no alcohol in the Green house, no television or music. At school he liked to paint and draw; senior year of high school he served as president of the Hunting and Fishing Club.

At eighteen he abandoned Kentucky and Christianity for California, where he'd been told the women outnumbered the men five to one. In San Jose, his odds weren't quite so favorable, but he never lacked for sex. ("I fornicated every woman I could jump on," he later said.) He served several years in the Army Reserves but left in 1968, perhaps because of a back injury. He smoked and sold marijuana along the beaches of Santa Cruz. He went nude surfing, drove a green VW minibus, and sold paintings of Native American life.

But limitless freedom would prove deeply unsatisfying. Now approaching his mid-twenties, Jim was as directionless as he was unhappy, as worn-out as he was untethered. He sank deeper into the drug culture. Even his contemporaries told him he'd "taken enough acid to fry" his brain, that he needed to "get it together."

His anguish deepened. Life was a rip-off, a nightmare, a joke. "Day and night were blended into one mirage of torment," he wrote. "I became well acquainted with the agonies of the damned." His depression worsened. He grew sick of parties, sick of women. Could yoga help? What about meditation? He tried both. Did Native Americans know the way? He moved into the woods, alone, and lived out of a tepee.

One day he met a man who told him about a commune outside Sacramento called the Bear Tribe. "It's a group of people getting back to the land the Indian way," the man said.

Lost, alone, and desperate, Jim decided to see it for himself. "Sounds like my kind of people."

In the wake of the Bear Tribe's collapse, Jim and Lila hitchhiked through Montana and Idaho, searching for new land where they could resuscitate the group. As the days and weeks went by, however, Lila grew frustrated with Jim, grumbling to herself about his relentlessness, his fanatical need to keep pressing forward. Sometimes she wondered if he'd been damaged by all the drugs she knew he'd taken.

In July, the couple attended a raucous concert at Farragut State Park in Idaho. It was a wild scene, with between twenty thousand and forty thousand attendees—young men and women enjoying alfresco sex, injecting their veins with mushroom tonic, and giving speed to sleepy stagehands. Young women openly hawked drugs ("Cocaine, cocaine for sale, come get your cocaine!"). According to a report, one man advertised his availability for sex "by means of balloons tied to his penis."

The concert also attracted a raft of hippie Christians, ambassadors of the Jesus Movement in all its loopy sincerity. "The Lord is really moving all over here," a twenty-year-old woman told a journalist. "Yeah, yeah, there's been drugs, but a lot of kids have turned on to Christ, too." The event was described as "a gathering of early Christians" where "the masses took care of each other, rejoiced in each other's presence and provided drugs, food and shelter to all who asked."

For Jim and Lila, however, the event only confirmed their sense of religious people as hypocrites. Not a single person evangelized to them as Lila, topless, sat listening to music with Jim in the amphitheater—though plenty of men did gawk at her breasts.

From Farragut State Park the couple continued east, grabbing food and rides wherever they could. When they were approached by an evangelist one day, Jim grabbed the young man's Bible and ripped out a handful of pages. "This is what I think of this stupid book," he said.

At the end of the summer the couple moved into an abandoned cabin in a field near Seeley Lake, Montana, an hour outside Missoula. Jim made money by trapping beaver and muskrat and selling furs. When it got cold out, he and Lila insulated the cabin by hanging the furs from the walls.

As winter continued, Jim and Lila only grew more and more unhappy. They were unprepared for the difficulty of life on the landscape and took out their frustrations on each other. Lila said she was sick of eating muskrats, sick of being "snowed in with a maniac." She announced she was going back to Sacramento. Instead, she sank deeper into a depression.

At the laundromat one day she picked up an illustrated booklet promoting Christianity. The booklet said nonbelievers were doomed to hell, a claim that didn't frighten Lila so much as it enraged her. The arrogance of it all! The presumption! "The more I read the angrier I became," she later wrote. "I was a volcano."

For the next several days she remained preoccupied by the booklet. It was at this point that Jim announced he was going to Missoula to buy hash. He left Lila alone in the cabin, hitching a ride with a man who started talking to him about Jesus. Jim held his tongue and stared at the passing landscape as the man prattled on. *I would have to get picked up by a religious nut*, he thought.

He spent the next three days smoking and drinking in Missoula. On the way home, he got a ride from a man in a truck—yet another Christian, it turned out.

"You don't have to live in darkness," the man said as they passed through the snowy landscape.

Jim usually dismissed evangelists out of hand. But something about the young man, or his message, or Jim's state of mind began to work on him, and Jim responded with uncharacteristic sincerity. He wasn't a church person, he said. He "didn't fit in with the crowd." And it was true. Jim's hair and beard were thick, ratty, and unkempt. He looked more like a mountain man than a churchgoer.

But the evangelist said none of that mattered. Jim didn't have to belong to a church; accepting Christ was all that mattered. It was one of the driving messages of the Jesus Movement writ large, that God could meet people wherever they were, even and especially outside the institutional Christian church.

Jim pondered the man's message as he looked out at the mountains. Eight years had passed since he'd left Kentucky and the religion of his youth. He'd ventured west in search of new gods—but where had that gotten him? He was now a washed-up hippie, a deadbeat drug user. His relationship with Lila all but over.

What if redemption was possible? What if it didn't matter what he'd done in the past?

When they arrived at the cabin, Jim invited the young man inside. Lila was in bed, under the covers, hungry, bedraggled, and upset. She'd clearly been crying.

Jim told her to listen to the evangelist. Lila was indignant. She and Jim didn't need God, she said. Religion was for the weak.

But the young man was insistent. "What you need is a personal relationship with Jesus."

They debated back and forth, Lila and the evangelist. But eventually she, too, started listening—*really* listening—to what the man had to say.

Like Jim, Lila had found little in the way of lasting satisfaction or happiness. Back in West Sacramento, she'd been at the top of her class. Now she and Jim were "hippie wanderers, desolate, chasing false gods, and living only for darkness." Much as she'd despised the booklets at the laundromat, they also highlighted how far she'd fallen, how miserable she'd become.

She sat down and looked at the floor.

Then something switched—in the room, in Jim and Lila. It was time.

"Repeat this prayer after me," the young man said.

Jim and Lila took each other's hands.

"Lord Jesus, take this garbage that is my life and fill me with you."

"*Lord Jesus,*" they repeated, "*take this garbage that is my life and fill me with you.*"

"I accept you as my savior."

"*I accept you as my savior.*"

A kind of brightness filled the cabin. Lila raised her hands to her face: It was as if someone had lifted a heavy burden from her back. She felt like singing. Jim, too, felt the release of a great weight, the presence, throughout his body, of an ecstatic, radiant love. Goose bumps prickled his arms. Then, suddenly, he was speaking, not in a language he'd ever known, but in God's own holy tongue. Tears fell down his face. He clasped his hands in thanksgiving.

"I'm free," he said. "I'm free."

Lila was crying now, too—crying and smiling as she looked out the window. The snow was so fresh, so white. How beautiful it was. How beautiful and pure.

CHAPTER 5

Jim and Lila might have sincerely regretted the lives they'd led prior to conversion. But for the purposes of narrative—for the stories they would tell about who they'd been and how they'd transformed—they couldn't have planned things any better. The couple had been drowning in "a slimy cesspool of wickedness," a pit of "fervid lostness." And yet still God had saved them. This was the Road to Damascus by way of the Haight-Ashbury, a spiritual U-turn that was all the more compelling for being so dramatic and unexpected.

Lila and Jim pursued their new faith with the same intensity they'd brought to the Bear Tribe. They were disappointed, however, by the leniency of the Jesus Movement churches they encountered. In Missoula they visited a congregation that served low-alcohol beer. *I don't need this*, Jim thought, scanning the red-lit, nightclubbish space. *I'm trying to walk clean. What are you going to do, have fornicating in a corner over there in the name of Jesus?* One day they met an Episcopal priest on his way to a conference; but when Jim and Lila asked about the event, the priest turned sheepish. "If you want to know the truth," he said, "we just get good and smashed." Another pastor they admired turned out to be gay—further evidence, as they saw it, of the hypocrisy of the church.

They got married and by late 1972, a year after becoming Christians, they'd moved to an old farmhouse in Kentucky, near where Jim had grown up. Lila gave birth to a daughter shortly after Christmas. The baby was sweet and good-natured. She had blue-green eyes, big lips, and wispy blond hair. Her name was Sarah. Jim called her Sissy Bug.

Jim did landscape work while Lila stayed at home with Sarah, all part of Lila's effort to "submit to her husband," as directed by scripture and social convention. But this was a difficult transition for Lila, who'd been largely self-sufficient since childhood. In early 1975, she gave birth to a son, Josh, in an excruciating delivery that resulted in a C-section. Though she lost a great deal of blood in the operation, she refused to get a transfusion. She said she didn't want someone else's tainted blood flowing through her veins.

In months and years that followed, the Greens moved several times throughout the South and the Lower Midwest, sampling and rejecting churches as they went. Increasingly, however, they felt unsatisfied and discouraged in their faith. They were still "hungry for God," as Jim put it, "vexed in our soul" that they hadn't experienced "the peace that transcends all understanding." Something was missing.

Eventually they landed near Jeffersonville, Indiana, where they joined a massive church led by a booming-voiced female preacher named Berniece Hicks. Christ Gospel was one of many congregations under Hicks's leadership: By the mid-seventies she ran what one journalist described as a "vast empire" of churches nationwide and abroad.

As a Pentecostal church, Christ Gospel was part of the charismatic renewal that reinvigorated American Christianity in the 1960s and seventies. The modern Pentecostal movement had begun in the early twentieth century among marginal communities in Los Angeles before spreading to the South, Southwest, and beyond. Some mainstream believers looked down on these "Holy Rollers" and "snake handlers" who flailed on the floor and picked up venomous snakes to prove the protective power of their faith. But by the 1960s, as many Christians began to seek a more emotional, embodied connection to God, Pentecostalism had begun to grow in popularity. Like the Jesus Movement, which was frequently associated with Pentecostalism, this spike in interest functioned as a corollary of the counterculture more broadly. Some people found meaning in sex, psychedelics, and tarot card readings. Others found it in this highly physical, experience-driven subculture of Christianity.

Christ Gospel was Pentecostal to a P. Berniece Hicks issued prophesies during services, interrupting herself with sharp verbal outbursts triggered by the Holy Spirit: "*alabahaya,*" "*akabahaya.*" Parishioners responded by speaking in tongues, calling back in a sacred cacophony, whirling and whooping in the aisles.

Jim and Lila took to the place quickly. After years of wandering, they'd finally found a church whose sensibility matched their own.

But Berniece Hicks had her critics. In 1979, several years after the Greens joined the congregation, the Louisville *Courier-Journal* ran an explosive multipart investigation under the provocative headline "Southern Indiana Church More like a Cult, Some Say."

"It was as though a spell was on me," a woman told the paper. "You just can't believe the control [Hicks] has over people." Ex-members said that Hicks encouraged the breakup of families divided over their allegiance to the church. One person claimed Hicks ran a counseling program that engaged in "mind control." "She asks people to describe, in detail, their sexual problems or sexual relations," the woman said. "I've had people tell me, 'Even if I found out she was wrong, I'd still believe her.'"

The allegations were coming at a moment of especially intense cultural interest in—and concern about—cults. The desperation of families who'd lost loved ones to separatist, authoritarian religious organizations had led to a rash of media coverage and political action. A California State Senate subcommittee held hearings on the issue in 1974; Illinois, New York, and Maryland, too, tried to address cultish groups via regulation. These efforts extended all the way to Washington, D.C., where in 1976 Kansas senator Bob Dole held a public hearing on cults. But there were major setbacks in the effort to hold cults to account, too. In 1976, the New York State Supreme Court dismissed a "brainwashing" case brought against a pair of Hare Krishna leaders. Religious activities "cannot under our laws—as presently enacted—be construed as criminal in nature," wrote the Court. After the 1976 presidential election, the Jimmy Carter administration effectively took the same position. And yet the hunger for action was acute: By 1977, up to 750,000 Americans were "involved in" cults, according to one estimate.

When Senator Dole held further hearings in 1979, a brass band of "Moonies" congregated outside the Senate Office Building and played "We Shall Overcome." Other inquiries bore limited fruit—a House investigation ultimately found the "Moonies" had engaged in "tax, banking and immigration fraud," and members of the Church of Scientology (long trailed by accusations of cultism) were convicted of crimes related to the group's successful infiltration of the IRS and other government agencies. Still, anti-cult activists consistently found it difficult to get around the First Amendment and its unequivocal religious protections.

"I don't know what a cult is," US attorney general Griffin B. Bell said in 1979, adding, with a dash of irony, "I am a member of the Baptist Church. I suppose I am in a cult."

And so, despite ample public attention and even outrage, Christ Gospel and other groups accused of being cults continued operating largely without prosecution. The "cult wars" had begun.

Lila and Jim spent the mid- to late seventies on mission trips organized by Christ Gospel. Around 1976 the couple moved briefly to Mexico, where they worked at an orphanage and, later, a Christian college. Sarah was a happy, rambunctious four-year-old, unbothered to be living in a squalid shack once inhabited by pigs. She made friends easily. Soon she became proficient in Spanish.

During the day, she and Josh were cared for by a seventeen- or eighteen-year-old male student at the college. Every afternoon he would put Josh down for a nap and took Sarah on a walk. One day he brought her into the empty school church. When they sat down in a pew, the student opened his pants and showed Sarah his penis.

She should rub it, he said.

It happened the next day, and the next. After several weeks of this, the student brought along a friend. Together they led Sarah into a cramped space below the altar, the sound of organ music filtering down as they raped her.

At bathtime that evening Lila spotted blood in Sarah's underwear, quickly piecing together what had happened. Horrified, Lila told Sarah she would make things right. The family returned to the United States shortly thereafter.

Back at home, Lila told Berniece Hicks what had happened, but as Sarah recalls it, Hicks didn't believe her. Naturally, this response angered the Greens, who'd been growing increasingly dissatisfied with Christ Gospel. Jim and Lila particularly hated that Hicks lived such a notably extravagant lifestyle: clear proof, as they saw it, of her hypocrisy.

Eventually the Greens decided to leave the church to seek God on their own. They packed their green panel truck, strapped their faded suitcases to the roof, and headed south, through Mexico and into Central America.

They visited churches. They distributed Spanish-language Bibles. They ate cans of pork and beans they heated in fires alongside the road. Sarah was still a version of the bright, bubbly girl she'd always been. But the pain of her experiences in Mexico remained deep within her, a shard of glass that cut away at her from the inside. At night she slept in the front of the truck, terrified she was going to get kidnapped.

It was around this time that Jim Jones organized his mass murder-suicide in Guyana. The shocking episode drew attention from people worldwide, the Greens included. Jones's warped version of Christianity had little in common with their own. But the couple could recognize an organizational and spiritual master when they saw one.

Jim and Lila discussed Jones as they continued through Guatemala and Honduras and into Nicaragua, where a full-blown revolution was in progress. Rebuffed by locals, the couple sold their truck and left the country, ultimately flying to Miami, the cheapest American destination they could find.

In Florida, Jim and Lila got counseling jobs at the Salvation Army, an organization founded in the late nineteenth century by a married couple not at all unlike the Greens. In 1880, cofounder Catherine Booth ("Mrs. General Booth") had advocated for what she called Aggressive Christianity: "Oh! people say, you must be very careful, very judicious. You must not thrust religion down people's throats. Then, I say, you will never get it down."

Almost a decade had passed since Jim and Lila had first met. Though the intervening years had been filled with struggle, they had also provided, for the couple, an uncanny education in the art of radical leadership. Sun Bear had shown how to launch a separatist commune. Berniece Hicks had modeled what a powerful female preacher could look like. Jim Jones had demonstrated, from afar, it was possible to recruit people to a bold, outlandish vision. Even the Salvation Army had proven instructive, alerting Jim and Lila in the hawkish ways of Aggressive Christianity.

Month by month, year by year, it was all coming together.

In 1979, the Greens moved west, to Missoula, Montana. Sarah was six. Josh was four. The family attended a few prayer meetings around town, but mostly they avoided more established congregations. They would worship and pray at home, away from the hypocrisies and degradations of the church.

In the fall Sarah started second grade. She was a scrappy child, small for her age. Her favorite subject was history. After school, she and Josh liked to play with Cowboy, the family Pekinese, or go roller skating in the basement.

One day, however, Lila told Sarah and Josh they weren't allowed to play there anymore.

"Why not?" Sarah asked.

"It's our prayer chamber now," Lila said.

Sarah was upstairs several days later when she heard a strange, guttural noise coming from the basement. It was a woman's voice. It was her *mother's* voice.

"*Hoo, hoo, hoo, hoo. Huh, huh huh. HAA HAA MAA!*"

Sarah crept down to the basement, where she found Lila curled in a fetal position on the floor. Jim sat next to her, praying silently.

Sarah walked back upstairs. She tried to ignore the noises as they continued, at various rhythms and pitches, for the next hour.

Lila kept moaning in the basement in the days that followed. Then one afternoon she invited Sarah and Josh downstairs to join them.

Lila explained what was going on. She said she was birthing new souls into God's kingdom.

From then on, Sarah and Josh joined their parents in the basement for prayer, their foreheads pressed against the concrete for up to two hours at a time.

"*Gahhhhhhhh*," Lila screamed, as if in the throes of childbirth, her face scrunched in agony. "*MAH, MAH, MAH, MAH, MAHHHHH!*"

Weeks went by like this. Then Lila started making prophecies. The end of the world was coming, she said. A time of purification was at hand.

Sarah remained indifferent to her mother's pronouncements. Sometimes she fell asleep as Lila groaned on the floor next to her. For Jim and Lila, however, this was wildly exciting stuff. For years they'd felt unfulfilled in their faith. They'd fasted. They'd prayed. They'd begged God to intercede in their lives. And yet mostly he'd stayed remote, silent, and unresponsive. They'd never been able to figure out why.

Now they understood.

God was pulling them out of the institutional church. He was calling them to build an army of spiritual soldiers who would prepare the world for Christ's return. What this meant in practice they didn't yet know. But everything was clicking into place. They could see it. They could feel it.

"The battle cry has sounded," Jim wrote. "The time of war is at hand."

May 18, 1980, a Sunday afternoon.

Sarah is hanging out around the house when the dog starts whining outside.

"Shut up," Jim yells from the couch, where he lies resting his bad back. Lila is at work cleaning houses.

When the whining continues, Sarah steps outside. Immediately she understands the reason for the dog's distress. The sky has turned a dark, incandescent gray. A kind of ashy snow is falling to the ground.

Sarah puts the dog in the garage and summons Jim outside. Together they stare out at the dimming landscape.

When they go back inside, Jim retrieves a black-and-white television from the basement. A newscaster says a volcano has erupted in

Washington State. Mount St. Helens, dormant these past 123 years, is belching out a toxic plume of ash, gas, and smoke. Already the ominous cloud is extending across Oregon, Idaho, and Montana.

Strange things are happening in the areas beneath the ash cover. Cows are lying down to sleep. Automatic streetlamps are flickering on. A journalist says the splintery ash gets everywhere, "in our hair, our ears, even our mouths." People can feel it "grinding between our teeth."

Sarah stares out the window, rapt, in awe.

It is almost biblical, this midday darkness. Just like the crucifixion, when the afternoon sky went black for three hours. Just like the Exodus plague, when Moses cast a three-day darkness over the people of Egypt. Just like the final judgment still to come, when the sun is to become as "black as sackcloth of hair," the moon "as blood." To see a daytime darkness is to experience a foreshadowing—literally, an early shadow—of the world's annihilating finale.

It can hardly be a coincidence that Mount St. Helens is erupting now, just as Lila has begun to have visions. God has told her the end is near; that the forces of Satan are pouring forth across the land; that she and Jim will lead the way into a mighty spiritual conflagration. The volcano, then, is a grimly poetic illustration of the underworld let loose: a chthonic cloud of sin.

Or maybe it isn't a metaphor at all. Maybe it is the gates of hell flung open, a spew of *actual demons* let loose upon the world. Maybe this is the opening of the war Lila has been predicting. Maybe the principalities of evil are on the move, transforming the world into "a dungeon horrible on all sides round," as Milton writes of Hades, "As one great furnace flamed; yet from those flames / No light; but rather darkness visible."

CHAPTER 6

Back in the fifties, when Maura Aluzas was still a child, her mother would take her and her sister to McDonald's for dinner most Friday evenings. The girls would order burgers, fries, and milk shakes—vanilla for Maura, chocolate for her sister. It was a fun little ritual. Maura looked forward to it every week.

When Maura was in third grade, her parents converted to Roman Catholicism, which meant they weren't permitted to eat meat on Fridays. At the end of the week, Maura, her sister, and their mother would wait until midnight to make the one-mile pilgrimage to the golden arches that hung, steeple-like, in the dark Sacramento sky. It was technically Saturday now, and they could eat whatever they wanted.

Maura's parents soon soured on Catholicism. But they continued to send Maura and her sister to Mass, where the girls passed the time by staring at the women parishioners' hats. With the modernizing reforms of the Second Vatican Council still several years away, the liturgy was conducted largely in Latin. Religion struck Maura as a tedious affair, and it was a relief when, eventually, her parents allowed her and her sister to drop Catholicism, too.

Then, when Maura was in fifth grade, she and her family were invited to a service at a more informal church. A guest preacher there spoke vividly of hell and its torments. The underworld was no myth, he said. It was *real*.

Maura never returned to that church, but the sermon was to stay with her in the years that followed. It stayed with her as she entered high school. It stayed with her as she started having sex. It stayed with her as she grew her hair out, tried LSD, and experimented with marijuana. Mostly she didn't think about hell. But occasionally she could feel the old fear stirring, as when she passed cautionary Christian billboards on the side of the road.

"DO YOU KNOW WHERE YOU'RE GOING TO SPEND ETERNITY?" the billboards asked.

Well? Did she?

In the years following their departure from Medicine Rock, Maura and Iantha lived with a small group of young people out in the woods and along the ocean. Away from the overly devoted members of the Bear Tribe, Maura came to a kind of happiness. She was finally living a version of the life she'd imagined for herself as a girl.

In 1972, she gave birth to a daughter she conceived with a musician several years her junior. She named the baby Sarah: Sarah Chelew. Maura subsequently got involved with a handsome blond-haired handyman named Steve Schmierer. By 1975, when she turned twenty-seven, she and Steve were expecting a baby, Maura's third.

Maura, Steve, and the kids moved to a yellow one-bedroom house in French Gulch, a small, remote town three hours north of Sacramento. In August, Maura gave birth to a boy, Nathaniel; she and Steve got married the following May. Steve didn't make a lot of money with his carpentry and tree-pruning work, but he and Maura didn't *need* a lot of money. Things were mostly perfect. For a long time it felt that way.

One day Maura was driving her beige VW Bug through the mountains when a curious thought occurred to her. What if she and Steve converted to Christianity?

Religion hadn't been a part of Maura's life since her brief foray into Catholicism two decades prior. But she'd always felt drawn to what she called signs and wonders, flares of truth that pointed to some deeper spiritual significance. Perhaps Jesus was the answer.

Fear, too, informed her thinking. Maura still wondered if the fire-and-brimstone preacher of her youth had been right. Back in the woods she had dabbled in astrology until someone had warned against drawing star charts ("The Bible says that's evil"). Another person might have shrugged off the comment, but not Maura. She put the charts aside.

Then Maura heard from an old acquaintance named Don Beattie, or Bear Marks as he'd been known in the Bear Tribe. In the years since leaving Medicine Rock, Don had converted to Christianity, and now he was looking for a place to hold a Bible study. Here it was, precisely the kind of sign Maura had been looking for. She offered Don the use of her house in French Gulch and started attending the Bible study herself. Occasionally Steve did, too.

It wasn't long before Maura and Steve decided to accept Christ. When it came time to get baptized, Don walked them across their backyard, past the apple tree, and into the creek. It was spring. The water was cold.

So they were Christians now. For Maura, conversion wasn't some radical recalibration, as it had been for Jim and Lila. It was merely another step forward in her search for truth and meaning. Some small changes were in order, though. To announce her new faith, Maura put a Christian bumper sticker on the back of her car. It said, "PRAISE THE LORD!"

It was 1976, a year of tremendous religious importance, not just for the Schmierers, but for the entire nation.

In the 1910s and twenties, Christian fundamentalism had emerged as a potent force within the American Protestant church: a reaction, in part, to new scientific discoveries about the origins of the world and humankind. The fundamentalist movement came to a climax in 1925, when the State of Tennessee banned public schools from teaching evolution. The ensuing Scopes "Monkey" Trial dramatized the growing conflict between scripture and science, between religion and modernity. Supporters of the law initially emerged victorious, but press coverage was firmly on the side of science. Many commentators believed fundamentalism to be all but finished.

And yet it would find new prominence after World War II thanks in part to revivalist preacher Billy Graham. When Graham sought to expand his conservative coalition to include more religiously moderate followers, he started describing himself as an "evangelical." The term, not widely used at the time, referred to reformed Protestants from a range of denominations. Evangelicals proclaimed the inerrancy of the Bible, the importance of a decisive conversion experience, and the need to spread the Gospel (*evangel* in Greek), among other beliefs.

But a checklist description could hardly encapsulate the full meaning of the word "evangelical." Its meaning was in some ways emotional rather than doctrinal. *Newsweek* would gesture at this definitional vagueness, while also providing a useful (if sardonic) appraisal, in 1976, when it proclaimed, "Evangelicalism is the religion you get when you 'get' religion." Here was an emphatic, deeply personal mode of faith that demanded to be spread, that was active and alive in the lives of its practitioners.

There was overlap, too, between evangelicalism and the Jesus Movement (and Pentecostalism, for that matter), the various religious movements of the era speaking to the great social changes sweeping the nation.

By the mid-seventies, when Maura and Steve converted, the movement had taken its place at the center of American life. Nineteen seventy-six was "The Year of the Evangelical," *Newsweek* declared in a major cover story. The *New York Times*, too, reported that the movement could have up to 78 million members—this in a country of more than 200 million people. A 1976 Gallup poll found that 34 percent of all adult Americans were "born-again," among them presidential candidate Jimmy Carter. Another poll revealed that attendance at churches and synagogues had gone up "for the first time in nearly twenty years." Evangelicals were an important driver in that shift. "No other sector of the Christian church seems as vibrant," reported *Christianity Today*, "and certainly no other is getting as much attention."

Many public schools had been desegregated; national abortion rights had been upheld by the Supreme Court. It was now illegal to pray in public schools. A counterreaction to these and other developments was all but inevitable. *Christianity Today* also cited disillusionment with science and technology as a factor in the rise of evangelicalism. "Many young people and some older ones are beginning to feel that humanity cannot be trusted after all, and that outside help is needed." God, in other words.

Maura Aluzas, now Maura Schmierer, had been a line-and-sinker participant in the counterculture. Now she'd joined a spiritual revolution that was, in part, a response *against* that same counterculture. As a young woman she'd followed the cultural winds of the moment, and now, slightly older, she was doing the same thing again.

Several years passed. Maura baked pies with blackberries she and the kids harvested from around the creek. At the library they checked out books by Dr. Seuss and Richard Scarry. Iantha, nearing adolescence, plowed her way through Judy Blume, the Hardy Boys, and Trixie Belden. Steve was a good husband, if a somewhat severe father, though he knew how to joke and play with the kids. He made them laugh when he referred to farts as "butt snorts."

In 1980, the year of the Mount St. Helens eruption, Maura turned thirty-two. She didn't go to church much these days, though she remained a Christian. Then, out of nowhere, she received a postcard. It was from Lila.

The two women hadn't been in touch since their departure from Medicine Rock nine years earlier. Maura had heard about Jim and Lila's conversion through the grapevine, but she'd never tried to find them. Her friendship with Lila seemed to have died in the Bear Tribe. Still, she sometimes wondered about Lila, particularly now that both women were Christians.

Lila's note was brief. She said she and Jim had found God. Now they lived in Montana and were thinking about coming back to Sacramento.

To write back or to ignore the postcard? Here it was, another decisive juncture in Maura's life, another contingency that hardly seemed like anything of lasting significance at the time. To Maura, the note seemed like yet another message from God. How else to explain how Lila had found their address? She decided to write back.

So began Maura's correspondence with Lila, and later Jim, whom Maura had barely known back in the Bear Tribe. Now he sent her long, grandiose letters pulsing with near-manic excitement. "These past fifteen months have been very precious and informative," Jim wrote. "The Lord has led us out of man's religious systems and brought us into his bosom."

Maura read the Greens' letters with interest, as did Steve, even though he'd never met the couple. Iantha, too, began to look forward to the envelopes Jim covered with colorful drawings of tepees, bears, and peace pipes.

That spring, Steve built a cabin on a plot of land outside French Gulch where the family could live closer to nature. The cabin had no electricity, no plumbing. The three kids, ages twelve, eight and five, slept in sleeping bags in the loft.

Then one day another letter arrived. Jim and Lila were moving back to Sacramento.

The Schmierers usually went trick-or-treating around French Gulch for Halloween. This year, however, someone had told Maura that Halloween was "the devil's holiday," so she'd decided to plan things differently. She would take the kids to Sacramento, where they could see their grandparents. On the way home they would swing by the Greens' place.

When the holiday arrived, Maura made the three-hour drive to Sacramento as planned. After some time with her parents, she and the kids went to Jim and Lila's house.

Jim answered when Maura rang the doorbell. He looked nothing like the moon-worshiping zealot Maura had known in the Bear Tribe. Now he wore regular clothes and spoke in complete sentences. When Lila appeared in tight jeans and with a face caked in makeup, Maura was startled—she'd expected to find someone who looked more like a spiritual guru than a woman getting ready for a party.

Inside the house Sarah and Josh bickered over Halloween candy as the parents chatted. Despite the excitement of her letters, Lila seemed distant, almost cold. Jim lay on the couch eating potato chips. It was a disorienting scene, and Maura and the kids stayed for only a few minutes before heading back to French Gulch.

Maura had little contact with the Greens in the months that followed. Then, in the spring of 1981, Jim paid a surprise visit to the cabin, his arms full of groceries. He said little about God or Jesus.

By his next visit Maura had given birth another baby girl, Lilly, who'd developed a frightening case of pneumonia. Jim prayed over the child, though Maura also took the baby to the doctor. When Lilly got better, however, Steve said it was Jim, not the doctor, who had healed her. Maura wasn't so sure.

Lila, Sarah, and Josh came along for the next visit. They brought Kentucky Fried Chicken, biscuits, and mashed potatoes—a major treat for the Schmierers, who didn't have a refrigerator. Steve took an immediate liking to Lila, who'd ditched the tight clothing she'd been wearing on Halloween. Now she looked like the woman Maura had met years earlier, with long hair, a flowy dress, and no makeup.

The two families spent the afternoon in easy fellowship around the cabin. Josh and Sarah Green, six and eight, caught tadpoles in the creek with Iantha, Nathaniel, and Sarah Chelew. Among the adults there was little mention of God's Army. Lila's Bear Tribe fanaticism appeared to have cooled.

It was only later, when the shadows had begun to lengthen and everyone retreated inside, that the visit took a peculiar turn.

Maura was in the living room when the moaning started.

"UNGHHHH. MAGHHHHH. GAHHHHH."

She, Jim, and Steve followed the noise to the bedroom, where they found Lila curled in a fetal position in the corner.

"*HUH huh, HUH huh, HUH*," Lila grunted, her voice falling into a low, pumping rhythm. Maura recognized these as the sounds of childbirth.

Suddenly Lila's voice broke into an eerie, trilling falsetto. "*Wah wah wah wah wah wah wah wah wah wah wah wah wah,*" she wailed, lips stammering. Then her voice dropped to resume its husky grunting.

"*HUH huh, HUH huh, HUH huh.*"

Jim turned to Maura and Steve. He said Lila was giving birth to souls in the kingdom of God—as if that explained anything.

Lila fell silent. The she stood up and walked into the living room. Maura, Steve, and Jim followed after her.

By now it had grown dark. Maura and Steve lit kerosene lanterns and placed them around the cabin. The children gazed down from the loft as the adults arranged themselves in the living room.

It was time to talk. To *really* talk.

Maura listened closely as Jim and Lila laid out their vision for a spiritual army. God had called them to leave the church, they said, to take up arms against the forces of secularism and mainstream Christianity. Maura struggled to follow along, but Steve, engrossed, started talking about his early experiences with religion. He'd "tried to live a Christian life," he said, but he'd "never felt the guilt of sins roll off my back."

Lila's voice turned harsh. "Why don't you just serve God?" she said.

"I don't know," Steve replied.

A moment passed. Then, without warning, Steve's eyes filled with tears. He began to weep. He slid off the couch and onto the floor.

No one said anything. The sound of Steve's sobs filled the cabin.

Then Lila jumped to her feet. "Come out of him, spirit of rebellion," she bellowed.

A spasm jerked through Steve's body, and he began twisting and contorting on the floor. He started making noises, too, wailing, howling, yelling, cursing. To Maura, he almost sounded like Lila back in the bedroom.

Lila roared at Steve from across the living room. "I command the spirit of the living God to come into him, and cleanse him, and be in him, and fill him.

"Come out of him," she continued, as if speaking to some force within Steve. "Come out of him in the name of Jesus!"

But Steve kept jerking, howling, and crying.

Then, just as swiftly as the bizarre scene had begun, Steve's body went limp. The cabin was silent except for the exhausted huff of his breathing.

No one but Steve can know what really happened that evening in the woods. Perhaps he was putting on a show. Perhaps he was actually possessed. Or perhaps his longing for transformation was so intense that the right provocation could send him into what felt like an involuntary spiritual convulsion.

For years Steve had been consumed with guilt, much of it sexual in nature. He'd lived a life of "fornication and all manner of filthiness in the flesh," he later said. He'd lusted after his preteen stepdaughter, enough that "I started leaking in my pants. That scared me to death and I thought then, 'Man, what is in me to feel and do such a thing?'"

Into this morass of self-loathing Lila had extended the possibility of release, not through a standard Christian rite like confession but through a kind of exorcism Lila called deliverance. Steve's sins were too big for a prayer in a pew: He needed something commensurate to his guilt, something *physical*. Lila "told me the truth about myself which no other minister would do," he later said. It was a relief, finally being seen as the sinner he knew himself to be.

The Greens spent the night at the cabin. The next morning Lila continued on her crusade. "There is a spirit of gold mining that lives in these parts," she said, in reference to the gold rush that had overtaken the area in the 1840s and fifties. "You must be on guard against it." She showed Maura and Steve how to drive out demons by stomping on the floor.

Maura didn't know what to think. She'd heard almost nothing about demons or possession in her years as a Christian.

Several weeks later Jim and Lila returned to French Gulch to baptize the Schmierers in a creek near the house bordered by daffodils. Maura, Steve, and the kids had been baptized once before, but this latest immersion represented the beginning of a new commitment to Lila and Jim's vision. Maura remained confused by what had happened to Steve the night of the Greens' earlier visit, but they were a couple, a team. Wherever he would go, she would go. Wherever he would stay, she would stay.

Anxious to have a spiritual experience of her own, Maura went out into the woods one day to try speaking in tongues. When a strange word bubbled up from within her—"*Shondalamahi!*"—she headed back to the cabin hopeful God was at work within her, too.

Steve communicated more and more frequently with the Greens as the summer continued. Then one day he proposed moving back to Sacramento to be closer to Jim and Lila. Maura wasn't altogether opposed to the idea. It would be nice, having her parents around, and she certainly wouldn't miss washing everyone's clothes in a pot on the stove. Sacramento would also be a new adventure, another chapter in her search for meaning and truth. She remained unsettled and confused by Steve's "deliverance," and wondered if his attraction to Lila was merely physical. But maybe he was right. Maybe God wanted them more intimately connected to the Greens.

Still, there were times when she was overcome with foreboding, an intuition that moving back to Sacramento was going to lead to the end of her marriage. She couldn't say why, exactly. But the feeling was there all the same.

On their last night at the cabin, Maura walked outside to the garden. She'd put so much of herself into this little patch of earth, coaxing tomatoes, zucchinis, carrots, and beets from the soil. Steve had even buried Maura's placenta following Lilly's birth: Maura was quite literally part of the land. Now she was saying good-bye to all of it, every fence post and grasshopper, every worm, flower, and cucumber vine.

She looked up at the sky. Another perfect night, another bedazzlement of stars. She listened as an owl hooted from deep within the woods.

CHAPTER 7

By the 1970s, fundamentalism had effectively become a socially and politically conservative subset of evangelicalism: a more uncompromising contingent of generally older white believers repelled by what they saw as the moral and spiritual failures of the era. Evangelicals more broadly, however, operated under a bigger tent of belief, one that had room for moderates, conservatives, and even some liberals. The rigid partisan boundaries that would later transform "evangelical" into a byword for "Republican" hadn't yet been drawn: In 1976, when Maura and Steve converted to Christianity, a majority of evangelicals favored Jimmy Carter, a Democrat and a born-again Christian, over his Republican opponent, Gerald Ford.

Many evangelicals, however, argued for the separation of politics and religion (though in practice they could be forthright in their patriotism, or even nationalism). As Virginia pastor Jerry Falwell said in 1965, "Preachers are not called to be politicians." For some Christians, staying out of politics was a biblical mandate. "Render to Caesar the things that are Caesar's," Jesus had said, "and to God the things that are God's."

Falwell's own perspective on the matter had changed by the mid-seventies. Patriotism was everywhere in 1976, not just the "Year of the Evangelical," per *Newsweek*, but also America's bicentennial. Falwell sought to capitalize on this public fixation by raising money for a Bible college he'd founded in Lynchburg, Virginia. "The school's colors changed from green and gold to red, white, and blue," writes journalist Tim Alberta. Falwell traveled the country with a song-and-dance "I Love America" tour.

But Falwell had bigger goals. In 1979, he met with conservative political leaders to discuss how Republicans might harness the largely untapped voting power of fundamentalists and evangelicals. He founded an organization, the Moral Majority, that raised the alarm about controversial issues like abortion, pornography, drugs, and homosexuality. In the 1980 presidential campaign, Falwell went all in on Republican presidential candidate Ronald Reagan, who won the White House by a staggering 440 electoral votes. Falwell and his allies played an important role in that victory, building an impressive electioneering apparatus to help rally Christians to the cause.

The long-term consequences of this new coalition would be significant, not just for the Republican Party, but for white American evangelicalism writ large. Falwell had tasted success, demonstrating the mutually beneficial effects of narrowing the separation between church and state. Finally integrated into the halls of power, he saw victory ahead.

"We are fighting a holy war," Falwell said, "and this time we are going to win."

Falwell's proclamation tracked neatly with Jim and Lila's own spiritual evolution. They, too, were embracing a new militancy, just as many Christians were entering the battle against "secular humanism." That Jim and Lila had been *part* of that foundational depravity made their new spiritual militancy all the more noteworthy. They were cause and effect, insurgency and counterinsurgency. They'd helped create the same America they now wanted so desperately to destroy.

By 1981, the Greens had been living in Sacramento for about a year. Initially Jim and Lila were hired to counsel orphaned children, but, as Sarah remembers it, when Jim was fired for being rough with a child, Lila left with him, taking an overnight job typing up patients' charts at the same medical center where her brother had died a decade earlier. Sometimes she told Sarah and Josh about the people she'd seen at work, imbuing her stories with an air of warning: *Be careful, or you too could end up like this....*

For all her intensity, Lila could be kind and caring when she wanted to be. She taught Sarah, now in third grade, how to sew and how to cook. She made fresh-veggie salads, tacos, and low-sugar coffee cakes. She attended parent-teacher conferences and stayed up with Sarah and Josh when they were sick. One day she made Sarah a red octagonal card with the word "STOP" inscribed in white letters on the front. Inside, Lila had written, "I want you to know that I love you."

But Lila was also a woman of great and growing contradiction. She excoriated a teacher who gave Sarah a book about witchcraft. She told Jim to destroy his paintings, drawings, and homemade moccasins—"works of the hands" that brought glory to Jim rather than to God. (Jim, unemployed and increasingly subservient, did as he was told.) Lila even became falsely convinced she was pregnant, as if willing to life a child that her body, ravaged by Josh's difficult birth, was apparently incapable of carrying.

The Schmierers moved to Sacramento in late August 1981, and Maura felt uncomfortable there from the start. She and Steve had always thought of themselves as different from the kind of people who lived in ticky-tacky neighborhoods, and yet here they were, settling down in a bland tract house with wall-to-wall blue carpeting and a leaky waterbed. The street was called Trail End Way, and for Maura, the name came with an ominous undertone: The end of what, exactly?

Steve worked at a sewing machine company while Maura stayed at home with the kids. At least twice a week they got together with the Greens to hear Jim and Lila preach and pray. People who went to regular churches were just "ten percent Christians," said the couple. Jim and Lila, however, were going to build an army of "one hundred percent Christians" who followed God without compromise or accommodation.

Lila and Jim practiced deliverance, too, on Steve, Maura, and even the children, who often cried whenever demons were summoned from their bodies. Maura never had anything but a minor response to the strange ritual, shaking slightly or coughing, but never with the same vigor Steve had shown back at the cabin.

One day Lila gave Maura a book to help her better understand the critical importance of deliverance. *Pigs in the Parlor* had been published eight years earlier amid an explosion of interest in exorcism—yet another spiritual trend the Greens had picked up on and incorporated into their own lives. (William Peter Blatty's 1971 novel, *The Exorcist*, and an Oscar-winning film adaptation of the same name were in many ways responsible for the upsurge.)

Pigs in the Parlor, written by married couple Frank and Ida Mae Hammond, argued that deliverance should be a regular spiritual practice like prayer or fasting. It could be a messy, savage business: Demons resisted expulsion by writhing, wailing, or burping from within their host subjects, the Hammonds said. There were demons for all kinds of sins and vices, too—not just obvious things like pride or envy, but for nicotine, even caffeine.

In its extreme, frenzied emotionalism, deliverance fit in perfectly with the charismatic movement of the 1960s, while also offering a version of the same frothy fervency many found in the hippie movement. And yet Frank and Ida Mae Hammond didn't see their ministry as an expression of the same forces that had produced the counterculture. Far from it. To them, deliverance was an explicit reaction *against* the social upheavals of the era. "It is no coincidence that beginning in the late 1960s the Holy Spirit began equipping the saints with more specific knowledge of deliverance," they wrote. Society's moral decline had led to a proliferation of "great Satanic activity"—and a corresponding need for deliverance.

For years Jim and Lila had practiced Christianity without any awareness of the strange spiritual rite. This unfamiliarity, they now believed, had been the root cause of the separation they'd long felt from God. Jesus had told his disciples, "In my name they shall cast out devils." And yet the church hadn't acted accordingly. The Greens weren't about to make the same mistake.

Around the time the Schmierers moved to Sacramento, Maura's nine-year-old daughter, Sarah Chelew, began spending more time with her father, Rick, who lived in Los Angeles. Steve objected to the arrangement—he said Rick spoiled Sarah, who in turn contaminated the other children with her worldliness. When Rick called the house to speak with Sarah one day, Steve snatched the phone from Maura's hand and told Rick he was no longer permitted to see Sarah.

"She's not your daughter anymore," Steve snarled. "She's mine." Maura looked on in stunned silence.

Maura tried to push back, but Steve said it was God's will. Several days later Maura was served legal papers; Rick was determined to have a relationship with Sarah Chelew even if it meant getting the courts involved.

As the court date grew closer, Steve coached Sarah in what she should say to the judge. Then, in a sudden reversal, he told Maura she needed to "let Sarah go." If Sarah couldn't spend *all* her time with Steve, Maura, and the Greens, she couldn't spend *any* time with them.

Maura was as confused as she was devastated. *This can't be God*, she thought. *God wouldn't do this to me.* But by now she was accustomed to suppressing her emotions, skilled at pushing aside her own doubts. The habit of compliance was becoming engrained.

About a week after Sarah went to live with Rick, Maura sent her a card for her tenth birthday. Lila told Maura she was to have no further contact. "You must relinquish Sarah fully." And so she did.

Was it happening? Was Jim and Lila's nascent ministry transforming into a cult?

Cult. A word heavy with fear and judgment, mockery and bewilderment. A swift, curt monosyllable stuffed with so much baggage that many scholars refuse to use it altogether, preferring instead wan, impotent terms like "emergent religion" or "new religious movement." But what these terms fail to imply, what the word "cult" so energetically suggests, is an air of mystery, zeal, even madness. People who speak ill of cults like to think of themselves as immune to their loopy, menacing ways. But embedded in that gleaming slash of a word—*cult*—is the faint suggestion, the fascinating possibility, that under the right circumstances, any "normal" person's defenses might fall. That they, too, might join.

The Greens' ministry, such as it was, remained too open, too integrated into the outside world, to qualify as a cult. Yes, Lila had separated Maura from her daughter Sarah. Yes, Lila claimed to have a singular connection to God. But she still had her job at the medical center. The kids still went to school. Whatever exploitation the Greens inflicted on the Schmierers was minimal. The two families didn't live together, or wear the same clothes, or perform the same duties. They didn't eat the same food or hold the same jobs.

Yet the trend line was clear, and it pointed ominously and decisively in the direction of cultism. When the ministry *would* become a cult—when its extremism would tip into Jim Jones territory—was hard to say. Change so often happens on a gradient: Blue is still blue until somehow it is purple, the shift hard to pinpoint but irrefutably *there*. That a precise threshold doesn't readily reveal itself hardly means a major change hasn't taken place. Because it has.

Despite Maura's ongoing misgivings, she felt as if she had "no reason not to believe." God had saved the Greens while on mission trips through South America, they said, and Lila's knowledge of scripture seemed so comprehensive—she clearly knew more about the Bible than Maura did. But perhaps the most important factor in Maura's acquiescence was that she *wanted* to believe. She *wanted* to perform deliverance with the same vigor as Steve, if only to repair her fraying marriage. It was by eradicating her misgivings, she figured, by tamping down on her internal rebellion, that she might find her way back to her husband.

About a month after Sarah Chelew went to live with Rick, Steve told Maura to cut off contact with her parents.

"They're not your mom and dad anymore," he insisted. "They're not of God."

Maura suspected the instruction had come from Lila and Jim, but she felt she had no choice in the matter. What was she going to do, divorce Steve and move out? It was unthinkable. Maura was thirty-three, a mother of four. She would do as her husband told her.

Her mother was confused and saddened when Maura called to say good-bye. "I can't explain why," Maura said. "You wouldn't understand."

One day Steve discovered that thirteen-year-old Iantha had written a letter to Maura's parents and announced that she needed to go live with them: Clearly her heart wasn't in the ministry. When Maura pushed back, Steve threatened to divorce her.

For years things had been good between them. Steve had been Maura's handsome handyman, her caring lover. They almost never argued. Now he was becoming someone Maura didn't recognize.

Iantha lasted several weeks at her grandparents' place before asking to come home. Steve and the Greens allowed her to return but made her send back a box of gifts her grandparents had given her while she was living with them. "I'm doing this for Jesus," Iantha wrote in a careful cursive note she included with the box.

> I have to. I want to be closer to him. I covet too much. Don't take anything against dad . . . he's the greatest. These things are very hard to give up, I need to though. Sorry if I hurt you, the lord wants me to do this. The Garfield folders, shoelaces, feather clip and Chariots of fire tape are what I got with the allowance you sent. Here's all the stuff. I don't think I'll ever see you again.

Jim and Lila decided to call their budding organization Free Love Ministries, a surprising choice, given the couple's contempt for the counterculture. But to Greens, the name made complete sense. God's love was, after all, free. If the hippyish vibes scared away regular Christians, well, all the better. The Greens didn't want those "spiritual masturbators" around, anyway.

The two families began to make small illustrated booklets, or "tracts," to promote the ministry, distributing them at bus stops, in phone booths, and on campus at UC Davis. Before long, people were dropping by the Greens' and Schmierers' to hear Jim and Lila rail against the wantonness of the world, the iniquity of the mainstream church. Among the drop-ins was a short, soft-spoken man named David Gains. He had a wife and a daughter and owned several frame and art shops in and around Sacramento.

Which is to say, he had money.

Soon it was the fall of 1982, a year since the Schmierers' move to Sacramento. By now Maura was pregnant again; Steve said the child, Maura's fifth, would inherit Maura's demons if she didn't give them up during deliverance, a possibility that terrified Maura, even as her skepticism remained. *Lean not on your own understanding*, she told herself. *God's ways are far above your ways.*

The baby was born in November. Steve named him Steven, fawning over the child at the hospital with Lila as if Lila were the mother. The attraction between Steve and Lila seemed clear.

At Lila's instruction, Maura agreed to have her tubes tied. She was fine not having more children: Five was enough. After the operation, however, Lila forbade Maura from taking pain medication, which she said could open Maura up to satanic invasion. A doctor recommended that Maura spend the night at the hospital, but Steve insisted they leave. Someone was playing music down the hallway. If they stayed any longer, he said, the baby could be demonized by a spirit of rock 'n' roll.

CHAPTER 8

Sarah Green hops on a bike and races beneath the noisy elevated freeway. She glances back to see if anyone has caught her, but they haven't—not yet, anyway. She pedals as fast as she can, urging Nathaniel and Josh, also on bikes, to *hurry up, c'mon, let's go!* Sarah is ten. The boys are seven and eight. It is a temperate morning in early spring of 1983, and they are off to do some adventuring.

Within a few frantic minutes the kids have arrived at the old brick schoolhouse. The lower-floor windows are boarded up with plywood. A fence covered with No Trespassing signs circles the property. Sarah and the boys pay these prohibitions no mind, ditching their bikes and slipping through the same opening in the fence they always use. They sprint to the side of the building, where a dug-in stairwell leads them to a pair of basement-level exit doors. The doors are chained shut—but this is no impediment, not to these explorers, who give the doors a quick, decisive yank. A slim opening appears. One by one they squeeze inside.

They've been here before and have come prepared. They flick on their flashlights, filling the dark basement with a dim, Duracell glow. It smells damp and urinous down here. It smells *old*. Sarah hears the sound of dripping, or at least she *thinks* she hears the sound of dripping, though maybe it's just the effect of the Nancy Drew novels she's been reading at the library on the sly. Life for Sarah—and for Nathaniel and Josh—is now defined by an increasingly inflexible set of rules and restrictions. The Greens and the Schmierers have recently moved to a trio of adjacent homes half a mile from the schoolhouse. This relocation has corresponded with a host of other changes. Meetings take place daily. A growing number of strangers drop by to listen to Sarah's parents. The sense of strictness, of oversight, is growing ever more pronounced.

Sarah leads the boys up the basement stairs and into a classroom where the ceiling tiles hang haphazardly above them. There is a poignancy to the space, to the way it summons the spirits of the children who once studied here. That's how it feels to Sarah, in any case. She and the boys press their hands to the wall. *Can you feel anything?* The echo of a former teacher, maybe, or a student.

Sarah is enthralled. Her parents allow her only limited access to her friends outside school hours; whenever Sarah sees them, Lila denounces them bitterly: *Is she wearing pants? Is she wearing makeup? She's a whore, she's going to hell.* There is a kind of mystical companionship, then, in the specters Sarah feels in the schoolhouse.

She and the boys make their way back into the hallway and up another set of stairs. It is brighter up here, where the windows aren't obscured with plywood, and the sunlight casts the space in a dusty, apocalyptic haze. At the top of the tower they look down at the freeway, at the pleasant, humdrum neighborhood where they now live. Sacramento is the City of Trees, and from up here—one of the highest points in the area—the name seems wholly appropriate. City of sycamores. City of cedars. City of redbuds, elms, and palm trees.

City of bougainvillea, bushy green and pink.

City of governors, immigrants, and floods.

City of seekers.

On their way back down, the kids accidentally knock over some bottles that have been left on the steps. The clinking, crashing sound echoes throughout the building. Sarah and the boys shriek with gleeful terror.

It grows dark again on the first floor, where thin slits of daylight shine in from around the plywood. Nathaniel, blond and gentle faced, is the youngest of the three children and the most apprehensive. Sometimes he gets nosebleeds when he's nervous. Nathaniel is close with Sarah and Josh; their families are too intertwined for them not to be. But the Green children sometimes pick on him in a way that—can it be?—almost resembles the way their parents treat his mother. Like Maura, Nathaniel often has a slightly forlorn look on his face.

Josh is more easily ebullient. He makes jokes, mimics people, and speaks in an English or Scottish accent.

By now the kids have arrived in the dressing rooms for the auditorium. The sense of a spirit world is especially strong here; again, the kids press their hands against the walls, feeling out the current, listening, listening. They cover their ears with their palms and then pull them away, which, Sarah says, makes them more alert to the room's buzzy supernatural frequency.

She guides the boys out to the darkened stage, where they put their ears to the floor. *Is that the sound of tap dancing?*

They stand up, shine their flashlights into the auditorium at the hundreds of empty seat backs that are pressed together like so many headstones.

Who were the kids who once sat here? What were their lives like?

Did they play kickball?

Did they eat corn dogs?

Did they go swimming?

Were they allowed to watch television? Did they have sleepovers? Did they try on their mothers' makeup?

Did they read Nancy Drew in the open, without fear of being caught?

Sarah and the boys stand together in the weighted silence. They flick off their flashlights—and all is darkness.

CHAPTER 9

The three houses formed an unassuming cluster at the corner of X and 23rd Streets, within audible distance of the elevated freeway just a block to the north. The Greens took the main house, an old bungalow with steep entry steps and a wide, domineering porch. It stood maybe ten feet above ground—a relic of Sacramento's early days, when the city flooded with almost biblical frequency. The Schmierers moved into the first of the smaller adjacent Tudors; David Gains, who'd recently left his wife and young daughter to follow Jim and Lila, took the second. When they removed the fencing between the houses, the property was subtly but importantly transformed. No longer was this a modest street corner in an ordinary working-class neighborhood. Now it was "Fort Freedom," a military base with a "Citadel" (the bungalow) and a pair of "Barracks" (the Tudors).

David Gains almost certainly funded the purchase of the properties with his income from the frame and art shops. Lila's salary helped a bit at the beginning, but she soon quit her job to spend more time receiving visions in a "prayer closet" in the Citadel. Jim meanwhile spent his days holed up at a drafting board, drawing tracts to promote the ministry's message around Sacramento.

Sarah and Josh shared a bedroom on the main floor of the Citadel. They slept in low-clearance military bunk beds and stored their belongings in steamer trunks, the Spartan furnishings a marked contrast to the filigreed lighting fixtures and intricately carved brass doorknobs that filled the house.

Jim and Lila held meetings in a room just off the walnut-paneled parlor. By now their theology had come to a partial clarity. Members of Free Love Ministries were "Manifest Sons of God," elite believers who would reach a state of "sinless perfection" through prayer, deliverance, fasting, and missionary work. It was time to "raise up a people," Lila said, to prepare the way for Christ.

"You may not find it in the Bible," Lila said, "but you can know it is true, because we have heard it directly from God."

The Greens weren't content simply to spread their message throughout Sacramento, however, or even America. From the beginning they had ambitions to travel abroad and to recruit spiritual soldiers from throughout the developing world. Until they took an actual mission trip, they would mail tracts to churches and other organizations across West Africa and beyond. Maura had no idea how they'd established contact with these faraway believers.

For now the Greens and the Schmierers remained connected to the broader Sacramento community. The kids still attended public school. Sometimes they went to the library or even the ice-cream parlor. Sarah liked to visit an antiques shop near the compound where she bought cheap but beautiful artifacts: an old lace dress, a pair of baby shoes with tiny leather buttons sewn into the sides.

Steve earned his contractor's license and started taking jobs around Sacramento, plowing much of his income back into the ministry. Maura continued to suspect he was physically and emotionally attracted to Lila. When he gave Maura a bouquet of flowers, he gave one to Lila, too; when Jim bought Lila a bathrobe, Steve did the same for Maura. He was often off talking with Jim and Lila at the big oak table in the Citadel—about Maura, she often suspected.

Chief among Maura's sins was her reluctance to beat her children. Lila said six-month-old Steven was too loud and squirmy during meetings, and that Maura needed to whip him into submission, just as Jim had whipped Sarah and Josh when they were young. In an effort to appease Lila, Maura gave the baby a quick swat on the backside. Steve, however, did exactly as Lila directed, thrashing the baby with a belt until large welts were visible on his backside. (A former ACMTC member later confirmed that Steve inflicted "severe child abuse" on the child at Fort Freedom and that the boy was sometimes "covered with bruises.")

"God's love is not as man's love," the Greens insisted. "God's love is stern, hard."

Part of Maura wanted to believe this was true, if only to better align herself with her husband and the Greens. But another part of her remained confused, in turmoil over what was happening to her family. She thought about running away with her kids, but that seemed impossible. She wondered if Lila was right, if she really *was* leaning on her own understanding.

She was at home in Barracks 1 early one evening when Steve summoned her to the camellia bushes along the sidewalk, where Lila was waiting for them.

"Take off your wedding ring," Steve said.

Maura asked what he was talking about.

"It has demons," Lila said. The ring had once belonged to Steve's mother, whose husband, Steve's father, had possibly committed suicide. Now the ring was cursed.

"Take it off and throw it in the gutter," Steve said.

Maura looked down at the gold band on her left ring finger. She didn't want to throw it away. But she figured that keeping her family together meant doing exactly as Steve and Lila demanded. Resigned, she pulled the ring from her finger and tossed it down the storm drain.

Lila and Steve weren't finished. "That one, too," Lila said, pointing at the wedding band on Maura's other ring finger. It was the ring Carlo had given Maura all those years earlier, the ring she'd promised to wear forever.

Who could've predicted things would turn out like this? That Lila Green, radical hippie turned pseudo-Christian prophet, would command her late brother's caretaker to discard a ring he'd offered Maura on his deathbed? That Maura would feel she had no choice but to obey? That she would look down at her hand, pull the ring from her finger, and then toss it—*clink*—down the gutter?

* * *

At this point Jim and Lila held more or less equivalent leadership positions at Free Love Ministries, though Lila's status as a prophet gave her a certain special authority. Sometimes Jim asked why he didn't receive visions, too. "You're not the source," Lila hissed. "You're not the vessel." Jim generally accepted Lila's explanations, while also struggling with the nontraditional structure of his marriage—this in spite of his almost panting love for his wife. It was a remarkable shift from those days in the Bear Tribe a decade earlier, when Jim had displayed an unbending, even ferocious machismo.

Lila argued that biblical prohibitions against female priests had been misinterpreted. "I've got news for you," she wrote in an evangelizing tract.

> If God can't find any men who can do the job, then He will use women. If men are so stinking carnal minded and so dead in their trespass and so dead in their sins that they won't be spiritually minded, then God will raise up women who will obey Him.

As to the New Testament admonition that wives should submit to their husbands, Lila offered a withering rejoinder: "If you're not walking in God, don't expect any woman to submit to you. Why should she submit to a dog? Why should she submit to a blasphemer? Why should she submit to an adulterer? Why should she submit to a lying hypocrite? So she can damn her own soul like a hypocrite is damned?

"I'm not preaching feminism," she maintained. "I'm preaching righteousness." Still, it was impossible not to hear, in Lila's arguments, an echo of her time in college as a women's activist. This was second-wave feminism by way of Christian fundamentalism, a curious alliance of sensibilities that, to Lila, was hardly curious at all.

It was also part of a long tradition of female religious leaders in America—Ann Lee of the Shakers, Ellen White of the Seventh-day Adventist Church, Mary Baker Eddy of Christian Science, among others. Even in the colonial period the "most active [Quaker] preachers were often women," writes Philip Jenkins. Female cult leaders, too, have long been a staple of America past and present, from Bonnie Nettles (who cofounded Heaven's Gate in 1974), to Elizabeth Clare Prophet (founder of

Church Universal and Triumphant, 1975), to Nancy Salzman (cofounder of NXIVM, 1998), and Amy Carlson (founder of Love Has Won, mid-2000s). Scholars have argued that cults and cult-like groups can provide women with leadership opportunities otherwise unavailable to them: that these groups are in effect reactions against the restrictions of patriarchal society.

Lila was merely the latest entrant in this tradition. "Now as never before there is a need for women to return to their place of dignity which was originally given to them by God," she exclaimed in a tract. Women were "the most untapped natural resource left in the earth!!!!!!!!!!!!"

As the weeks and months went by, Jim and Lila only grew more fixated on demonization, another obsession that was reflective of trends in the broader culture. Three years earlier, in 1980, a Canadian psychiatrist and one of his former patients had published a book about the patient's "recovered memories" of child abuse. The woman, who went by the pseudonym Michelle, claimed that a group of satanists had confined her to a snake-infested cage and forced her to watch as babies and animals were murdered, among other sensational allegations. According to scholar Joseph Laycock, "Michelle" even said "her teeth had been removed and horns and a tail had been surgically grafted onto her body." *Michelle Remembers* was later discredited, but by then it was too late: The book was a huge bestseller.

With Jonestown only a few years in the past, cults still had a grip on the public imagination, thanks in part to the ongoing if diminished clamor of the "cult wars": the mostly fruitless efforts of distraught families to "rescue" loved ones through legislation, public pressure, and new methods of "deprogramming." Now, in the 1980s, the cult boom was on the decline. And yet *Michelle Remembers* still spoke to an ongoing anxiety that satanic cults could be hiding in plain sight.

That anxiety intensified in 1983 when a schizophrenic woman in Manhattan Beach, California, claimed her two-year-old son had been sexually abused at daycare. The ensuing media and law enforcement frenzy ignited other investigations around the country suggesting that a vast network of satanic cults had molested thousands of children "with drills, masks, and snakes," per one accusation, "in meat markets, bathrooms, and car washes," even forcing them "to throw babies against a wall."

"Today we have found Satan is alive and thriving," reported the prominent television show *20/20*, "or at least plenty of people believe it is."

There was only one problem. Almost none of it was true.

Investigators were "singularly ill-equipped" to interview the alleged victims, according to a child abuse lawyer consulted by the *New York Times*. The investigators asked leading questions, often refusing to believe children who denied abuse. "Anytime I would give them an answer that they didn't like, they would ask again and encourage me to give them the answer they were looking for," one former daycare student recalled years later. "I would try to think of the worst thing possible that would be harmful to a child." He said he drew on the rituals and iconography he knew from the Catholic Church to help fabricate especially lurid descriptions of exploitation.

"I'd just throw a twist in there with Satan and devil-worshipping," he said. Only then would the adults leave him alone.

The Satanic Panic, as this shameful episode became known, would ensnare hundreds of innocent adults and traumatize countless young children. Here was a modern-day witch hunt, a true moral panic that revealed the delusional capacities of otherwise reasonable adults. In the end, researchers found that "investigators could not substantiate any of the roughly 12,000 accusations of group cult sexual abuse based on satanic ritual," according to the *New York Times*.

In 1983, when Jim and Lila launched their ministry in earnest, the truth had yet to come out. Many Americans were actively worried that demonic cults had infiltrated their communities in precisely the kind of satanic overthrow Jim and Lila said they'd been called to fight. The irony, however, was that even as Free Love Ministries positioned itself in opposition to the demonic forces promoted by these alleged cults, the Greens were starting to display elements of the very cultism they denounced.

To help promote the ministry, the group purchased airtime on KFIA, a Christian radio station where Jim hosted a show called *Battle Cry*. Local pastors wrote letters objecting to Jim and Lila's increasingly frenzied broadcasts, and eventually KFIA kicked the Greens off the air. ("We didn't want to be associated with one of those cultish groups," the station manager told a reporter.) The Greens moved to an open-access radio station and started distributing tracts on campus at UC Davis, in bus stations, and around low-income housing developments. The booklets were filled with screeds against yoga, tight jeans, homosexuality, abortion, television, and, above all, the institutional Christian church.

At first the visitors came one or two at a time, drop-ins who'd heard about Jim and Lila from the radio, or from tracts, or through friends. Within a few months more than a dozen people were regularly stopping by the compound.

They were nurses and construction workers, alcoholics and veterans, punk rockers, college dropouts, and aspiring pilots. They lived on the streets, or went to college, or came from backgrounds of great privilege. They were in their teens, twenties, or thirties; they were white, Black, Hispanic, and Native American. Many moved on after a meeting or two. Others came by again and again.

Brenda Eutsler, for one.

She was seventeen, with Farrah Fawcett hair and a rose tattoo on her left ankle. Her parents had divorced when she was four. She moved frequently as a kid and had trouble making friends. At twelve, she tried to kill herself; in tenth grade, she dropped out of school. She had no structure, no direction. So when her boyfriend's brother told her about Free Love Ministries, she decided to attend a meeting. Maybe the group had something to offer.

It did. It had Lila. In the pulpit she could be a fearsome figure, cold and imperious, but one-on-one she knew how to perform kindness and consideration. One day she gave Brenda a sandwich with carefully chopped bits of bell pepper she'd mixed with the tuna fish. It was a small thing, but to Brenda, a young woman cast about by life, it didn't *feel* small. It felt like real care. Another time Lila returned from the bulk foods store with a flat of Kern's pear nectar drinks. She'd remembered (*how?*) they were Brenda's favorite.

Brenda attended services at the Citadel with growing regularity. Soon she began to feel something she'd never felt before. She felt like she belonged. So when Lila told Brenda and her boyfriend, who also attended meetings, they should move onto the compound, of course they said yes. Brenda started working at David Gains's art shop, as did several other new recruits, and even drew a small salary. It was an ideal setup in every possible way. Brenda had housing, community, a job. She had a *purpose*.

A version of this story would play out over and over again as the months went by. High schooler Julie Padilla left a life of booze, gangs, and parties to follow the Greens. Rachel Johnson, an alcoholic, quit her job as a psychiatric nurse to move to the compound. A former Air Force member came to the ministry consumed with guilt about his past: He said he'd slept with sixteen different sex workers while stationed in the Philippines. Derek and Lisa Dye were unemployed when they first arrived at the compound, but they quickly received jobs at the art shops.

The Greens bought a fourth house adjacent to Barracks 3 when it came on the market, almost certainly with significant financial assistance from David Gains. Fort Freedom now straddled a sizable portion of the block. Curious neighbors asked what was going on, particularly when Jim and Lila put up signage and raised a flag above the compound. But no one meddled. The Greens weren't doing anything illegal. They kept the property spotless.

Inside the Citadel, however, every evening the group exploded into a frothy, cacophonous frenzy. Members fell from their chairs, wailed in tongues, and convulsed on the floor. One day several boxes arrived at the compound containing military uniforms: collared button-downs, pleated khaki pants and skirts. Eventually all twenty or thirty members were given military ranks to match the outfits. Jim and Lila were Lieutenant Colonels. The children were Privates.

Group members signed loyalty pledges, burned old baby photos, and severed connections to unconverted friends and family members ("blood ties"). Sarah and the other children were pulled from school. Eventually Lila also encouraged members to change their names as an indication of their new lives in Christ. Steve became Philip. Iantha became Rebekah.

Not everyone was rechristened—Sarah, Jim, Josh, and Maura remained as they were—but Lila herself took a name from the Old Testament.

"Villagers of Israel would not fight," proclaims the book of Judges, "they held back until I, Deborah, arose, until I arose, a mother in Israel." So, too, would Lila arise. So, too, would Lila—would *Deborah*—call forth an army of holy chosen soldiers. Even the group itself received a new name to match its growing militancy. Free Love Ministries was over. In its place was born the Aggressive Christianity Missions Training Corps.

CHAPTER 10

It can be comforting to think of oneself as invulnerable to cults. But for decades researchers have studied the membership of extremist groups—not just cults but terrorist cells and other similar factions. And for decades many researchers have come to a similar conclusion. No clear personality profile exists. All of us are vulnerable.

The word "cult" may evoke images of bug-eyed lunatics, deranged people waiting on a hilltop for a spaceship to whisk them off to Jupiter. But the reality is that many cult recruits are far more conventional, far more *relatable* than we might care to admit. Two-thirds of cult members come from what clinical psychologist Margaret Thaler Singer describes as "normal, functioning families." There's an eerie banality to her finding that "the majority of adolescents and adults in cults come from middle-class backgrounds, are fairly well educated, and are not seriously disturbed prior to joining."

This is not to say that everyone is vulnerable to cults at all points in their lives. Timing appears to be a decisive factor: After a breakup, a job loss, or any other major life transition, the call of cultism becomes harder to resist. To the impossible, persistent question, "Who am I?" cults offer a clear, unambiguous answer: *You are a follower, you are a soldier, you are a member of the holy chosen few.*

Some clinical psychologists reject the "Not Me" myth, or the idea that everyone, no matter their history or personality, is at risk of joining a cult. Their studies find a higher incidence of troubled backgrounds, substance abuse, and psychological problems among cult recruits than in the general population. And yet the prevalence of "ordinary" men and women in many cults is as inarguable as it is unsettling. A German study from the eighties categorically rejected the stereotype of cult members as mentally unstable. "In fact," writes cult scholar Eileen Barker, "there was a higher proportion of 'not-normal' cases among the control group." Barker even goes on to suggest that a "happy, secure home background" can actually make a person *more* likely to join a cult. Having grown up in an ordered, loving environment, a person stymied by the difficulties of adulthood might be especially open to groups that promise to re-create the warm, ordered environment they once knew.

Most cult recruits are driven not by extremism but idealism. A cult may offer the chance to make the world a better place; and it is for this reason that many cult evangelists emphasize the social justice aspect of their ministries. Cult recruiters are furthermore disinclined to approach people with obvious mental difficulties: They want people who can *do the work*. Some cults "have attracted disproportionate numbers of highly educated, accomplished recruits," writes journalist Zoë Heller, as was the case with the Aum Shinrikyo cult, which released sarin gas on a Tokyo subway in 1995, killing thirteen people in the immediate aftermath of the attack and injuring thousands more. Education, in other words, isn't necessarily a defense against recruitment.

In 2008, *The Guardian* reviewed a restricted British government report that tried to determine who, precisely, is prone to joining a terrorist cell (perhaps the most extreme version of a cult). Recruits are "demographically unremarkable," the report found. They have families; they have jobs; they are of average intelligence. As *The Guardian* put it, there is "no more evidence of mental illness or pathological personality traits found among British terrorists than is found in the general population."

A shocking finding—but also one with a certain chilling logic. Cults and other "totalist" groups (as social psychologist Alexandra Stein calls them) speak to the most primal, most animal needs of our species. They promise love and community. They promise purpose and camaraderie: a kind of anti-loneliness. To widespread contemporary ailments like isolation, social atomization, and spiritual emptiness, cults also offer both an emotional panacea *and* practical assistance. They provide housing, employment, food, and childcare. They provide *clothes*. The thinness of the American social safety net may help explain the prevalence of cults in the United States: Why wouldn't a person consider joining a group that so comprehensively meets their material needs?

Most provocatively, cults promise a top-shelf, high-proof version of the spiritual fulfillment billions of people find in more conventional spiritual practice. Religion is the deepest answer to our own transience, an attempt to resolve the disunity at the heart of everything. Every human being "craves to be consoled in his very powerlessness," writes influential philosopher William James, "to feel that the spirit of the universe recognizes and secures him, all decaying and failing as he is."

And so we go to Mecca. So we go to synagogue. So we mythologize the stars and spill the blood of goats and make windows out of stained glass, God shattered into a thousand shards of color.

And so we join cults. Whatever religion promises, cults promise in excess. If devotion is good, more devotion must be better. If discipline is good, more discipline must be better, too. Moderation is nothing but watered-down decadence. All the way is the only way. It is God, neat.

Of course, no one ever really "joins" a cult. They join what they believe to be an alternative community, or an especially devoted religious group; only gradually does the organization's extremism reveal itself. The process of becoming a member, too, can be so slow as to appear nonexistent. It starts with a meeting or two. Then the leader invites the person to stay—temporarily, of course, while they get back on their feet. A month passes, then another. By now the recruit is too busy, too tired, to see friends on the outside; and anyway, their entire world is increasingly with the group. Alternate, opposing voices disappear. Daily life may be difficult, but it makes the member feel valued, important. Soon they become distrustful of the outside world, where people *just don't understand*. They work and pray, work and pray. Months pass, and then a year.

A year. The group is home.

Cult expert Robert Jay Lifton, a pioneer in the process of what he calls thought reform, says that becoming enmeshed within a cult often involves two key processes: confession and reeducation. When a recruit reveals, to a leader, the deepest parts of their soul, they hand over a kind of spiritual kompromat, an admission that can build an anxious loyalty to the leader, who rebuilds the person in their own image, creating a new sense of self oriented entirely to the group—reparenting, as this process is known.

People also join and stay in cults for non-nefarious reasons. Members may feel they are doing something important, or that they have been chosen by God. They may enjoy being surrounded by like-minded people, within a community that shares their values. Writer and scholar Amanda Montell notes that cults can be rewarding at the cellular level: "Our brains release feel-good chemicals like dopamine and oxytocin when we partake in transcendent bonding rituals."

But most of the factors that keep a person stuck—that pull them deeper into fanaticism—are more obviously malicious. A tightly controlled environment allows a leader to block information that doesn't suit the group's purposes. A lack of food and sleep can weaken a recruit's defenses, making it difficult to see the abusive reality of their situation. The recruit may have quit their job or abandoned their partner; they may have scorned their family, left school, or given up all their worldly possessions. Their entire community is *here*, within the physical and emotional confines of a group that may appear bizarre to an outsider but to the recruit is simply home. There is also the "sunk cost" factor: To leave a cult is to acknowledge the error of joining in the first place, an acknowledgment that may be too difficult, too painful, to accept.

This is to say nothing of the fear, the terror, that to leave a cult is to risk eternal damnation—to throw oneself into the hot blue flames of hell.

Leaders aren't, however, exclusively cruel to their followers. They can't be: It is often through the occasional burst of kindness that people are often drawn in. Just as Brenda Eutsler felt seen and appreciated by Lila Green, who gave her such carefully made sandwiches; who bought her pear juice at the bulk foods store, so, too, do many cult leaders alternate between harshness and love, between care and punishment.

Social psychologist and cult survivor Alexandra Stein argues that cults are built on so-called disorganized attachments, where a single authority figure serves as a source of both care and mistreatment, as when a parent provides food and shelter to a child while also abusing them. So it is with the cult leader and their followers. The result, says Stein, is "fright without solution," a state that can trigger dissociation, or a split between what a person thinks and feels. Recruits may be exhausted, or in pain, or starving, but they lack the capacity to fully examine *why* they are exhausted, or in pain, or starving. The disorganized relationship has effectively left them psychologically disabled.

And yet people do retain some element of agency through this process. Most cult scholars dismiss the concept of brainwashing, by which they mean a process of mental manipulation that categorically shuts off a person's decision-making capacity. Montell writes, "Simply put, you cannot force someone to believe something they absolutely do not on any level want to believe." The fascinating and disturbing corollary, then, is that some people may actually *want* to sacrifice themselves to the authoritarian leaders they follow. The mental coercion that appears so horrific to outsiders may, in fact, be part of a cult's appeal. "This moment of submission," writes Stein, "of giving up the struggle, can be experienced as a moment of great relief, and even happiness, or a spiritual awakening."

It feels good to follow. To join a group or to trust a leader is to absolve oneself of the burden of agency: which shoes to buy, which principles to believe. We may insist that we want to make these decisions ourselves, and on some level we surely do. But another part of us, a more unspoken part, *doesn't* want to accept the responsibility of action. We are like so many schoolchildren, running out onto the playground, gape mouthed, in search of a game to join, a friend to follow. *What should we do today?*

In the Old Testament, the Israelites beg God for a king to rule over them. He tells them a king will turn their sons into servants, their daughters into bakers. A king will take their fields, their vineyards, and their sheep. "Ye shall be his servants," God says. "And ye shall cry out in that day because of your king which ye shall have chosen you; and the Lord will not hear you that day." But the Israelites refuse to listen. They don't care about all they stand to lose. It is almost as if they *want* to lose it. "Nay," they insist. "But we will have a king over us."

And so they get one.

CHAPTER 11

The sky, dark. The freeway, quiet.

The bleary-eyed residents of Fort Freedom stumble into the basement of the Citadel, recently converted into a sanctuary. It is 5:00 a.m., a typical morning at X and 23rd Streets, where between twenty and thirty men, women, and children now live as soldiers in God's holy chosen army. They wear pressed khaki uniforms and black undershirts; the women sport deliberately uncomfortable leather shoes Lila calls pride busters.

Silently everyone files into the bland, brown-carpeted space. They sit in rows of metal folding chairs facing a simple wooden lectern at the front of the room.

Lila, now called Deborah, steps forward and launches into a prophecy. "I say that I the living God will vindicate myself upon those who plot against my beloved," she intones. "I say that I will crush them, I say that I will scatter them as dust in the streets."

Sometimes Deborah gets down on the floor, thrashing about in a wordless muddle of sound. Other times she stumbles around the room, gyrating and thrusting with an almost sexual fervor. Deborah is in her late thirties, a trim woman with a dramatic jawline, a tight uniform. When the Holy Spirit seizes control of her body, a shadow of her old hippie wildness emerges. Bobby pins go flying from her head. Her wavy hair whips and snaps in a brownish, libidinal blur.

After the service, members change into their work clothes and head to breakfast. The mess hall is located in the basement of recently purchased Barracks 3, adjacent to Barracks 2; members eat oatmeal, eggs, or potatoes, unless they eat nothing at all. "Ten times as much work gets done when we don't eat," Jim tells a reporter profiling the group. "And when you fast, you're more sensitive to God."

After the meal the adult members change into white shirts, black slacks, and black skirts. They struggle to stay awake as they commute to the art shops that largely finance the ministry, renouncing the demons of fatigue that tempt them back to sleep. At the art shops, they work with customers, build frames, cut glass, and bag hardware. In the back they listen to recordings of the Old Testament as they work. Store policy is to blot out satanic images that appear in artwork brought in for framing, like unicorns and frogs.

Back at the compound, Sarah, Josh, Iantha (now called Rebekah), and Nathaniel spend the morning in the small freestanding "schoolhouse" the group has built in the shared yard space behind the four barracks. The kids' instructor is a UC Davis dropout named Alberto; he is funny, a skilled pantomimist, but he seems to know nothing about teaching. Jim and Deborah remain uninvolved in the children's education—they are too busy listening to God and making tracts in the Citadel.

After lunch, the kids join the adults at the three frame and art shops where they work for a dollar an hour, or minimum wage when they're older. It is only here that group members have any meaningful interaction with the outside world. The broader Sacramento community, however, is well aware of the Aggressive Christianity Missions Training Corps, or ACMTC. The *Sacramento Bee* has recently investigated the group, noting that Alberto's parents have hired a lawyer in an unsuccessful effort to extract him from the group. (In response, Alberto tries to get a restraining order taken out against them.) Distraught family members have attended meals at Fort Freedom, falsely suggesting they are thinking about joining the group, but when Deborah picks up on their intentions, she bars them from the compound.

At the end of the workday, members return to Fort Freedom, where they shower, change, and then reassemble in the sanctuary. Again, they sit dutifully listening to Jim and Deborah, both recently promoted to Brigadier General. At one point Deborah confesses she is jealous of Mary Magdalene, how close she was with Christ. Members play the guitar and the drums, improvising songs through the power of the Holy Spirit. They open their Bibles at random to read whatever verses God has chosen for them.

Always, too, there is deliverance: the retching, the wailing, the jerking. "*You can't make me,*" shrieks a demon from within a young male subject, howling against all commands of expulsion. "*You can't make me, you can't make me!*" Jim says a person can be demonized with up to six thousand evil spirits at a time.

Members slash the air with invisible demon-slaying swords. They run in circles and stomp the floor to "put Satan underfoot." They crawl around on the carpet, noses pressed to the carpet, to learn about humility. By now Deborah can get her followers to do almost anything she wants. Brenda Eutsler has agreed to get the purple rose tattoo removed from her left ankle. Aspiring pilot Mike Spoerhase has burned his old flight log, an irreplaceable record of hundreds of hours of effort.

After the service it's back to the mess hall for dinner. Members make spaghetti, salad, and canned oyster soup on a rotation. When the meal is over, the cleaning crew gets to work as the others head back to the barracks to take care of household chores. Once a week Jim and Deborah conduct white glove inspections, searching for dirt in sock drawers, on the top of ceiling fixtures.

In the evening, members collate tracts in the Citadel, stapling and stacking the shouty, colorful booklets in an assembly line. "HEAVY METAL, KISS OF DEATH!" the tracts proclaim. "WHILE CHRISTIANS SLEEP, COMMUNISTS WORK . . . *TO DESTROY CHRISTIANITY!*" Some pamphlets include lifestyle tips, as when Deborah promotes a recipe for "travel bars" she says God told her to make. "Although the devil tormented me," she writes, "I obeyed the Lord and the results were delicious, nutritious, and kept very well under conditions of extreme heat and humidity."

The tracts are distributed throughout Sacramento and mailed across the world. Jim and Deborah have contacts in Uganda, Togo, Jamaica, India, Ghana, Ethiopia, Nigeria, Mozambique, and beyond, though the mechanism of this outreach remains mysterious. The couple has even led several in-person visits to their correspondents abroad, also almost certainly financed by quiet David Gains. Members have established a clinic to serve "primitive Negrito tribals" in the Philippines who are "addicted to a native narcotic plant," according to ACMTC literature.

The group receives up to fifty messages a day from far-flung letter writers. "Thank you for saving my life from Satan fire," a man writes from Ghana. Another Ghanaian follower says, "General Deborah, I have heard women preach before but your preaching has been one of the most anointed. Fire burns in my bones at any moment when I am listening to your sermons on cassettes." Members spend hours each night responding to these letters.

By ten o'clock the kids have crawled into their sleeping bags. The adults do the same at around eleven; everyone sleeps on the floor to prepare for the difficulties of the mission field. Even now, however, the day's work isn't complete. Members who have guard duty wake for hour-long shifts throughout the night, traipsing to the sanctuary or walking around the property to pray for God's protection. When they wake the next morning, they have gotten no more than four or five hours of sleep.

In its relentlessness, its exhaustion, its personality-destroying uniformity, everyday life at the Aggressive Christianity Missions Training Corps operated as a near-perfect mechanism of control. Denied all external perspective, members struggled to see their treatment as exploitative. There was no time to reflect on anything, not between the meetings and the meals and the shifts at the art shop. Jim and Deborah had carved out a core vacancy in their followers and filled it with a pernicious, soul rattling fear. Members wondered if they were doing right by the Greens, if they were doing right by *God*. The only way to address these anxieties was to try harder, to press closer, to retreat further into a prison that often felt, to its inmates, like no prison at all.

As the group descended further into madness, Maura's confusion only grew stronger. Whole weeks passed in an exhausted, uncertain haze; she still struggled to perform with the spiritual flamboyance that came so easily to Steve and many others. Deborah said Maura's difficulties with deliverance, and her reluctance to beat her children, indicated that her heart was full of rebellion. Deborah reminded Maura what Jesus had said: "If any man come to me, and hate not his father, and mother, and wife, and children, and brethren, and sisters, yea, and his own life also, he cannot be my disciple."

The Greens' frustration with her only grew more pronounced as the months went by. Steve, too, was becoming even angrier, as if her attempts at improvement only highlighted her ongoing failures. He told Maura she was holding him back; if she didn't pull herself together, he was going to divorce her. She was terrified of losing her family, terrified of what lay beyond the walls of Fort Freedom. Deborah told her she would be a shopping cart lady if she couldn't hack it at Free Love Ministries. And Maura believed her. She knew that without the group, she would have nothing. She would *be* nothing.

Was she a true believer? Against the heavy mudslide of her fear, the question was almost irrelevant. "He wears a mask, and his face grows to fit it," writes George Orwell. For so long Maura had worn that mask. Now, at last, her face was growing to fit it.

Reality was warping. Maura could barely see beyond the next hour, or, at most, to the end of the day. Uniforms, Bibles, chairs, tracts: The world had narrowed to a limited and repeated refrain of textures, sights, and sounds. One day she had a daydream where Jim got into an argument with a stranger outside Fort Freedom. Maura imagined the stranger pointing a gun at Jim's chest; in the daydream she ran from the house and hurled herself between the two men just as the stranger fired. Maura survived the imaginary shooting, but with an injury significant enough to win back Jim and Deborah's favor. She had sacrificed herself for them. She had bled on their behalf. Perhaps now, finally, they would love her.

CHAPTER 12

It was 1986, three years since the move to Fort Freedom, and two years since Jim and Deborah had pulled Sarah from school. She was thirteen now, and still felt the loss keenly—no more friends, no more history class, no more afternoons spent snacking on ice cream and chatting with the boy at the convenience store. Before things had become so fanatically regulated, she'd hung out with a Catholic girl down the street from Fort Freedom, but the girl's parents had found out about the group and barred their daughter from seeing Sarah. When Sarah showed up at the girl's house anyway, the friend handed Sarah a tortilla made by her grandmother. The tortilla was a farewell: Their friendship was over.

At one point Sarah swallowed a handful of Tylenol in a semi-serious attempt to kill herself. Another time she decided to run away, and even went through with the plan, calling a taxi and spending the night at a friend's house. When she arrived at the local high school the next morning, however, the police quickly took her back to Fort Freedom. Sarah remembers Lila expressing false motherliness when the cops appeared with her on the front porch of the Citadel, thanking them, and assuring them that Sarah *just needed to get back on her medication.*

Jim and Deborah were supposed to go to the Philippines that very day for a mission trip, but Sarah's attempt at running away had caused them to miss their flight. As punishment, the Greens decided to take her with them—and to make her stay there for several months, long after the primary crew departed. Sarah would live with married members Julie Padilla and Bernie Gudino, who'd been assigned to spread the Aggressive Vision in Cagayan de Oro. When Sarah returned to California, she would be a changed young woman, chastened and obedient.

Mindanao is a majestic place, an island full of rainforests, beaches, and waterfalls. There are skinks and geckos, lemurs and water buffalo, egrets, herons, and crocodiles. On arrival, however, Sarah is too filled with anger to appreciate any of the natural splendor. She starts getting cramps on a bumpy Jeep ride away from the coast, but her mother is unsympathetic. "This is God judging you," Deborah says. "You're feeling this pain because of what you did to us."

Sarah hands out tracts and listens to her parents preach at the local churches. This is among the group's first excursions abroad since a fateful trip to Malawi several months earlier, when twenty-nine-year-old ACMTC member Brad Rankin died after contracting malaria. Rather than taking the young man to a doctor right away (he was ultimately admitted to the hospital), Jim and Deborah had performed deliverance on him; they couldn't send people home "just because they don't feel good," they said. The Greens have always said war is a bloody business, that they need to be prepared for the worst. Brad's death is merely proof of this unavoidable fact.

Deborah and Jim leave the Philippines after several weeks of work, leaving Sarah with Julie and Bernie in a house with spotty electricity and no running water. It is a basic existence. And yet as the days go by, Sarah is filled with a slow-building elation. Her parents are more than seven thousand miles away. Julie and Bernie are often busy giving medical help to people in rural areas. Sarah has far more independence here than in Sacramento.

There's homeschooling to do, and plenty of chores, but when Sarah's daily duties are complete, she goes down to the street to hang out with a group of sisters she has befriended. She watches them massage avocado through their hair until it gleams with an oily black radiance. She meets the local boys, too, among them a young man named Gabriel. He is fifteen, dark haired, and speaks near-perfect English.

Gabriel and his friends ride BMX bikes for fun, and sometimes Sarah hops on with him, careening down the street under the dappled shade of the mahogany trees. They go to an indoor food court where they buy ice cream, cake, and deep-fried plantains rolled in turbinado sugar. They eat in an open area where a large television plays MTV—as foreign an experience as Sarah has ever had in her life. She doesn't spend time alone with Gabriel, though they do hold hands.

One afternoon Gabriel arrives at Sarah's house on a bike. He tells Sarah to come watch the arrival of a massive rainstorm now approaching the island.

When they get to the beach, the sky has turned into a multitude of grays: ominous, majestic, alive. Sarah and Gabriel look at the unsettled water. Should they jump in? They could get swept out to sea or struck by lightning. Of course they shouldn't jump in.

They jump in.

They are still swimming when—*crack! boom!*—the clouds split open. For a moment there is no division between sea and sky, the world a single watery swirl. Sarah and Gabriel find their footing in the sand. They clutch each other tightly. The moment is not quite romantic, and they do not kiss, but still, Sarah has a thrilling realization.

So this is what it's like to have a boyfriend.

She stands with Gabriel, their bodies united in the roaring din, until eventually the rain begins to lighten. Below them the fish coil and flick in the water.

CHAPTER 13

Scattered snowflakes blew against the window of Maura's brown Volvo station wagon as she drove through the quiet Sierra foothills. It was January 10, 1987. Sixteen years had passed since Maura had moved up here to join the Bear Tribe, but the landscape was just as beautiful as ever: hawks circling overhead, pine trees standing mute and majestic against the sky. ACMTC had recently opened a frame shop in Placerville, forty-five minutes east of Sacramento. As manager of the store, Maura made the drive there and back often. She liked having the time by herself to think.

There was plenty to think about, namely a whole new set of regulations Deborah had just announced. Maura had accepted most of them without complaint, but the rule that most frustrated her, the one that had actually made her cry, was on its face relatively minor. Deborah said all female group members had to wear their hair pulled back in a bun—a look that flattered Lila, with her hawkish face and piercing emerald stare. Maura, however, had always felt self-conscious about her tall forehead, hiding it with bangs since childhood. But when Maura told Steve she was upset, he'd been as biting as ever.

"Grow up," he said.

Steve. Despite everything that had happened between them, Maura still loved and desired him, and held out hope that he would come back to her. The evidence was not in her favor. If anything, Steve's contempt had only grown more palpable. Maura didn't beat their children hard enough, he said, didn't prioritize God over her family. She had a demon of motherhood, an evil spirit that was making her favor her family over God and the group.

It was evening by the time Maura arrived back at X Street. Steve ignored her when she entered Barracks 1, same as he always did. Maura showered, put on her uniform, and hurried across the backyard to the sanctuary, where the evening service was already in progress. Everyone was seated in the metal folding chairs, their uniforms crisp and clean.

Jim was in the midst of an unexpected announcement. "God's doing a new thing in our midst," he said from the front of the room. "He's taking us off the deep end."

The Greens frequently made grand, sweeping pronouncements, but this seemed like something different. "We're entering a new dispensation," Jim continued, "and no uncleanness, no rebellion, will enter into it. Tomorrow morning, one of you is going to be judged by God. That person is going to wish they'd never been born."

A tremor of anxiety passed through the room.

Deborah then launched into an especially venomous prophecy. The object of God's forthcoming wrath was a "stiff-necked person," she said, "a thorn in his side. . . . Ye, they shall be judged by God's hand. Ye, they shall lie down in sorrow; ye, they will be put to shame."

At dinner, no one spoke except for Jim, Deborah, and Steve, who sat at their own table, chatting among themselves with jarring lightness. The silence among the rest of the group was only broken when David Gains looked up from his spaghetti. "You just don't know," he said. "You wonder, like Peter, 'Am I the one, Lord?'"

Members glanced at each other as they tried to eat. Who had Jim and Deborah been talking about? Was it Rebekah, eighteen and recently pregnant? Was it her husband, Mike? Was it Brenda, Alberto, Jacque, John, or any of the others?

Maura knew they had nothing to worry about. It was her—it had to be her. Now Steve's growing cruelty made sense. He'd known what was coming all along.

After the meal Maura left the mess hall and stumbled back to Barracks 1, speechless with dread. She curled into a fetal position on the bedroom floor. The entire world had fallen away. Nothing remained for her but the appalling certainty that all was lost.

Steve came in about an hour later. By now Maura's fear had curdled into terror.

"Is it me?" she said through tears. "Is it me? Am I the one?"

"I don't know," Steve said, leaning against a cabinet with untroubled, paternalistic ease.

"I don't understand," Maura replied. "I don't understand where I'm missing God."

Steve suggested she go speak with the Greens. Perhaps they could beseech God for mercy on her behalf.

Filled with a rush of resolution, Maura got up off the floor. She would make this right: She would humble herself before Jim and Deborah. She walked across the backyard and entered the Citadel.

If Maura had felt even a modicum of hope, it disappeared the moment Deborah opened the door to her office. Immediately Deborah pulled back, repulsed, as if Maura were drenched in sewage. "Wait here," Deborah said. "Let me go get my husband."

So it really was her.

Deborah returned with Jim and ushered Maura into the office, where Maura fell to the floor. "I don't understand," she said. "I don't understand what I've done."

Without speaking Deborah walked to her desk and pulled out Maura's most recent donation to the ministry: twenty-seven dollars, a biblically mandated 10 percent of her last paycheck. Deborah threw the bills to the floor and spit on them. Then she launched into a prophecy. Maura needed to repent, Deborah said, or she would die on the vine, would perish in body and spirit.

When Deborah was finished, Jim told Maura she could leave.

"Go in shame," Deborah said.

Maura gasped her way back across the compound to Barracks 1, where again she collapsed to the floor and wrapped herself in a blanket.

"What did they tell you?" Steve asked.

"I am the one," Maura moaned. "I am the one." Her face was dry. By now she'd passed the point of tears.

* * *

The next morning Steve ushered Maura into the sanctuary, where Deborah addressed the group from behind the lectern. "God's judgment has fallen on Maura," she said. "In outright stubbornness she has rejected God—and thus he has rejected her."

Maura was to serve as the camp's cleaning woman. That was her punishment: to wash the floors and scrub the cars and clean the dishes. She was effectively a nonperson now, Deborah said, and if anyone encountered her around the compound, they should turn their head away from her. Even Maura's own children were to avert their eyes. If Maura proved her obedience, she might be permitted back into the group. But there were no guarantees. In the meantime, she would be called Forsaken. To illustrate her status as a fallen woman, she would wear a white sack dress and a navy headscarf.

In the evening, Maura gathered everyone's dishes from the mess hall and took them back to Barracks 1 to wash them in the sink. Lilly, Nathaniel, and Steve watched her from the living room.

"Daddy, what's wrong with Mommy?" Lilly asked.

"She's not your mother anymore," Steve said.

Maura looked at him in horror. "Steve?"

"Shut up," Steve snapped. "Turn around and do the dishes."

And so it began—a Grand Guignol of suffering that would continue for six impossibly hellish months. Maura spent her nights in the chop shop, a prefab metal structure behind Barracks 3. She spent morning services at the back of the sanctuary, face pressed into the corner. During the day, when the chop shop was in use, she tried to hide behind an oak tree; when it was too cold outside, she tucked herself next to a flimsy plywood clubhouse where Sarah, Josh, and Nathaniel liked to play. She cleaned the floors, washed the vans, chopped wood, and picked dead leaves from the camellia bushes.

The Greens told her to write letters confessing her wretchedness. "I have taken God too lightly and my repentances have been fake," Maura admitted. "No lasting change. I've been a drag on [the group]. I've been stupid. I deserve to be spit upon. How I long to be re-enlisted. If Captain

Schmierer would be pleased to take me back, I would be a good wife & mother."

At night, shivering on the concrete floor of the chop shop, she dreamed of Jesus. She dreamed of Steve. She dreamed of Rebekah, Nathaniel, Lilly, and Steven. She dreamed of her second daughter, Sarah Chelew, whom she hadn't seen in years. Now Maura was on the verge of losing everyone else, too, and it was this awareness, coupled with her own clawing terror of hell, that kept her from running away. She considered killing herself but knew that suicide would only guarantee eternal separation from God and her family. Better to endure this living death for the chance, however small, of being readmitted into God's Army.

One day a ruddy-faced blondish woman appeared in the door of the chop shop. It was Jacque, a fellow ACMTC member whose brother, Brad, had died in Malawi. Maura had known Jacque for years. And yet when Jacque spoke, it was as if they'd never met.

"Hello," Jacque said. "I'm Barren." She, too, had been cast out of the group for the sin of idolizing her family; she, too, had been given a degrading new name.

As the days passed, the two women washed and painted the houses. They woke at 3:00 a.m. to scrape putty off Steve's tarps below the freeway. Eventually they were moved to the plywood playhouse—just five feet tall, with no windows, just a peephole in the door and a single fluorescent light. It rained for several days after the move, water seeping up through the floor and into their sleeping bags. Whenever Maura looked through the peephole to watch her children, Jacque chided her for giving in to temptation.

The privations grew even more excessive as the weeks went by. Maura used old napkins for sanitary pads. She urinated in a tin can when the chop shop was locked. When her shoes grew ragged, she wrapped her feet in plastic to stay dry.

In February, a month after Maura's judgment, a male group member appeared at the clubhouse with a stack of forms for Maura to sign. They were divorce papers.

Crying, Maura asked if there was anything she could do to save her marriage. The man shrugged. "Keep looking to Jesus," he said.

"Everything precious to me is gone," Maura wrote the Greens. "A position in [God's] Army, my spiritual family, my husband who now abhors me and is devorcing me, the beloved children of my womb, my job—all rightes and priveledges—but most cutting is the seperation from God."

Eventually Maura signed the papers. When Jacque received divorce papers, she signed them, too.

Sarah Green returned from the Philippines in late January. She and Maura had never been close, if only because of the twenty-five-year age gap between them. But whenever she dropped off the women's meals—six peanut butter sandwiches a day—she also brought an illicit snack. Maura was especially moved when Sarah sneaked her a chocolate chip granola bar. She'd remembered they were Maura's favorite.

Maura didn't know it at the time, but Sarah was struggling mightily, too.

The judgment was still ongoing when a male member maybe ten years her senior approached Sarah in the sanctuary. His ACMTC name was John Green: He'd taken Jim and Deborah's surname as a marker of his devotion to the group.

"I have to get something off my heart," he said.

Sarah asked what he was talking about.

"I spoke to your parents and they approved. I'm asking you to be my wife."

Sarah scoffed. She'd just turned fourteen. Obviously this was a joke.

But John was insistent. Deborah and Jim had approved the match.

Sarah stood still, betraying no additional response. "I need to talk to my parents," she said, heading upstairs.

Sarah's body had changed while she'd been in the Philippines, and the men around the compound had noticed. She had hips and breasts now. Her face was increasingly angular. She tried to make herself seem unattractive by acting like "one of the guys," cracking jokes and even eating less. But the act was getting harder to pull off. The unstoppable march into adulthood had begun.

Jim and Deborah seemed to be expecting Sarah when she appeared outside their bedroom.

"What did you say?" Deborah asked before Sarah had a chance to speak.

So it wasn't a joke.

"I don't think this is legal," Sarah said.

"It's God's will," Deborah said. "He came to me and told me you were going to be the Mother of Nations. I foresee you having six to eight children."

A hot rage rose to Sarah's face. The situation was suddenly clear. If her parents could marry her off and force her to produce children, she would remain lashed to the ministry forever. A husband was just another way to prevent her from running away again.

"*This is illegal,*" Sarah replied. "*This is illegal, this is illegal.*" Deborah had arranged marriages within the group, but never with anyone as young as Sarah.

"*I hate you,*" Sarah screamed, turning and running to her bedroom.

Deborah proudly announced the engagement to the group the next morning. Sarah's face turned red. She felt like she was going to vomit.

In the days that followed, Sarah ignored John or shot him a withering stare. If she had to get married, she wasn't going to make it easy for him.

She was in the chop shop one afternoon when John appeared from behind her, wrapping his arms around her with wolfish satisfaction. "You can't run from me," he said. "We're meant to be."

Here it was, Mexico all over again, the memory of the rapes lodged within her, not so much a memory as part of her body.

But Sarah wasn't four years old anymore. Now she could fight back.

Quickly she scanned the chop shop. It was scattered with hammers, saws, screws—and razors.

She pulled herself from John's grip and grabbed a blade from the table. Then she whipped around and plunged the razor into John's arm. She went deep.

John fell back, stunned, his face white, blood dripping down his arm. Still gripping the razor, Sarah turned around and marched back to the Citadel.

* * *

That Sarah could fight back, not just against John but against her parents—against the entire project of ACMTC—was something of a mystery. Certainly, she was fully a member of the group, living, working, and praying as the others did. She spoke with the same faith-inflected vernacular that reflected her birthright citizenship in ACMTC: Failed Christians were "backsliders"; law enforcement officials were "persecutors." But this linguistic allegiance didn't correspond, in Sarah, with the same fervency of belief demonstrated by many of the adult members. "Belief" wasn't even much of a consideration for her—she figured it didn't matter what she thought of her parents' teachings, they simply formed the fundamental infrastructure of her life. Sarah was a member of the group by virtue of her bloodline, and if this didn't necessarily protect her against cultism, it did help explain why she felt indifferent to the most deranged proclamations of her parents. She hadn't chosen this life: *It* had chosen *her*. She knew what things were like on the outside; she knew what she was missing. In this way, her desire for something different wasn't a turnaround. It was, instead, an intensification of the same curiosity and world-hungriness she had shown since childhood.

At Fort Freedom, that world-hungriness expressed itself in small ways, namely her antiques collection. Her favorite item was an old rectangular brush that had stiff boar bristles and an embossed silver handle. Sarah loved that brush, loved it so much that she never once ran it through her own hair. She didn't want to disturb the ghosts of the women who'd owned it before her.

It was only a matter of time, however, before Deborah condemned the collection as idolatrous. One day several members took everything into the backyard, where they smashed, ripped, and chopped it all to pieces. From her place in the clubhouse, Maura could hear Sarah's screams.

Early one evening in late February, almost two months after Maura's initial judgment, Steve knocked on the door of the clubhouse. "At seven o'clock, you're coming to the sanctuary for court," he told Maura and

Jacque. The two women were confused but also excited. Perhaps Jim and Deborah were about to admit them back into the group.

At the appointed hour, the two women entered the sanctuary. Everyone sat stoically uniformed, same as ever. But something was different. A table had been placed at the front of the room. Gradually Maura understood. The table was a witness stand, and she and Jacque were on trial.

The two women took their seats at the table, facing out toward the group. Steve and Deborah sat next to each other in the front row, their backs turned to Maura and Jacque. Jim walked to the lectern and called the room to order.

He'd only just started speaking, however, when a young woman with a baby was ushered into the space. Maura recognized the woman as Lisa Dye, one of the ministry's few Black members. Lisa and her husband, Derek, had just returned to Sacramento after a nine-month mission trip to the Philippines. On their arrival back at the compound, Jim and Deborah had ordered the couple to get divorced for the sake of their "spiritual betterment." Their commitment needed to be to the group, not each other.

The baby was taken from Lisa's arms as Jim directed her to the third chair at the witness stand. Forsaken and Barren had been through a difficult test, he said. Now they would be allowed to eat the leftovers from the mess hall. But their trials were far from over.

Jim said the three women were on trial for what he called spiritual adultery. They'd been unfaithful to God, had cheated on their heavenly father by prioritizing their husbands and their children. They had made an idol of the family, and now it was time to "smash that idol." Henceforth Lisa was to be known as Despised. She would live with Forsaken and Barren in the clubhouse.

Spiritual adultery. The term neatly distilled so much of the psychosexual energy that animated the Aggressive Christianity Missions Training Corps. Jim and Deborah were obsessed with the erotic, perpetually raging against the "whoredoms" and "harlotries" of the world. But the effect of these denunciations was to cultivate a kind of backward fixation on sex, if only to denounce it. The Greens' screeds against fornication, homosexuality, promiscuity, and other sins of the flesh expressed an almost pornographic glee, a kind of imaginative indulgence in the very sins Jim and Deborah so fervently condemned. To disavow impurity was, in fact, to *fixate* on impurity, to turn it over in one's mind, to picture its many expressions in all their thrusty glory.

It rained for four days after Lisa's judgment. There wasn't enough room in the clubhouse for the three women to sleep stretched out, so they lay on the floor with their knees pulled up to their chests. Maura's despair ballooned into a kind of manic frenzy. "I've always prayed for a vision of Hell believing it would give me an aggressiveness to fight for the soul of men," she wrote. "Praise God; He's answered my prayer. I have literally been dangled over hell and I feel such fire inside to fight the devil and lay down my life in the Lord's service."

Lisa was disturbed by Maura and Jacque's deterioration. "They seemed to slip in and out of insanity," she later recounted. "At times they were incoherent."

Lisa was also deeply concerned about her one-and-a-half-year-old daughter, who'd been diagnosed with "primary complex tuberculosis" back in the Philippines. The baby needed treatment.

Five days after the trial, Lisa sneaked into the chop shop to call an acquaintance for help. The friend called the police, who arrived at Fort Freedom later that day to give Lisa an escort off the property. Lisa told the officers "the ministry had her baby," though Jim said Lisa "could have her baby," and that he'd told the three women "they were free to leave at any time." After further negotiation with the Greens, the police reunited Lisa with her daughter—and not a moment too soon. The girl's eyes rolled back into her head. She moved listlessly, as if drugged.

Maura and Jacque still longed to return to the ministry, but not Lisa. That afternoon she and her daughter left Fort Freedom once and for all. A doctor later said the baby's arm was abscessed. Any further delay in treatment could have required amputation.

Maura's tribulations, however, were just beginning. She would remain under the judgment for the next four months, her punishments only growing in their gothic extravagance. She wheelbarrowed cinder blocks. She pulled nails out of old lumber. When she was moved to Barracks 1, she noticed her children's old yellow and white crayon scribbles in the closet. Now her kids turned away from her whenever they encountered her in the backyard. Rebekah's baby was due soon, and Maura wondered if she would ever see it herself, or even learn if it was a boy or a girl. At the peak of her misery Maura was driven to a notary, where she signed over custody of her children to Steve. She barely understood what she was doing.

"Oh, how I've grown to abhor my self!!" she exclaimed with operatic but still authentic misery.

One day Steve stormed into Barracks 1 with four-year-old Steven, whose normal kidlike behavior around the compound had earned him the nickname Steven the Demon. The boy was Maura's now, Steve said, this in spite of his custody rights to the children. Maura had been an adulterous wife, Steve said, not just to him but to God.

Some time later Steve came to Maura with the command she'd been dreading. She and the boy needed to leave Fort Freedom that evening—it was over.

Quaking with the near certainty of her future in hell, Maura called her mother, whom she hadn't seen or spoken to in about five years. Her mother picked them up at the compound that evening and took them home with her; the next day, Maura called Fort Freedom and begged Deborah to let her return. She would be better! She would be so much better! Deborah said she would consider Maura's request but also accused her of flirting with her four-year-old son.

Maura waited another agonizing day before calling again. No Deborah. She took a bus downtown, where she found a pay phone, and again tried fruitlessly to reach Deborah. Frantic, she checked into a hotel with Steven and called Fort Freedom yet again. This time she managed to reach Deborah, who said she would allow Maura one last chance at redemption. Ecstatic, Maura thanked Deborah for her extraordinary generosity.

But the next several weeks at the compound were to prove excruciating. Deborah said demons were waking up Steven in the middle of the night and ordering him to deface the compound, so Maura tied the boy to her wrist to keep him with her at all times. In the midst of all this, Jacque was permitted back into the group, but Deborah seemed to have no intention of extending this same grace to Maura. She was a witch, Deborah said, a sore on the group. She could kill herself now or wait to die, it didn't matter in the end. Hell was surely in her future.

Then, on July 6, 1987, almost six months to the day since Maura's banishment to the chop shop, Jim came to her room with the final verdict. "God told us there's no place for you in his army," he said. The Greens had done everything they could for her. Their efforts had failed. Now it was time for her to leave.

Maura had been an eager and devoted nurse's aide when, at twenty-one, she'd met Lila Carter in the Sacramento Medical Center. Now she was thirty-eight, ruined in every possible way, disgraced in God's eyes and her own. As a young woman, she'd set out in search of signs and wonders. What she'd found instead had been a kaleidoscope of suffering.

She called her mother again and packed her few belongings—a clock, a Bible, a fan. Brimming with despair, she left Fort Freedom for the last time. Her one consolation was that Deborah had allowed all her children to remain at the compound. Maura might be damned, but there remained some hope for the kids. At least there was that.

PART TWO

THE BLESSING

CHAPTER 14

They howl and they screech. They tremble and they moan. They hurl themselves to the floor, close their eyes, shake their limbs, and speak in "Indian" tongues. They pick invisible berries from invisible fruit trees and run naked through the woods. They draw circles in the dirt, curse the circles, jump inside them, and pound their feet like pistons. At night they break into the neighbors' homes, yelping and screaming until everyone in earshot area is awake.

During worship, they stamp so forcefully that the floorboards have to be reinforced. The men bang their heads against the rafters when they jump up and down, enough that their faces become covered in blood. To illustrate the extent of their persecution, they "[hang] a woman by the neck"—but only briefly, before she expires.

At the center of this mayhem is a rawboned mystic, illiterate and blue-eyed, the daughter of an English blacksmith. She and a handful of followers are on the run, fleeing mobs who attack them with horse dung and fire hooks. The woman's name is Ann Lee, but her followers call her Mother, for that is what she is to them: a caretaker, a leader, a teacher. A creator.

It is the early 1770s, in and around Manchester, England. Mother Ann's followers have dissolved the bonds of their earthly families—wives are no longer wives, husbands are no longer husbands. They believe in pacifism, collective ownership, and the equality of the sexes. They are celibate. They are called the Shakers.

In the 1740s, when Ann Lee was a girl, her family's squalid home was so cramped she could hear and perhaps even see her parents having sex. According to historian Chris Jennings, Lee "chastised her mother for submitting" to the lust of her father, who whipped her for meddling: the opening skirmish in a lifelong war Lee would wage against the erotic. As a young woman, Lee was "constantly pregnant," per Jennings. All four of her children died in infancy or not long thereafter; the youngest was wrenched out of her with forceps. Clearly, the wages of sex was death.

By this point Lee had joined up with a group of celibate, renegade Quakers known derisively as the Shakers. They worshiped by "trembling, shaking, and screeching in the most dreadful matter," reported one commentator. The intense physical expression reflected the presence of God working within them, and their reaction to his majesty in their lives.

In the early 1770s, Ann Lee and several other Shakers were locked up for disturbing a local church service. On Lee's release from jail, she was a woman transformed. God had given her a vision of the Garden of Eden, she said, and now she knew the truth. It was Adam's lust, not Eve's rebellion, that had brought sin into the world. Did not the snake bear a striking resemblance to a certain male sexual appendage? Had not Jesus died a virgin?

The book of Revelation foretold of "a woman clothed with the sun, and the moon under her feet, and upon her head a crown of twelve stars." Ann Lee was that woman, the flesh-and-blood manifestation of a returned Christ-Spirit. Under her leadership the group would build a new church, an embodiment of the Kingdom of God on earth.

For these heresies, and for their shaking rituals, the Shakers faced severe persecution. In 1774, when Mother Ann had about thirty followers, one of them received a vision of America and the church of Christ, so represented by "a large tree" that "shone with such brightness as made it appear like a burning bush." The reference to Moses was surely self-evident. It was time for several of the Shakers to make their Exodus, to pass through the Red Atlantic Sea, to find a new and better Promised Land of their own.

The story of American religion is the story of separatism and dissent; of fanatics and factions; of factions *within* factions; of cranks, shamans, hucksters, visionaries, wisdom mongers, and truth-tellers. Americans are always writing treatises, claiming persecution, insisting on purity, and then spinning off still further factions: groups that insist on even greater forms of purity, more radical modes of worship.

So it has been since the early 1600s, a century and a half before the Shakers' arrival in America, when the Puritans sloshed their way across the Atlantic to flee the Church of England (itself a breakaway faction from the Catholic Church). Puritans wanted to create a "City on a Hill," as leader John Winthrop called it, a society that could model Christian values and practices to the world. But the Puritans, too, would throw off their own share of rebel sects, each helping to build what historian Frances FitzGerald has called a "marketplace of religion" that would ultimately make America "the most religious country in the developed world." Unlike in Europe, where state-sponsored churches were dominant, American religious leaders had to compete for converts. Here was a kind of spiritual capitalism, an economy not of finance but of faith; a free market of the sacred where competition helped lead to the creation of flashy denominations, sects, and—slightly further down the gradient of extremism—cults.

Ann Lee and her handful of followers arrived in America in 1774, a year before the start of the Revolutionary War. It was a moment of especially vigorous spiritual diversity in the colonies. A raucous jumble of sects had emerged in the wake of the First Great Awakening, an influential series of revivals that unfolded up and down the East Coast in the 1730s and forties. (A "sect" is a group that emerges out of a schism with an established religion. "Cults," by contrast, are generally seen as "more innovative, more conspicuously deviant," according to Philip Jenkins.)

A cross-eyed English evangelist named George Whitefield preached outdoors to thousands of people at a time, imploring audiences to cultivate a personal relationship with Jesus, away from the intermediary meddling of the establishment church. It was a radical message, all the more so because of Whitefield's emotional, bombastic delivery. Whitefield's assistant wrote, "Sometimes he exceedingly wept, stamped loudly and passionately, and was frequently so overcome, that, for a few seconds, you would suspect he could never recover." Whitefield's style would set the precedent for the anti-hierarchical churches, sects, and cults that followed in his pounding footsteps.

The First Great Awakening faded in the 1750s. But in the late 1770s, shortly after the Shakers arrived in America, a follow-up movement known to locals as the New Light Stir flamed across New England. Dozens of sects sprang to life—the Merry Dancers and the Come-Outers; the New Israelites and the Annihilationists; the Universal Friends and the New Lebanon New Lights. These and other groups were usually led by charismatic figures, among them a woman named Jemima Wilkinson, who preached to a region devastated by the Revolutionary War, attracting followers with "the Voice that spake as never Man spake." A pipefitter named Shadrack Ireland led a sect outside Boston, where he lived with a "new spiritual wife and a retinue of other female disciples," according to scholar Stephen A. Marini. Ireland claimed to be immortal, though when it became clear death was imminent, he told his followers not to bury him because he believed Christ was about to return. (After Ireland died, his followers made it ten months before finally interring the decomposing corpse.)

In 1787 a poet remarked, not incorrectly, "How many sects entirely new, / Are daily springing into view, / Claiming exclusively a sight, / To Christ and heavenly glory bright."

The word "cult," as we use it today, is generally applied to groups that emerged in the twentieth century (though many scholars avoid the term altogether). But sects of early American history often demonstrated cult-like elements; as Jennings writes, Shadrack Ireland's sect "might more properly be called a cult." There were groups led by strange, charismatic leaders; groups that operated outside mainstream society; groups with startling and novel belief systems; groups that placed members in exploitative or abusive situations. Like cults and sects through American history—through world history—they reflected the social anxiety of the moment, a sense, particularly strong in these post-Revolutionary years, that humanity was approaching a kind of apocalyptic culmination. Many sects sprouted near the far reaches of what was then the American frontier, and the accompanying sense of remoteness, the proximity to the far reaches of colonial knowledge and experience, helped these groups proliferate as they did. At the edge of the world, so much remained unsettled. In this expansive mountain range of uncertainty, this big blue question mark of a sky, people sought out faiths that could match the novelty of the society they were trying to create.

In 1774, following their arrival in America, the Shakers migrated to upstate New York, living and farming on a homestead northwest of Albany. Mostly they kept to themselves. All that changed on May 19, 1780, when a strange midday darkness rolled across the New England sky. Bewildered colonists ate their meals by candlelight, or else ran outside, wailing that the Day of Judgment had arrived. Bats emerged from their roosts. Sheep lay down to sleep. One commentator wrote, "It is not recollected from History that a darkness of equal Intenseness & Duration has ever happened in any parts of the world"—except, he noted, when Moses cast a plague of darkness over Egypt, and when the sky went black following the crucifixion.

Smoke from Canadian wildfires was responsible for the unsettling cloud cover. But for Mother Ann and her followers, this otherwise inexplicable eclipse was a sign from God. It was time for the Shakers to expand their ministry.

In the months that followed, members of the small but growing sect evangelized in town after town, often under threat of violence. And yet the Shakers' manic intensity—and, crucially, Mother Ann's gravitational charisma—would prove irresistible to many, and before long, Lee had gathered more than a hundred followers. The very totalism that scared off some potential members proved attractive to others.

The shaking rituals remained as extravagant as ever, if not more so. Members performed exorcisms and spoke in tongues: "*Hiero devo jirankemango, ad gileabono, duren subramo.*" They scorned mainstream churches, deriding them as the Antichrist. They wrote and sang songs proclaiming their disgust with the world they'd spurned to follow Mother Ann:

> Of all the relations that ever I see
> My old fleshy kindred are furthest from me

So bad and so ugly, so hateful they feel
To see them and hate them increases my zeal
O how ugly they look!
How ugly they look!
How nasty they feel!

The Shakers' denunciations of sex remained equally vehement, but also had the effect, however inadvertent, of training the group's focus on precisely the kind of eroticism they'd forsworn. Mother Ann said sexually active spouses would go to hell, where "their torment appears like melted lead poured through them in the same parts where they have taken their carnal pleasure." Mother Ann herself danced naked, according to some Shaker apostates, including one who claimed, "I have seen her slap the men, rub her hands on all parts of their bodies, press the men to her bosom and make them suck a dry breast." Once, three young women were ordered to "strip themselves naked . . . and whip themselves, and then whip each other." Their crime? "Attending to the amour of two flies in the window."

When Mother Ann died in 1784 at the age of forty-eight, the group's more fanatical customs died with her. Under new leadership the group gradually took on the gentle, slightly twee sensibility for which it is known today. Worship became as ordered as once it had been unhinged. Shakers wore bonnets and oval glasses. They sold seed packets, vegetables, and ladder-back chairs. They invented the clothespin.

The Shakers prospered under the next generation of leadership, and by the turn of the century, there were more than a thousand Shakers and eleven Shaker villages in New England. If not for its post-Lee overhaul, the faith might have faded into history. And yet those early years had been marked by a fiery volatility, an extreme version of the emotionalism that, with the First Great Awakening and the New Light Stir, had become definitive markers of American spiritual expression.

"Sectarianism was not aberration, an inexplicable breakdown in the life of otherwise healthy churches," writes influential religious scholar R. Laurence Moore. "It was normal. It was a constant, not a disappearing factor in American religious life." The first Shakers had been rejected by one town after another; the group was deranged, people said, blasphemous, even satanic. And yet despite all this—even because of it—the group embodied the beginnings of a distinctly American mode of worship. The Shakers and other sects like them had injected a charismatic, sweat-and-tears bravado into the religious bloodstream of the young country. That ecumenical flamboyance would pass down through the decades, from one church to another, from one magnetic leader to another—until, eventually, it would arrive in Sacramento, California, in the 1980s, in the form of another female prophet; another self-proclaimed vessel of Christ; another woman with klieg eyeballs, who knew, as Mother Ann had known before her, that she was the way, and the truth, and the life. A woman named Deborah Green.

CHAPTER 15

In the days following her expulsion from the group, Maura Schmierer went looking for work. She got a job at a nursing home, a grim, smelly place filled with "old, feeble-minded, helpless, demonized, incontinent forsaken people," as she put it in a letter to the Greens. "Everywhere I look people are headed toward hell. It appears as tho [sic] I am also." She begged to rejoin the group. "Could I receive Battle Cry? Tapes? Is there anything I can do for you? Paint? Clean sidewalks? Anything? Thank you again for your long suffering towards me."

It was July 1987. With a $500 gift from her parents she rented a modest studio apartment behind a barbershop. The apartment came with a futon, but Maura slept on the floor, as she'd done in the group. She wore her hair up, too, even though she hated the way it looked, hoping God might see her sacrifice and accept her back into his favor. One day she bought a half gallon of ice cream but only ate a few bites before dumping the rest into the sink, ashamed and guilty, convinced she didn't deserve anything so luxurious.

She missed her children, though she knew it was in everyone's best interest she'd been expelled. "As much as I long for Fort Freedom," she wrote Deborah and Jim, "I am glad for you that I'm no longer there to problem you." It was an extraordinary statement, a chilling demonstration of how fully Maura, the consummate victim, had come to see herself as a spiritual criminal who deserved every ounce of the punishment the Greens had inflicted on her.

She read her Bible before work, after work, during lunch, on breaks—whenever she could. While in the group, she'd relied on Jim and Deborah to interpret scripture for her. Now she was forced to parse the text herself, searching for clues about how to win back God's favor. It was hard work. "Repentance seems so complicated to me," she wrote. She knew that if she didn't get back to Fort Freedom, she would never see her children again, to say nothing of her future in hell. Her old misgivings about the group hardly lessened her desperation to rejoin it.

But then something curious started to happen. As the days went by, Maura began to notice inconsistencies between scripture and ACMTC teaching—nothing major, just a verse here or there that went against something Deborah or Jim had said. At first Maura gave these contradictions little thought, shrugging them off without any deeper consideration. But they kept piling up. Eventually they became impossible to ignore.

Divorce, for example. Except in certain circumstances, Jesus seemed to condemn the practice. But Jim and Deborah had thought little of breaking up marriages within the group, Maura's included. On the subject of love, too, the Greens were utterly at odds with the Bible. "Love thy neighbor," Jesus had said. And yet Deborah had shown only contempt for those who lived around Fort Freedom—for anyone, really, outside the purview of the group.

Maura was on a bus one day about three weeks after her excommunication when a verse from the book of Matthew floated, unbidden, through her mind. *You shall know them by their fruits.* The verse got Maura thinking: What were the Greens' fruits, the products of their ministry? There were the converts, of course, in Sacramento and around the world. At Fort Freedom, too, Jim and Deborah had built a self-contained community, an entire world that interacted with outsiders only when strictly necessary. It was an impressive achievement.

And yet ACMTC had also left a trail of wreckage. All those families, fractured. All those relationships, destroyed.

Maura opened her Bible to the book of Galatians, where the "fruits of the spirit" are enumerated: virtues like love, joy, peace, gentleness, and self-control. Deborah and Jim hardly lacked for self-control. But were they loving? Were they joyful? Were they peaceful?

No, Maura realized with a start. They were not.

It was such a glaringly obvious insight. And yet it had actually taken leaving Fort Freedom for Maura to see it plainly.

In the days that followed, Maura read scripture with even greater intensity than before. She bought another Bible at the Salvation Army, cutting out verses the Greens had taken out of context and then pasting them together on blank sheets of paper. Jeremiah 51:20 for example: "Thou art my battle axe and weapons of war: for with thee will I break in pieces the nations, and with thee will I destroy kingdoms." The Greens had always presented this verse as justification for the group's militancy. But Maura discovered that the passage didn't refer to the Israelites, as she'd been told—a minor misrepresentation that nonetheless suggested other, more serious falsifications might have been at play.

About a week after her revelation on the bus, Maura called Lisa Dye, who, as Despised, had spent several days with Maura in the cold, drippy clubhouse. Deborah had said Lisa was controlled by a "big African witchcraft demon," and would find only misery on the outside. But the opposite was true: Lisa and her daughter were doing fine.

The two women started speaking regularly on the phone, often late into the night.

By now it was August. Only weeks earlier, Maura had been asking to sweep the sidewalks of the compound. Now she was increasingly convinced the Greens were false prophets. It was a shocking shift, and yet in some ways it also made perfect sense. "When the fruit is ripe, a touch will make it fall," writes William James of sudden conversion. A change that appears instantaneous may, in fact, be the product of a slow ripening. Maura had been through an almost unthinkable crucible of suffering, but the judgment had also tilled the soil of her spiritual life, had planted the seeds of her transformation. "Emotional occasions, especially violent ones, are extremely potent in precipitating mental rearrangements," writes James. Maura's time as Forsaken had been nothing if not emotionally violent. If there was an upside to all that suffering, it was the extent to which it had positioned her for a dramatic change.

For years Maura had struggled with Jim and Deborah's teachings—the angry intensity, the obsession with demonology. Even as Maura had accepted the group's ideology, she'd also pushed back against it, at least at first, in ways that had caused her tremendous psychic distress. For years belief and doubt had warred within her, until the fight had grown too exhausting, and she'd all but given herself over to the Greens. Through all this confusion, though, Maura had never wavered in her commitment to Christianity, a commitment that dated back to her conversion in the mid-seventies. It was all the added stuff—the retching, the wailing—that had brought her such torment.

Now it seemed possible, even likely, that the faith of her earlier life, not the fanaticism of the group, was the real pathway to salvation. She was "so excited about what was being revealed to me in God's word that many nights I stayed up late devouring truth."

Maura started attending a nondenominational congregation where Lisa worshiped. New Hope Christian Fellowship was an evangelical church, filled with precisely the kind of conservative believers who'd helped elect Ronald Reagan in 1980. But politics wasn't central to worship, and certainly wasn't central to Maura. She liked New Hope because it made her feel welcome, like she belonged.

In many ways, life remained difficult. She had barely any money. She was still separated from the kids. But in barely a month and a half, after nearly a decade of suffering, Maura's entire worldview had been transformed. She still wore her hair back, and would for some time to come. But eventually she started sleeping in an actual bed.

It was such a small thing, this—but it was everything.

People leave cults for a variety of reasons. Some, like Maura, are kicked out, while others leave voluntarily. In the seventies, some people were forcibly removed from cults through a controversial process known as "deprogramming." Families hired people to effectively kidnap their loved ones from cults and subject them to a barrage of mistreatment that could surpass the abuse the person suffered while in the cult—detention, threats, food and sleep deprivation. The idea was to "wake up" the cult member, to alert them to the reality of their situation.

Some people who escaped the deprogramming process successfully sued their families and the deprogrammers who'd been hired. For their part, deprogrammers argued they were protecting cult members from harm; they, too, found some success in the courts. But as the lawsuits piled up, many families began to pursue different strategies, seeking out conservatorships to grant them legal authority over their cult-ensnared loved ones. These efforts had mixed results, as in 1981, when New York governor Hugh Carey vetoed a bill that would have granted temporary guardianships to families of cult members.

"Exit counseling," the process that became dominant in the years that followed, has the benefit of being voluntary. Friends and family members attempt to make nonconfrontational "mini-interactions" with loved ones, as expert Steven Hassan puts it, reaching out to them by letter, email, phone call, text, or even in person. The idea is to set the stage for a more substantial conversation with an expert away from the group.

To arrange such a discussion, a family may invite the targeted individual to lunch, or even express an interest in joining the group. Then, when the person is physically off the cult property, an exit counselor asks them about their life in their group. Rather than prescribing a certain line of thinking, the counselor tries to get the cultist to connect the dots of their mistreatment themselves. It can be helpful having friends and family members on hand, along with photos, music, movies, magazines, and books the person loved in their former life—anything to help them "reconnect with the authentic identity," per Hassan.

Exit counseling can be startlingly effective, and very quickly; one researcher estimates that 90 percent of cultists who spend three days in exit counseling leave the groups they've joined. (Reintegrating oneself into society is a far longer and often more arduous process that usually takes about two years.) The encouraging fact of the matter is that a shift in circumstance can facilitate a shift in thinking. The ice cube that has remained steadfastly frozen in the freezer begins to melt the very moment it is placed in the sun.

Maura Schmierer didn't participate in anything like formal exit counseling, but her experiences in the weeks and months post-expulsion amounted to an independent study in the practice. Through her readings she realized Jim and Deborah had mischaracterized parts of the Bible; through Lisa Dye she saw it was possible to build a fulfilling life away from the group; and at New Hope Christian Fellowship she found a community that had her best interests at heart. The result was that by late summer of 1987, not two months after being banished from Fort Freedom, Maura had effectively weaned herself off the group.

Only one major issue remained: the kids.

Maura reached out to a former District Attorney and state prosecutor named Bob Blasier who'd previously worked with several parents who'd tried (and failed) to extract their children from the group. Blasier was intrigued by Maura's story and referred her to a colleague who worked on custody issues. Maura quickly won weekend visitation rights with twelve-year-old Nathaniel, six-year-old Lilly, and four-year-old Steven. (At nineteen, Rebekah was now an adult and free to do as she wished.)

In September, Maura arrived at the compound to pick up the kids for the first time. Steve greeted her on the porch of Barracks 3, an arm around another ACMTC member he'd taken as his fiancée. When Maura said Deborah and Jim's teachings around divorce weren't biblical, Steve called her a religious fanatic who'd "opened up [her] legs to every man that walked by."

Maura eventually got the kids off the compound and took them to the state fair, where Bob Blasier's secretary paid for them to take the rides. Everyone had fun. On the way back to Fort Freedom, however, the mood darkened. Nathaniel started calling Maura Forsaken.

Maura was at home not long thereafter when the police arrived to tell her they were bringing Lilly and Steven to live with her—not for the weekend, but forever. As with Maura's second daughter, Sarah Chelew, the Greens and Steve refused to share custody. If the kids couldn't stay at ACMTC all the time, they had to leave entirely. (Steve wanted Nathaniel to remain on the compound to participate in group mission trips.)

Maura went back to court and won weekday custody with Nathaniel. Lilly and Steven had reacted well to their new living situation, but not so for Nathaniel. The Greens told him to wreak havoc at his mother's place, and he did, cutting the electrical cords, pouring coffee and honey onto the floor, breaking lightbulbs, burning Maura's legal papers, and ripping up her phonebook, which, he said, was full of "backsliders." When he refused to go to school, Maura grabbed a switch; he in turn smacked her with a stove poker, punched her, ran outside to a pay phone, and called Steve, who reported Maura to the police for child abuse.

It was chaos. A counselor from Family Court Services expressed serious concerns about ACMTC but also allowed that "continued contact [between Nathaniel and Steve] in many respects remains appropriate," given Nathaniel's loyalty to his father. For Maura, however, the situation was untenable. In the end she decided to relinquish Nathaniel to the group. She hoped that as he grew older he would start to see the light.

Maura reconnected with her now sixteen-year-old daughter, Sarah Chelew, who still lived with her father. She went on public assistance, took nursing classes at a local community college, and quit her job at the nursing home to take care of the kids. She also enrolled in a speech class where she talked about her experiences at ACMTC; the teacher, gobsmacked, arranged for her to speak at the Sierra Club and at churches around town. The Greens were false prophets, Maura told rapt audiences. People needed to be aware of them.

Maura had always longed to have a purpose and now she had one. But her crusade was about more than just exposing the Greens. It was about making sense of those years she'd spent in the group, a way of giving narrative shape to a period that had been marked by so much pain and upheaval. The speeches helped Maura recast the difficult times as part of a redemptive arc: the rising action in a plot that had, with the judgment, reached its climax; and was now, in its post-cult dénouement, coming to a powerful resolution.

There was truth to this framing. Maura *had* suffered, *had* gotten out, *had* found a social utility to her time in the group. But no amount of public exposure could get back the time Deborah had stolen from her. Those years were gone—irrevocably and completely.

As the weeks went by Maura's fervor only increased. "The heresies that men do leave / Are hated most of those they did deceive" writes Shakespeare, and so it was with Maura. How, though, to find spiritual justice?

She prayed about it. She spoke with the leaders at her church. Soon God's calling felt clear.

Maura would sue Jim and Deborah. She would try to shut down the Aggressive Christianity Missions Training Corps.

Up to now the Greens had experienced little in the way of meaningful opposition. On several occasions a group of parents had demonstrated outside the compound, but Deborah mocked their efforts as "the Burrito Wars," in reference to the Mexican food they ate while protesting. Other families had sought advice from lawyers, pastors, and anti-cult organizations that had emerged as part of the "cult wars" of the seventies and eighties, but had mostly gotten nowhere. Child Protective Services appears to have visited Fort Freedom on two occasions, but no one evidently found anything objectionable. "Congress shall make no law respecting an establishment of religion, or prohibiting the free exercise thereof"—there it was, right in the Constitution, ACMTC's most ironclad of defenses. The Greens and their followers were free to worship as they wished, no matter how bizarre their practices.

Still, the First Amendment was hardly license to break the law with impunity, and it was this fact that Maura sought to exploit in a lawsuit. "How can I put into words the horror of what I experienced?" she said in a statement. "It's hard for most people to understand how anyone can become so much out of their mind to fall prey to and believe such erroneousness. I have no clear answers myself."

Bob Blasier agreed to take Maura's case, and on March 15, 1988, more than a year after the Greens had exiled Maura to the chop shop, he filed a complaint in Sacramento County Superior Court. Blasier alleged four separate but interconnected causes of action: intentional infliction of emotional distress; deceit; false imprisonment; and negligence. For each alleged violation Blasier sought $5 million in damages. Maura would be happy to have the money, of course, but it mattered less to her than did the prospect of bringing down the group. A settlement could drain ACMTC of its assets and resources. Without money, the whole operation might collapse.

Jim and Deborah were served papers but refused to respond. "The Lord did not want us to appear in court and be dragged into years of costly and emotionally damaging litigation," they later explained. Rumor had it they buried the paperwork in the backyard.

That summer Jim and Deborah purchased an idyllic twenty-acre farm an hour north of Sacramento, where group members could train for the mission field and dodge the "persecutions" of life in Sacramento. Only a few people went to the property at first, mostly on weekends, but as the weeks went by, the group's center of gravity began to drift away from Fort Freedom.

Sarah was fifteen now, with a bright smile that hid an increasingly turbulent interior life. She hated being even further away from the real world than she'd been in Sacramento, though with time she came to appreciate the beautiful farm property, with its apple trees, blackberry bushes, peaches, figs, and kiwis. By now the group's homeschooling efforts had mostly ended, so Sarah spent much of her day harvesting prune plums and driving the old Chevy around the property. Sometimes she daydreamed about attending midwifery school: an ambition that felt as out of reach as everything else Sarah wanted.

For much of her life Sarah had seen Deborah engage in disordered eating, and at the farm Sarah started doing the same. She purged her meals not just to exert some kind of control over her life, but also to ward off the hungry glances of the men in the group. In the chaos of the move to the farm, her "engagement" to John had faded into the background, but she knew it was only a matter of time before Deborah would force her to get married—if not to John, then to someone else.

Soon it was 1989. A year had passed since Maura had filed the lawsuit. After repeatedly trying to engage the group, Bob Blasier submitted a motion for default judgment, effectively asking the court to issue a decision without the participation of the Greens.

A hearing was held March 9. The next day, the Court awarded her a judgment of just over $1.2 million.

Maura had won. She had actually won.

When she learned of her victory, Maura didn't feel much of anything—for her it had always been more of a spiritual battle than a legal one. And yet the sheer facts of the case were remarkable. Two years earlier, Maura had sat confined in a shed, cold, wet, in despair over the eternal fate of her soul. Now she was an independent woman, struggling to get by but also buoyed by an abiding sense that she was beloved—by her church, her community, her god. The ruling only added to the poetry of it all. Two years earlier, the Greens had placed her under a "judgement" for the crime of "spiritual adultery." Now it was Maura's turn to punish Jim and Deborah with a judgment all her own.

Several weeks later, evening.

Sarah, Josh, and a handful of adult members drive from the farmhouse down to Sacramento. For days now the group has been quietly gutting the four houses, ripping out sinks, toilets, tubs, doorknobs, and lighting fixtures: anything that might give the property added value.

Law enforcement will soon be seizing and selling the compound, with the proceeds of the sale going to Maura, in partial fulfillment of the judgment. It is an astonishing development, and, for Deborah, an unthinkable one. Not only is she losing Fort Freedom, she is losing it to *Maura*, a spiritual adulterer who rejected all the Greens' attempts to save her.

And so Deborah has done the unthinkable. She has called for the compound's destruction.

Wrecking ACMTC's most valuable asset means the group will have to work that much harder, and that much longer, to pay off the judgment. But this apparently matters little to Deborah. Fort Freedom is a holy place. Maura cannot, *must* not profit from its sale.

Sarah and the others throw their axes, crowbars, and sledgehammers over the back fence. Josh cuts himself climbing into the yard, but urges Sarah onward: They don't have much time, and must do as much damage as possible.

Other members fan out into Barracks 1, 2, and 3. Sarah and Josh take the Citadel. They have lived here longer than in any of their other homes, have experienced so much within the confines of these wood-paneled walls. And yet if Sarah feels a twinge of regret at smashing up such an elegant house, where she has always admired the craftsmanship, it doesn't stop her from lifting her sledgehammer and bringing it down against the floors; against the counters; against, yes, those beautiful walnut-paneled walls.

If anything, it feels good, taking out the years of frustration that have been building up inside her.

Within an hour everyone has reconvened in the backyard. The compound is now a ravaged shell of its former self, Barracks 3 in particular. Group members have sawed through the wooden foundation, thrust spikes into the roof, ripped up the floors, and exploded the walls as if with hand grenades. The damage is so extensive that the house will eventually have to be torn down.

The sanctuary, too, on the ground level of the Citadel, lies ruined beyond recognition. The floor is covered with rubble, the ceiling no longer a ceiling but an inverted combat zone, all smashed and gouged. On the wall someone has spray-painted a Hebrew name, and below it, an English translation. "ICHABOD," it says, "THE GLORY HAS DEPARTED."

CHAPTER 16

The months following the ruling were filled with a flurry of bizarre, manic activity—Jim and Deborah's effort to hold off the "judgment terrorism" they said Maura had unleashed upon them. The couple held a press conference at the farm to denounce Maura ("We dismissed her for sexual misconduct"), and to defend the ways of the group ("We are merely Christians, hardworking, disciplined Christians"). But the art shops were seized in May; facing imminent expulsion from the farm, Deborah appears to have given the property back to the previous owners, who allowed ACMTC to remain there for the time being. It was yet another inexplicable move that conceded the group's most valuable remaining asset just to spite Maura.

David Gains remained in the group, but the loss of his art shops was a huge financial blow. Members tried to fill the shortfall by peddling vegetables, frames, furniture, and expired Hostess-style desserts on the side of the road. But by the end of the summer, life at the farm had grown unsustainable. Neighbors shot at the property and attacked Steve Schmierer with beer cans. Deborah, too, became increasingly erratic. When she called for the execution of a "rebellious cow," members hit the cow in the head with a sledgehammer, hung the carcass to drain the blood, and cut it down the spine with a chain saw.

For the first time since the group's founding, members began to peel away in significant numbers. From a peak of about thirty-five people, ACMTC dropped to around twenty-five members—though Deborah claimed, in an absurdly exaggerated denial of reality, the group still had "roughly 800,000 to one million" followers worldwide.

Deborah's disciples had suffered all manner of exploitation. But for many, the daily unpredictability, and the involvement of the legal system, proved too much to bear, even if members still believed, as some did, that leaving meant condemning themselves to hell.

Deborah considered fleeing with the group to a Native American reservation, and told Julie Gudino to search census records for information about her alleged Indigenous heritage. But when Deborah said God had told her to abandon these efforts, she decided to relocate the group to Klamath Falls, a smallish logging city in southern Oregon where Steve had gone to school years prior. In July, the parents of member Mike Brandon purchased an old Victorian there for $55,000, for reasons that would remain mystifying. (Brandon very likely came from money: His maternal grandfather founded a successful citrus packing company in Riverside, California.) The group moved into the house shortly thereafter.

These were "desperate days," Deborah later wrote. "Many times I would find myself weeping hot tears in the night for the mercies of God's provision to us for the day just passed."

Even twenty-year-old Iantha, now called Rebekah, was growing disillusioned. Unable to discipline her two young children with the force the Greens demanded of her, she and her husband ran away with them in the middle of the night—a classic illustration of how salient so-called "escape hatch" relationships can be (to use Alexandra Stein's term). Even if a parent cannot appreciate the extent of their own manipulation or abuse, they may recognize if their sons or daughters are being abused; and it is this recognition, this sand in the soup, that can make a person capable of leaving.

So it was with Rebekah. When she started to cry on a bus ride out of the city, her husband asked if she'd changed her mind, if she wanted to go back.

"No," Rebekah said. "I'm just leaving all my friends."

By September 1989, ACMTC had just nineteen members. Sarah, sixteen, was as unhappy now as she ever had been. Her weight continued to drop. No longer did she think about running away—her previous failure felt like a foreclosure on any future attempts. Sometimes she imagined dying in her sleep.

Jim and Deborah showed little apparent concern about their daughter's distress. Their focus was on a restaurant they opened in downtown Klamath Falls in an old Moose Lodge that Mike Brandon's parents purchased for $80,000. The restaurant was a place for "hungry people" to "congregate for the bread of life," per a local advertisement. "Come for more than just a meal . . . come for the total experience."

The name the Greens chose for the restaurant, Shaker Square, gestured at Deborah's growing fascination with the Shakers. She'd read about Ann Lee back in Sacramento, and began incorporating Shaker practices into daily life in the group. ACMTC members made Shaker chairs, Shaker tables, and Shaker herb boxes. Deborah even suggested she was the reincarnation of Ann Lee herself.

The similarities between the two leaders were striking. Both were radiantly charismatic women who'd convinced a group of people to take up an all-consuming new way of life. There were the visions, too, and the condemnations of the establishment church; the half-messianic claims, and the highly physical, even violent worship services.

In their understanding of sex, too, the two women displayed meaningful similarities. Even as a child, Ann Lee had raged against the erotic—in part because of her childhood exposure to her parents' sex lives, in part because of her own horrific experiences with pregnancy and childbirth. Lee believed that purity required the suppression of all lustful energy, and the redirection of that energy into the creation of Christ's kingdom on earth. Deborah hadn't ordered her followers to stop having sex, though, as Sarah remembers it, she tried (and failed) to impose celibacy on Jim. Still, Deborah shared Mother Ann's backward obsession with sex, and used worship as an erotic valve to give dramatic, if still confined, expression to the carnal impulse. Deborah liked to flail, thrust, and gyrate her way through meetings, and so did Ann Lee, as if out of some primal need for a sexual outlet—despite or even because of her pornographic condemnations.

"There are no slovens or sluts in heaven," Ann Lee had insisted, sounding an awful lot like Deborah Green.

Shaker Square stood as a monument to Deborah's fixation with Lee, her vague ambition to complete the work the Shakers had begun two centuries prior. Up above the restaurant, in the old second-floor ballroom where the group worshiped, ACMTC members performed Shaker dances. They "rolled over their pride" by literally tossing around on the floor, crawling around on their hands and knees to demonstrate their submission to God. Deborah even made them line up before her so she could slap them for being what she described as rebellious children.

These and other practices weren't Shakerism, not really, but neither were they entirely unrelated to it. They were, instead, a convergence across the centuries of two women who believed, with equal certainty, they knew the one true pathway to God. That they *themselves* were the pathway to God.

It was 1990, a year after Maura's victory in court. Maura received some money from the sale of Fort Freedom but hadn't come after the group for the money they still owed her. Shaker Square did excellent business, plates used at such a rapid pace they had to be rushed through the dishwasher and returned to the salad bar while still too hot to touch. Customers might have reconsidered their patronage, however, if they'd known that much of the food they ate came from dumpsters outside local grocery stores and restaurants. (Deborah only cut back on the dumpster diving when members found used condoms and a dead dog among the more useful provisions.)

Sarah was given some small amount of autonomy at the restaurant, planning meals and leading food preparation. She was almost eighteen now, her face a striking blend of her mother's sloped cheekbones, her father's tart smolder. This could only mean one thing. It was time for her to get married.

The only group member who struck her as halfway tolerable was twenty-seven-year-old Mike Brandon, a former punk rocker who'd taken a new biblical name, Peter, as well as Jim and Deborah's surname. He was a head taller than Sarah, with a jutting chin and the soft, compliant face of a Boy Scout. That his parents had paid for the Klamath Falls properties couldn't have been lost on Jim or Deborah; and although Peter had previously been married to another member, this appeared not to matter to the Greens, who'd told Peter to get rid of his wife several years earlier, even though she was pregnant, by dropping her off on a random street corner in Susanville, California. Ever obedient, Peter had done as he was told.

Up until the marriage announcement, Sarah had felt mildly intrigued by the prospect of a wedding and the children who would inevitably follow. But as the ceremony approached, Sarah's interest turned to despair. Marrying Peter and becoming a mother would make it that much harder to have a life outside the group, that much more difficult to make good on her midwifery ambitions.

The ceremony took place in the auditorium above the restaurant dining room. The couple exchanged no rings, signed no marriage certificate; Deborah said the government had no business in their private affairs. After the ceremony Sarah posed for photos wearing a frilly white dress with gray-blue sleeves and a matching bib collar.

That night, covered in blankets but still shivering, Sarah stared at the ceiling as Peter smothered her with his body. She cried—from the pain, from the brutal reality of it all, from the memory of what had happened to her in Mexico all those years earlier.

She was on her way home from the restaurant several days later when she ran into a Christmas parade. It was full of young people in uniforms, teenagers marching and playing music and just—*being*. She stood and watched in silence. The lightheartedness, the sense of unconsidered freedom: It was like something from another universe. The music and the yelling intermingled in the cold air, and still Sarah kept watching, inhaling the scene with fascination and envy.

She stood there until the entire parade had passed. Then she continued on her way home.

CHAPTER 17

From the beginning, Bhagwan Shree Rajneesh was a collector. He grew up in the 1960s, in Bombay, India, where he gathered stones from along the beach—"so many that his mother sewed extra pockets into his clothes," according to psychiatrist and writer Anthony Storr. In adulthood he turned his eye to watches, bracelets, cuff links, and Rolls-Royces. It was with people, however, that Rajneesh's talent for collecting shone most brightly. By the mid-seventies, when he was in his forties, he'd accumulated six thousand followers who lived with him at the Shree Rajneesh Ashram in western India.

Rajneesh and his disciples practiced a jury-rigged combination of Christianity, Hinduism, Sufism, Judaism, Taoism, and more niche practices like "psychosynthesis" and "bioenergetics." Members of the ashram engaged in ecstatic "Dynamic Meditation" ceremonies, too, panting to the point of hyperventilation and hurling themselves to the ground, sometimes with so much force they suffered bone fractures. Female members inserted mangoes into their vaginas and fed them to the men. Girls wore see-through clothing and nothing else to help facilitate the "passage of energy." Storr writes, "[Rajneesh] used to give out boxes containing cuttings from his hair or nail clippings in case carrying his photograph was not enough to persuade his disciples that he was always with them."

The Indian government, however, was less enamored with Rajneesh, and in 1981, he moved to the United States ("I am the Messiah America has been waiting for," he declared). He ultimately landed in upstate Oregon, on a sixty-four-thousand-acre ranch, where yet again he attracted followers, some twenty-five hundred by 1985. Eighty-three percent of his acolytes had been to college. Twelve percent had doctorates. They were doctors and lawyers, engineers and professors. The heiress to the Baskin-Robbins fortune was a member, as was the daughter of a congressman who'd been killed while investigating Jonestown.

Rajneesh and his chief consigliere, a woman named Ma Anand Sheela, envisioned the commune as a back-to-the-land utopia that could model an ideal society to the world. They called it Rajneeshpuram. Members worked long, punishing hours, quickly developing the ranch into what was effectively a full-fledged city; it had "water and sewer systems, [a] hospital, shopping mall, and police force," according to historian Carl Abbott. Members planted organic barley, oats, and summer wheat. Abbot writes that "they encouraged chickens to lay eggs by piping in classical music and tapes of the Bhagwan's monologues."

But Rajneesh and Sheela had bigger ambitions. The group purchased property in Antelope, a nearby town with just a few dozen residents, and attained municipal status for Rajneeshpuram, allowing them to get around county land-use laws. Concerns were raised by state officials, among them Oregon attorney general David Frohnmayer, who said Rajneeshpuram violated the separation of church and state, given that only Rajneesh's followers were permitted to live on the commune. In November 1982, group members used their substantial voting power to take over the Antelope City Council. They renamed the town Rajneesh and gave the garbage trucks names like Kermit and Miss Piggy. The dump was christened in honor of Adolf Hitler.

The situation escalated even further in 1984, when members of the commune tried to take over the county government, too. They bussed in homeless people to help amass additional electoral capital and sent three thousand voter registration cards to the county clerk. Then, shortly before the November election, they sprinkled salmonella-spiked water on seven restaurant salad bars in and around the county. More than seven hundred people became violently ill; the idea was to execute an even bigger attack in November, debilitating enough local voters to swing the election in Rajneeshpuram's favor.

That attack never came to fruition, and on Election Day outraged residents swarmed the polls, successfully defeating the cult at the ballot box. When Rajneesh was arrested while trying to flee the country, he took a plea deal for immigration fraud, and agreed to leave America. Only with the express permission of the US attorney general would he be allowed to return.

About a year after ACMTC's move to Klamath Falls, Brenda Eutsler, who'd taken a new biblical name, Esther, arrived at Shaker Square to find a brown paper bag hanging from the front door handle. She opened the bag and looked inside. It was full of dog feces.

By this point locals had begun to grow suspicious of the group, in part thanks to newspaper coverage of Maura's lawsuit that had followed them north. ACMTC wasn't some cutesy Amish group, it turned out. It was a menace to the community—a cult.

Business at Shaker Square slowed. To make up for the loss of income, group members sold baked goods around town, but eventually that business dried up, too.

There were other problems. Julie Gudino's mother, Virginia Padilla, traveled from Sacramento with several other families who'd lost loved ones to the group, protesting outside the Victorian house where everyone lived, shouting and waving signs. "Look at your brother," Virginia yelled when her daughter briefly stepped outside. "We love you!" But in a videotaped recording of the exchange, Julie's face remains stony and unyielding, as if she hasn't heard a thing.

The most serious potential threat remained Maura, who knew the group had fled to Klamath Falls but hadn't yet made an attempt to collect what remained a substantial portion of the judgment. She wouldn't wait forever, however. In dire need of cash, Deborah sent Virginia Padilla a ransom letter claiming (falsely) Julie had been kidnapped by pirates while doing missionary work in South America. According to Julie, Virginia reported the letter to the Sheriff's Office, which reported it to the FBI. When federal agents came to interview Julie, however, she was emphatic. She *wanted* to be a member of the group.

The protests continued, not just from members' families, but from people in and around Klamath Falls. At one demonstration, Brenda-turned-Esther saw someone waving a sign that said: "REMEMBER ANTELOPE, OREGON."

Locals hardly could have forgotten. The salmonella attack had taken place five years earlier, just a few hours north, in a once-ordinary town much smaller than Klamath Falls, but just as distinctly Oregonian. True, ACMTC was nowhere near the size or sophistication of Rajneeshpuram. And yet the similarities between the two groups were undeniable. Both were run by domineering, charismatic leaders. Both operated out of closed-off, self-made communities. Both attracted followers who had subjected themselves to obvious manipulation and exploitation.

The 1984 salmonella attack had been an unthinkable, brazen act of bioterrorism—to this day the largest ever committed on American soil. ACMTC hadn't indicated any interest in a similar kind of attack, at least not yet. But things could change. Shaker Square had a salad bar of its own. If the group wanted to poison its patrons, it would have little difficulty doing so.

Business at Shaker Square continued to dwindle. Then, on New Year's Day 1992, little more than two years after moving to Oregon, Deborah, Jim, Sarah, and about ten other members piled into the ACMTC fleet and headed south. On its face this was a missionary trip to Native American communities across the Southwest. But the Greens also had another, more urgent reason for the excursion. It was time for them to find new land.

Rusty bluffs. Wide-acre skies. Faraway mountain ranges: There was so much for Sarah to look at as the caravan wound its way through Nevada, Utah, Colorado, and Arizona. Through everything Deborah pressed onward, possessed by the conviction that "the Lord wanted us to do something in New Mexico."

It was an impulse with ample precedent. In the early twentieth century, groups of painters and writers had established communes across the state, making art and rejecting the strictures of society. In the mid-1960s, a generation of hippie wanderers had done much the same thing, more than thirty-five communes and alternative communities sprouting from the arid, gritty soil. Not all of these groups qualified as cults, but many did. According to one study, by 1979 New Mexico had more cults per capita than any other state except Nevada.

The Aggressive Christianity Missions Training Corps was now joining this long and curious heritage. By heading to the desert, it was entering a mythos of the American West—not just a place but a disposition, one of "coarseness and strength," of "a restless, nervous energy," a "dominant individualism, working for good and for evil; and withal that buoyancy and exuberance which comes with freedom." In 1893, Frederick Jackson Turner, the preeminent scholar of the American frontier, had written of the pioneer mentality that, he argued, defined the national character. In a land without (white) precedent, without (white) infrastructure, frontiersmen and -women were forced to build society over and over again, cultivating within themselves a "freshness, and confidence, and scorn of older society, impatience of its restraints and its ideas."

In strictly geographic terms, Jim and Deborah were and long had been residents of the American West. By venturing into New Mexico, however, the group was passing into a deeper kind of west, a frontier defined not so much by longitude but by landscape and sensibility. Out here, an explorer who ignored Indigenous history could gaze at what they might perceive to be a tabula rasa, a vast nothing waiting to be tamed, occupied, and exploited.

The cults and communes of the 1960s had seized on this opportunity—as, for that matter, had Bhagwan Shree Rajneesh, who'd come to Oregon in 1981 in explicit pursuit of an "empty West" to accommodate the made-from-scratch community he envisioned. "Rajneeshpuram was a *western* community from start to finish," writes Carl Abbott, "and its history is a western story just as much as it is a story about spiritual quests and new religious movements."

"We were sure that we would change things," Jim would write of his time in the counterculture, "not only in our nation, but around the world!" Even if the Greens had long ago rejected the mores of their previous lives, the couple was still engaged in a similar project, forever pressing forward, seeking the edge of not just a geographic frontier but also a spiritual one. The outfits had changed, and so had the guiding morality. But the re-creative impulse remained much the same—in California, in Oregon, and now, especially, in New Mexico.

In early February, after a month on the road, ACMTC arrived in the Mesilla Valley, a kind of Fertile Crescent of far southern New Mexico. Driving near a remote pinhead of a town called Berino, Deborah noticed an old brick schoolhouse sandwiched between a vegetable field and a pair of train tracks. The building was two stories tall, with wide, ceremonious entry steps and little more than a dusty, barren acre for a "yard." It looked abandoned, perhaps even uninhabitable. But Deborah said she had a feeling.

"Let's pray," she said. "I think this is the place God wants us."

Deborah went to the local post office to inquire about the owner, who ultimately agreed to lease ACMTC the building for about $300 a month.

It was decided, then. God's Army was moving south.

Notwithstanding Deborah's snap decision to rent the property, full relocation took several months. In Klamath Falls, members shut down the restaurant and packed up the group's belongings. In Berino, they repaired the building's plumbing and heating systems, sweeping snakes and spiders from the toilets. On the lower level, where most of the walls had been removed years earlier, they hung black sheets of plastic to create "rooms."

In Oregon, Brenda Eutsler's name had changed to Esther. In New Mexico, her name changed yet again, to Johanna. She and Sarah led up the baking operation in the newly outfitted kitchen, churning out cookies, pies, and fruit breads that members peddled in Las Cruces and El Paso, half an hour to the north and south, respectively.

As ever, the Greens conducted twice-daily prayer and worship sessions on the second floor of the schoolhouse, in what had once been the auditorium. Deborah's sermons and prophecies still vibrated with fury: "Consider what I am saying unto thee, if a man were to wallow in a dead carcass the stench that would be upon him. When my people wallow in the world, they wallow in death." Members rolled on the floor, wailing and weeping for the sodomites, the communists, the abortionists.

In the spring, Sarah, nineteen, decided to build a garden behind the schoolhouse. She gathered manure, cotton burr, and flower trimmings from nearby farms, mixing them in garden beds she made from old railroad ties.

Summer came and went. So did fall. By the spring of 1993, the soil had turned a soft, worm-wriggly black, its scent so rich and pungent that Sarah came to crave it with a force that felt like hunger. She planted roses, clematis, trumpet vine, and other flowers with no discernible purpose beyond her own enjoyment. Butterflies and hummingbirds swarmed the perfumed oasis, their pendant bodies atremble in the hot summer sun.

Another fall passed, another winter, and again, the garden bloomed, this time with even greater exuberance. In a world otherwise defined by restriction and severity, this was Sarah's refuge, her place to dream. In her free time after lunch, she lay in the shade, gazing up at the fluttery tangle and basking in the oasis she had summoned, godlike, from the ground.

In those brief but wonderful moments of respite, she was happy.

She was also pregnant.

Ever since getting married four years earlier, Sarah had known it was theoretically possible for her to have a baby, though her disordered eating had usually kept her periods at bay. In Berino, however, some of her old weight returned, and with it, more regular periods. Then, in early 1994, the periods stopped. Her breasts grew tender. She started throwing up in the morning.

Now twenty-one, Sarah had been dreaming of attending midwifery school for years. Deborah repeatedly forbade it, but that hadn't stopped Sarah from purchasing *Midwifery Today* magazine on visits to the health food stores. She knew the signs of pregnancy—and yet still it took her weeks to admit to herself what was actually happening.

Deborah was elated when a pregnancy test came back positive. Even if she herself couldn't have more physical children, the holy dynasty was, at last, to continue.

Sarah's feelings were more complicated. It wasn't that she didn't want to be a parent—she didn't want to be a parent with *Peter*. Theirs would be a baby born to a loveless marriage, a child condemned to live in a world Sarah knew to be cruel, restrictive, and brutal. For years Sarah had pushed back against the confines of the group, and yet here she was, sentencing an unborn child to the same prison she longed to escape.

Still, a baby. *Her* baby.

Months passed and her belly grew. By summer she'd developed painful varicose veins up and down her legs; soon it hurt to walk. Deborah said God was punishing Sarah for being insufficiently submissive to Peter—and, eventually, that she was being punished for her "sins," almost two decades earlier, as a four-year-old in Mexico. Sarah had wanted those boys to rape her, Deborah insisted. Her present pain was the result of her girlish harlotries.

Weeks passed and Sarah's misgivings about the pregnancy grew stronger. She became despondent, then depressed, as depressed as she'd been years earlier, when she'd tried to kill herself. But it didn't matter. The baby was coming, whether Sarah liked it or not.

She awakes in pain. It is as if there is an anvil within her, pressing, demanding she pee. When she goes to the bathroom, however, what comes out is not urine but a blob of mucus, orange and terrifying. She flushes the blob down the toilet and tries to ignore the gathering storm within her. The baby isn't due for another six weeks. Perhaps she is merely sick.

In the kitchen she tries to pace away the pain. The anvil is heavier now, sharper. A huge industrial fan whooshes hot air from the ovens out into the backyard, but still Sarah feels a wet fire bellowing within her, enflaming her pelvis in a slow, surging rhythm. Rivulets of sweat run down her neck, her breasts, her thighs.

After morning worship, Sarah tells Deborah she may be in labor. Perhaps they should contact the midwife Sarah has been seeing for checkups? Deborah demurs, concerned the midwife will force them to go to the hospital, drawing unwanted attention to the group.

The pain worsens as the sun arcs across the sky.

By late afternoon Sarah is dizzy, hot, convinced she is going into labor. Eventually the pain is so intense, so obvious, that Deborah agrees to take her to a clinic in El Paso, though not the one where their own midwife is based—going there might raise questions.

At the clinic, an employee informs Sarah she can expect to give birth within the next twelve hours. Labor has begun. Sarah and Deborah exchange a look of mutual terror, a rare moment of unity between mother and daughter.

When they return to the schoolhouse Deborah places a vague call to their midwife, telling her that something *might* be going on, that Sarah *could* be in labor. Unaware of the situation's growing urgency, the midwife agrees to drop by later. It is an absurd exchange, one caught between Deborah's desire to have a healthy grandchild on the one hand and to keep away from the medical establishment on the other.

By now the sun is starting to set. Sarah retreats to her room. She paces, vomits, wipes the sweat from her body. Then somehow she is naked, an animal, feral with pain. It comes faster now, blowtorching itself between her legs.

Time: What is time? It is *pain pain pain pain*. It is her mother, frantic, crouched on the floor in front of her. It is Josh, flipping through a birthing manual, asking if he should boil a shoelace. A shoelace! Absurd. Irrelevant to the *pain pain pain pain*.

Wet, all over. Wet, between her thighs. Her back, pressed against a futon; Jim at one leg, Peter at the other. She is a tunnel of pain now, incandescent, obliterating. A crescendo, everything worse, her body no longer a body, but a bonfire, the whole world aflame—

And then, silence.

In her mother's hands, a small opalescent sac.

More stillness. More silence.

The sac is an oblong orb, smooth and wet—an enigma, both human and not.

What is this? Where is the baby?

The scent of hay, damp and musky. The sound of breathing, in out, in out.

Then, from within the sac, a small shudder. A liquid "pop"—and there he is, a tiny boy-creature far smaller than any baby Sarah has ever seen.

A moment. He rests, aloft in Deborah's hands.

Is the child breathing? Hard to say. Then (how much longer?) he lets out a cry, though to Sarah it sounds less like a cry than a meow, weak and plaintive.

Sarah takes the baby into her arms. She presses it—presses *him*—to her chest.

He is so small. So very small.

They are still connected, mother and son, by a fleshy rope that loops back inside Sarah. Should she pull it out? Should she tie it with Josh's boiled shoelace?

She is cold. She starts to shake. She wonders if the baby will die. She wonders if *she* will die. She hopes not. For now, they will lie atop the futon, skin on skin, time suspended, everything between them still to come.

CHAPTER 18

In 1784, fast approaching death, Ann Lee made a prophecy about the future of the Shakers. "The next opening of the gospel will be in the southwest," she declared. "It will be at a great distance; and there will be a great work of God."

Whether out of luck or providence, Mother Ann's prophecy was to prove correct. In 1801, seventeen years after Lee's death, an explosive revival roared to life, one that would expand the ranks of not just the Shakers, but a motley jumble of denominations, sects, communes, and cults. It would also scramble the distinction, already muddy, between fringe and mainstream faith practice in America.

The initial spark arrived in the woods of Cane Ridge, Kentucky, not far from the western rim of the frontier. In freshly cut forest clearings an estimated twenty thousand men, women, and children listened to self-ordained preachers who evangelized from portable pulpits, tree stumps—or, in the case of a twelve-year-old boy preacher, from the arms of two men who raised him before a spellbound crowd. Dropping a sweaty handkerchief to the ground, the boy bellowed, "Thus, O sinner! shall you drop into hell, unless you forsake your sins and turn to the Lord." ("At that moment some fell," records one listener, "like those who are shot in battle.")

Cane Ridge preachers performed with the same energy and emotionalism as those of the First Great Awakening and the ensuing New Light Stir. Revivalists responded to the emphatic sermons by laughing, weeping, tearing at their clothes, and barking like dogs, the intensity of the response an indication (perhaps) of how deeply the revival participants longed for spiritual transcendence. "The deliverance must come in as strong a form as the complaint, if it is to take effect," writes philosopher William James, "and that seems a reason why the coarser religions, revivalistic, orgiastic, with blood and miracles and supernatural operations, may possibly never be displaced. Some constitutions need them too much."

From Kentucky the movement expanded south, east, and north—all across the new country, promoted by frontier ministers who lived forever on the move, spreading God's word to congregations across the young country. This was the Second Great Awakening, a bottom-up spiritual crusade that unfolded outside the mainstream Christian church. A prominent preacher of the movement, Peter Cartwright, articulated its populist energy when he wrote, "I have seen so many of these educated preachers who forcibly reminded me of lettuce growing under the shade of a peach tree. I turn away sick and faint."

But Cartwright and his ilk weren't lettuce. They were evangelistic kudzu: hearty, fast-growing, and increasingly dominant.

As with every revivalistic heyday in American history, the Second Great Awakening spun off an exotic range of sects and splinter factions. (One irritated clergyman wrote, "Every theological vagabond and peddler may drive here his bungling trade, without passport or license, and sell his false ware at pleasure.") Many whiz-bang groups emerged in central and western New York: the "Burned-Over District," as it became known for being so aflame with religious fervor. In 1827, twenty-one-year-old Joseph Smith unearthed a set of golden plates near Manchester, New York; the plates set out the precepts for what became known as the Church of Jesus Christ of Latter-day Saints, or Mormonism. Smith's seedling faith found noteworthy success, and could boast twelve thousand members by the 1840s. Fleeing intense persecution, the Mormons headed west, ultimately landing in present-day Utah, where the church flourishes today.

Mormonism illustrated the difficulty of drawing a clear line between marginal and mainstream religious practice. Joseph Smith and his followers had been spiritual outliers in their early days, but their descendants were far less marginal by the late nineteenth century, when no less an observer than Leo Tolstoy called Mormonism *the* American religion—an apt if controversial label for a faith that embodied the inventiveness and ambition of America's ongoing expansion. Mormonism stood as a striking embodiment of the country's frontier spirit: the innovation, the self-sufficiency, the relentless push west. Tolstoy's use of the word "religion" here was noteworthy, too; for by the time of his observation, Mormonism had, in many ways, escaped the backwaters of sectarianism to become a full-fledged religion.

In doing so, Mormonism had demonstrated how counterintuitively central marginality is to the American identity. "Outsiderhood is a characteristic way of inventing one's Americanness," writes R. Laurence Moore. This was the subtext of the Tolstoy quip, that there could be nothing more American than standing *separate* from America, a country that so consistently valorized the iconoclast, the pioneer, the self-made man.

So many churches were born during the Second Great Awakening that it became difficult for the male ministry to keep up with demand. Women helped fill the void—more than a hundred, per scholar Catherine A. Brekus, traveling to preach "in barns, schools, or in fields." On the ever-expanding frontier, where pioneers daily created the world anew, there was a remarkable openness to something so revolutionary and controversial as female preaching. There had been women religious leaders before, of course, Ann Lee prominently among them; but in the wake of that vanguard, an unprecedented explosion of female evangelism, among both Black and white women preachers, came to extraordinary new prominence.

A pair of sisters, Kate and Maggie Fox, claimed it was possible to communicate with people from beyond the grave, thus igniting the popular "spiritualist" movement. Phoebe Palmer and Sarah Lankford, also sisters, helped spearhead what became known as the Holiness Movement; Palmer argued that the human spirit was capable of reaching a state of perfection, and that female preaching was permitted by the Bible. She pointed to a woman prophet in the Old Testament to make her point, writing that "the holy zeal of this mother in Israel nerved her for the conflict, and, with a faith and courage out-braving every difficulty, she led forth the armies of God to glorious conquest." The prophet's name was Deborah.

The widespread sense of social improvisation that emerged from the Second Great Awakening also found expression in a host of communes born in the mid-1800s. At the Oneida Commune, in central New York (again, the Burned-Over District), members shared their belongings and practiced gender equality; women were free to sleep with any of the men they wanted. There was an explosion of similar groups in this period, among them the Harmony Society, Brook Farm, and Fruitlands, a kind of proto-hippie commune founded by A. Bronson Alcott, father of *Little Women* author Louisa May Alcott.

The Second Great Awakening faded in the mid-nineteenth century. But its enduring influence was to prove character defining for the United States: a precedent for the movements, communes, and spiritual ingenuity of the century to come.

And what of that century? There was to be a Third Great Awakening in the mid- to late nineteenth century, a smaller but still influential uprising of social reform efforts, many of them led by women. There was to be the rise of fundamentalism, too, the wrenching clash between technological and biblical authority, and, ultimately, the Scopes "Monkey" Trial of 1925. Decades later, in the late sixties and seventies, there was to be the counterculture, or what scholars like William McLoughlin refer to the Fourth Great Awakening, not just a staging ground for the continued social change of the decades to come, but also a culmination of all that had come before. When hippies ditched society for the woods, sought out radical new forms of belief, or lived together in communes or cults, they were mining a deeply American tradition. They were defining themselves as outsiders, as spiritual pioneers, as exceptions to the mainstream rule. But they *weren't* exceptions. Their ambition to begin again, to find God where never he had been found before—here was an idea so particularly and identifiably American as to be woven into the very star-spangled fabric of the United States.

CHAPTER 19

In months leading up to the birth of her son, Sarah struck up a friendship with a deliveryman named Wally. He was tall, with brown hair. He made Sarah laugh. He worked at a florist wholesaler outside El Paso where Sarah got flower clippings for her garden. Sometimes he ribbed her for wearing what he referred to as "Amish clothes." Sarah matched his mockery with a sarcasm all her own.

"What?" she asked in mock horror, gesturing at her drab khaki skirt. "I love to dress like this!"

Was it an emotional affair? Sarah had never flirted, never engaged with a man except out of fear or obligation. She had no aptitude for the choreography of adult romance. Wally never placed a hand on her thigh, never held Sarah's gaze longer than a friend might have done. Still, there was something between them.

By fall Sarah had grown hugely pregnant. Knowing that a baby would foreclose the possibility of further visits, she came to say good-bye, handing Wally a note she told him to open when she'd left. It said, "In another world, I wish you could've been the father of my child."

Shortly thereafter, a group of ACMTC members came to Deborah with a strange discovery. They'd met a woman while peddling—Wally's wife, it turned out, who said she'd found a note in her husband's truck. The note was from someone named Sarah, who the woman suspected was part of ACMTC. The woman said Sarah should back off: Wally had a wife and children.

Deborah, disgusted, unleashed a torrent of fury on her daughter. "You're going to lose the baby," she said. "It's going to hell."

Sarah hadn't realized Wally was married. But she wasn't particularly upset by the revelation. It wasn't as if she'd ever thought anything would come of their friendship—she just wished Wally had been the baby's father. It was a simple statement of fact.

Then came the birth: the pain, the futon, the boiled shoelace. Sarah's son was a rare "caul baby," whose amniotic sac had remained intact on its journey down the birth canal. In ancient times, caul babies were said to have special powers—it was impossible for them to drown. Eventually the midwife had arrived, though her chief contribution had been to insist they go to the hospital, as they did, despite all Deborah's efforts to go under the radar. At the hospital, a doctor told Sarah the baby was going to be fine. She just needed to feed him every two hours.

And she did. Sarah fed him and fed him and fed him some more, her earlier ambivalence forgotten in the face of this tiny-fingered creature: her son. Deborah named the child Josiah, Hebrew for "God heals," and although Sarah didn't think of the baby in such explicitly spiritual terms, she did feel somewhat healed, if not by God, then by the child. Peter, an infrequent and unwanted visitor, expressed a kind of studly pride at having sired a son. But Sarah paid him little mind. It was just her and Josiah, a universe of two.

The baby was about a week old when Wally came by the schoolhouse to see how Sarah was doing. Deborah intercepted him at the front door and excoriated him for making a Jezebel out of her daughter. From behind her mother, Sarah mouthed the words, *I'm so sorry*. She watched as Wally stepped back from the door, got in his truck, and retreated into the distance. Later, she heard he'd taken a job on an oil rig off the Gulf Coast. She never saw him again.

At night, Sarah and Peter slept on the floor, the baby sandwiched between them. They had sex infrequently: yet another benefit of motherhood. The intensity of her love for Josiah threw into even sharper relief how little she felt for the boy's father. If there was anything she didn't like about the child, it was that he reminded her of Peter.

Deborah took over much of the baby's care as the weeks passed, as she always did with children born into the group. Sometimes she "nursed" Josiah in the kitchen, pressing his mouth to her breast, in much the same way Ann Lee had done with her male Shaker followers.

Windy season arrived, gusts of sandy air rattling the windows of the schoolhouse with banshee vigor. At night, bats squeaked in Sarah's garden, now more lush, more vibrant, than ever. By this point the group had settled into an equilibrium of between twenty and thirty men, women, and children. Many were holdovers from Klamath Falls and Sacramento, though some had been recruited in El Paso and Las Cruces.

About a year after Josiah's first birthday, when Sarah was twenty-three, she discovered she was pregnant again. She felt a version of the same excitement and foreboding that had marked her first pregnancy. But now there was something different. Introducing a baby to the group had made her see its limitations with fresh eyes; she didn't want to raise yet *another* child in such a restrictive, unhealthy environment. She hadn't decided to leave, not in any conscious sense. All the same, an invisible, silent clock had started ticking within her.

Like his brother before him, Sarah's second son arrived several weeks early. Deborah named him Isaiah. He was as hefty and robust as Josiah had been delicate and frail. Sarah called the boys "the bull and the bird."

It was late 1996. Almost no one had joined the group for several years now. The peddling teams sometimes recruited people in the parks and cafés in cities along southern New Mexico, but progress was slow. And yet still Deborah prophesied that ACMTC would be a world-dominating spiritual force.

How, then, to grow?

In recent years Deborah's focus had shifted from Ann Lee to contemporary figures like Bill Clinton ("a homosexual"), Hillary Clinton ("a lesbian"), and Jane Fonda. Still, she remained inspired by the Shakers' example, particularly when it came to recruitment. Because the Shakers were celibate, there was no simple way for them to produce new members. And so, in the mid-nineteenth century, they'd begun to take in orphans.

Deborah was aware of this history and had long dreamed of doing the same. To build an orphanage, however, ACMTC would need more space. Fortunately, by now the group had acquired more land five hours north of Berino. The 320-acre property was located in central-western New Mexico, in an area where the nearest "town," Fence Lake, was little more than an intersection. The property had come with a small ranch house but mostly it was pinyon pines and junipers.

ACMTC was still setting up in Berino when the Greens were "given use" of the land near Fence Lake, as Deborah put it. The Greens went to great lengths to shroud the details of the acquisition; subsequent investigation would reveal a collection of trusts Jim and Deborah allegedly created to cover their tracks. The Fence Lake property was to be the group's Zion—not a replacement for the schoolhouse, but an extension of it, a place where children from around the world could grow in the embrace of the Shim Ra Na Holy Tribal Nation, as the Greens sometimes referred to the group. (The name meant "God's goodness has come" in a mysterious language Jim said had come from God.)

The Fence Lake property was also where Jesus was going to appear when he returned to earth—that was what Deborah claimed.

While Sarah and much of the group went about their lives in Berino, Steve Schmierer and a handful of other members went to the new property, which Jim and Deborah called Cedars of the Sun. They cleared land, poured a huge concrete foundation, and put up an imposing steel prefab warehouse where members could work, worship, make tracts, and sleep. Where, precisely, the orphanage fit into this plan remained unclear. But there was no lack of space. Space was all they had up here—vast, secluded, sky-dominated space. The issue would be finding the children.

Julie Gudino had always been one of Deborah's most devoted and reliable followers. She was a highly efficient seller, too, and often had extra time at the end of her peddling shifts to search for new members. One of Julie's recruits, a woman named Rebecca Melson, later recalled how Julie had approached her at a coffee shop in Albuquerque. Julie was wearing a beret and selling incense and pies from a small metal cart. She walked up to Rebecca and told her she could hear Jesus.

"If you can hear Jesus," Rebecca replied, "what is he saying to me right now?"

Julie's face went solemn. "He's telling you that he wants to make you a flower of the field where he is your only protection."

It was a powerful response, so powerful the woman followed Julie back to ACMTC.

Bringing in children wouldn't be quite so easy. But then a way forward presented itself. In mid-1997, Julie told Deborah about the women she often saw begging around El Paso, mothers who brought their children across the border from Juárez.

Julie's observation gave Deborah an idea. Julie should befriend one of the women and ask her to give Julie her baby. Julie would explain that at ACMTC, away from the crime and poverty of the street, the child could flourish. God had called Deborah to create what she called the Children of Nations, a brigade of international child soldiers who would live and fight Satan at Cedars of the Sun. A Mexican baby could be the initiative's first member.

Even for someone as obedient as Julie, this was an extreme proposition. But she believed in Deborah's singular connection to God. She would do as she was told.

Later, out peddling along the border, Julie, who was Hispanic and spoke Spanish, struck up a conversation with a woman who appeared to be pregnant. But when Julie asked the woman to give up her baby when it was born, the woman said she wasn't pregnant—she had a tumor. Julie would have to find someone else.

It was at this point that Deborah is said to have concocted a scheme even more drastic than the first. She allegedly told Julie to kidnap one of the children she encountered on her rounds.

On an evening soon thereafter, Julie drove to a bridge where she often saw Mexican mothers with their children. It was dark out. When Julie spotted a woman with a toddler in her arms, she let down her hair and got out of the van. She started following the woman. Then, as she grew closer, Julie was overtaken by a kind of hardness. She would *get that child*.

Just before she jumped forward and took the child from the woman, however, she felt a sudden burst of moral clarity. In that moment she felt as if she'd woken up. She couldn't go through with the mission.

She turned around and walked away from the woman, back into the darkness.

Julie had failed in her mission to kidnap the child. But what if she'd succeeded? Who, for such a crime, would have been ultimately responsible, her or Deborah?

It was a question with broad implications for the group. Though Deborah steered the ACMTC ship, she and Jim often off-loaded their most egregious tasks to their followers. During the judgment Steve Schmierer and Julie's husband, Bernie, had overseen the day-to-day-particulars of Maura's punishment. After the lawsuit, Deborah had ordered the destruction of the compound without ever lifting a crowbar. She'd kept her name off various real estate records, too, and had even ordered Sarah to buy the money orders they'd used to purchase Cedars of the Sun.

And yet Deborah's followers had responsibility, too. Cult experts say it is impossible to wholly switch off a person's decision-making capacity: There always remains an element of choice. We are certainly much more pliable than we like to think, but neither are we automatons, manipulable down to the smallest link of mental circuitry.

International law has largely taken the same position. After World War II, in a series of trials conducted in Nuremberg, Germany, Nazi defendants argued they'd merely been following orders during the war, and thus had no (or limited) liability for whatever crimes they'd committed. The courts had largely rejected this claim of "superior orders," now commonly known as the Nuremberg defense. Even within an authoritarian regime, people have agency.

So it is for the obedient, dull-eyed cult member. That a person was ordered to commit a crime may prove helpful during sentencing, but they still have at least some responsibility.

* * *

Deborah, naturally, was furious when Julie returned to the schoolhouse empty-handed. She gave her extra chores and refused to speak with her. But she didn't force Julie to go back, to find another mother, another baby. God was going to "make another way."

Several years had passed since the Greens' last major mission trip abroad. Now that the heat of persecution had lessened (Maura and her lawyer had not yet made an attempt to seize the New Mexico properties), the couple began to plan an ambitious trip through Uganda, Nigeria, Ghana, Tanzania, and Kenya.

The extent of the group's reach remained extraordinary. Though membership remained flat at about twenty to thirty members, Jim and Deborah could claim, with evidence, to have a global audience in the hundreds, perhaps even thousands. These "soldiers" might engage with the group only through the Battle Cry Sounding tract series, or through *Words of the Spirit*, an international shortwave radio program the group broadcast four times a day, Monday through Friday. Still, people were listening.

For this latest trip, scheduled for the fall of 1997, Jim and Deborah decided to keep the group small. Sarah would remain in Berino to take care of Josiah, almost three, and Isaiah, almost one.

Deborah, Jim, and Josh headed to East Africa in September. Sarah spent the next six weeks as she always did, cleaning and praying and working. When Jim and Deborah finally returned, it was clear the mission had been a success. "The fields are indeed ripe for harvest," they wrote. "The hearts are hungry and the move of God has indeed started."

In Kenya they'd passed out tracts at the Nairobi airport. In Tanzania they held outdoor meetings in Dar es Salaam and Morogoro. In Nsawam, Ghana, they connected to the Aggressive Youth Fellowship, an offshoot of a local ACMTC association the Greens had set up on an earlier mission or inspired through mailings. Though Jim and Deborah were known to exaggerate the scale of the ministry, evidence of their travels through Africa indicates widespread allegiance to the group: In photos, the couple stands with large groups of locals, many of them wearing ACMTC uniforms. Perhaps the outfits were put aside the moment the Greens disappeared, displays of Potemkin faith and nothing more. Likely these "soldiers" saw ACMTC as a kind of spiritual extracurricular rather than a totalizing way of life. Either way, however, Deborah's message was clearly galvanizing.

The most important visit on this latest mission trip had been to Kampala, the capital city of Uganda, where "the Lord issued the call to REVOLUTION AGAINST RELIGION," the Greens later reported.

At the end of a gathering led by the Greens, a young woman had come forward to ask Deborah for a blessing. The woman was pregnant, unmarried, and, Deborah later claimed, sixteen years old. The young woman's brother, also present, said their mother had recently died. In the wake of that loss, his sister had gotten involved with an older man. Now her dreams of going to culinary school and becoming a caterer were over.

That, in any case, was the story as Deborah reported it back in Berino.

After listening to the two siblings explain their situation, Deborah had bowed her head and offered a blessing. The woman's name was Ruth. The brother's name was Omondi.

What happened next is hard to say. Ruth and Omondi may have invited Jim and Deborah back to their home. The Greens may have joined them there for several days. What is certain, however, is that something momentous, something fateful, transpired the moment Ruth first stepped forward to speak with Deborah.

Breathlessly Deborah reported these events to her followers. Then she outlined the plan she said she had concocted with Ruth and Omondi: a shocking plan, a plan that made all Deborah's previous schemes seem like child's play.

Ruth would give her baby to ACMTC when it was born. The group would then sneak the child out of Uganda and back to Fence Lake.

In November, immediately following the birth of the baby, a female ACMTC member would fly to Uganda to receive the baby through what Deborah referred to as a "closed adoption" involving no government or agency oversight. The ACMTC member would take the child to the US embassy, pose as the mother, and get the child an American passport. Fraudulent paperwork in hand, the ACMTC member would fly the baby back to New Mexico, leaving Ruth to pursue her career as she wished.

(Ruth may have planned to follow the child to America, but this remains uncertain.)

Ruth had indulged in what Deborah described to the group as the "lust of the flesh." Giving the baby to ACMTC was her best chance to get right with God, to fall into *his* arms rather than into the arms of a man. And what a privilege it would be, giving birth to the baby that would launch the Children of Nations!

As for the group member who would actually retrieve the baby, it had to be someone strong and resourceful. Someone young enough to pass as the baby's mother. Someone who was in fact still nursing: irrefutable proof of a blood connection.

It had to be Sarah. There was no other choice.

Soon it was mid-fall. Workers at the farms around the schoolhouse harvested kale, peppers, spinach, and radishes. At night, when the doors to the schoolhouse were left open, the smell of chicken manure filled the building.

At first Sarah thought little of the scheme or her place within it. It was all too wild, too implausible, to be real. Perhaps Deborah had spoken to a pregnant woman in Kampala. Perhaps she had even proposed taking the woman's child back to the United States. But no one would have agreed to Deborah's terms. And anyway, how was Sarah, a white woman, supposed to convince anyone she'd given birth to a Black baby? It had to be a fantasy.

But then the faxes started coming—infrequently at first, then more regularly as the days and weeks went by. Sometimes Sarah sneaked into her mother's room, where the fax machine was located, to get a look at the messages herself. The words "baby" and "child" were never used; in their place the siblings wrote "gift" or "blessing"—"All is well with the gift"; "we are eager to give you the blessing." The Greens used similarly coded language in their own messages.

Soon Sarah was convinced. This was a real plan to pick up a real baby.

Later, at different points, Sarah would offer somewhat contradictory explanations for how she felt about the plan. She would say it made her uncomfortable, and nervous about getting caught. She would say she had misgivings about separating a newborn child from its mother, even if the mother had consented to the handoff. But she also said it was "a great idea" to bring the child to ACMTC: "We were going to build a tribal nation." Her phrasing here gestured at the ongoing loyalty she felt to the group, even as she longed to leave it. "I would love to adopt a child. I would love to have more children, sure." She also figured that if she refused to go to Uganda, Deborah might separate her from Josiah and Isaiah, as Deborah had done with other disobedient parents in the past. Most significantly, Sarah felt as if she had no choice in the matter. It didn't matter what she thought about the plan. Her mother had told her to do it, and so she would.

Sarah was working in the kitchen one morning when Deborah angrily summoned everyone to the second-floor auditorium. As the group assembled, Deborah writhed on the floor, wailing and speaking in tongues—"*sheba bi, ibogo, lababa, yababa.*"

Eventually she got up to explain her rage. Ruth had given birth to a baby girl, she said, but had decided to keep the child herself. The plan was off.

"How dare she do this," Deborah boomed. "That child is going to suffer."

Sarah was mostly relieved she wouldn't have to attempt the strange and complicated "adoption," but another part of her felt disappointed. She'd begun to look forward to caring for the child, as she knew she would be expected to do on her return.

Several days after the explosive fax, however, another message arrived with a simple, curt imperative: "Please come pick up the gift." Ruth had changed her mind again. Neither she nor Omondi explained why.

From here things moved quickly. Deborah bought Sarah a last-minute plane ticket, and Sarah rented a large breast pump from a store in a nearby town. She packed a duffel bag, bringing along a stack of tracts to explain her trip to border agents, if need be. She would tell them she was a missionary.

Sarah had been to Africa twice before, on ACMTC mission trips through Mozambique, Uganda, Kenya, Ethiopia, and Nigeria. This trip was something else entirely—a criminal conspiracy to commit a brazen act of international child trafficking.

The day of her departure, Sarah put several thousand dollars' worth of cash in a pair of Ziploc bags and strapped the bags to her inner thighs with a roll of plastic wrap. When she put on her leggings and her skirt, the money was invisible.

A bullet round of questions shot through her mind on her way to the airport.

What if I can't find Ruth or Omondi?
What if the baby doesn't like me?
What if I get arrested?

She was twenty-four years old.

CHAPTER 20

Sarah's plane lands midday at the Kampala airport. In the arrivals gate, she finds a tall Black woman holding a toddler and a sign with Sarah's name on it. Sarah introduces herself, but the woman speaks little English. Is this Ruth? A relative? The plan had been for Sarah to meet Omondi. Confused, she follows the woman to a bus station outside, where they board a bus.

Sarah grows nervous as the crowded bus rattles out of the city. The smell of diesel fills the air. Ruth and Omondi live in Kampala proper—that's what Sarah has been told. She looks out the window at jacaranda trees, at children playing in the road. The bus stops for a toilet break and she buys some mangoes.

Time passes. An hour? Two? The bus stops and the woman beckons Sarah to get off with her. By now the city is far beyond them. It is late afternoon.

Sarah follows the woman to a small hut. There is no baby here—no "gift"—nor anyone else. The woman hands Sarah a bucket and directs her to a lean-to at the back of the hut. In the lean-to Sarah strips, unwrapping the Ziplocs from her inner thighs. She tucks the money into her bag, below a stack of tracts. She moistens the towel and cleans herself.

"I am ready to receive the blessing," she says when she goes back into the hut. The woman stares back with a blank expression and gestures for Sarah to wait.

A man appears. Is this the woman's husband? Is it Omondi? The man seems confused by Sarah's presence. He drills the woman in a language Sarah does not understand, growing angrier with every response. He turns to Sarah and she tries to explain: the faxes, the "blessing," the "adoption." The man seems to understand, at least in part. He turns to the woman and shouts at her.

The woman retreats to the back of the hut and returns with a stack of faxes. In broken English the man translates between Sarah and the woman, piecing together something like an explanation for what has happened. The woman is not Ruth. Or, rather, she is not the *correct* Ruth. The *correct* Ruth apparently shares the same first and last name with the *wrong* Ruth, this woman in the hut. It appears the *wrong* Ruth has picked up several of the faxes intended for the *correct* Ruth at a public fax machine in Kampala apparently used by *both* Ruths. *This* Ruth thinks Sarah is a foreigner who has come bearing medical supplies, clothes, money: a "gift."

It is an explanation that makes no sense, not now and not later, when Sarah recounts it in court, under oath. Why would *this* Ruth believe that a random American couple wants to give her a "blessing"? The Greens have never met her; she has never met them. And Jim and Deborah have clearly been getting faxes from the *correct* Ruth, the *correct* Omondi: That much is clear from the birth and pregnancy subtext of the messages. But if *this* Ruth has been intercepting faxes meant for *that* Ruth, how has *that* Ruth come to understand the particulars of the scheme as Deborah has laid them out—euphemistically—in her messages? Perhaps there have been so many faxes, so many repetitions of the plan, that both women understand, or they think they do. Perhaps *this* Ruth thinks Sarah is a representative from one of the Christian aid organizations that operate in the area. Or perhaps Sarah is simply too exhausted, too confused by everything, to understand what is actually going on. Perhaps she is as mixed up as the woman in front of her.

Sarah begins to panic. She is far outside the city. She has no cell phone, no means of contacting Ruth and Omondi. The sun is starting to set.

The husband motions for the woman to take Sarah outside. Distressed, the woman guides Sarah back to the bus station and points her to a bus bound for Kampala Then she turns around and walks away.

Sarah arrives in the city several hours later. By now she is deranged with fatigue, ravenous for sleep. She tells a taxi driver to take her to a hotel, somewhere close to the US embassy. Deborah will be furious when she learns that Sarah has wasted God's money, but Sarah feels she doesn't have a choice.

She checks into a hotel, collapses onto the bed, and cries. She places a long-distance call home. No answer. She leaves a voicemail. She takes a bath and then blacks out in bed, waking briefly when the phone starts to ring. It is someone from ACMTC. The person says Omondi had been waiting for her at the wrong part of the airport. Sarah says to contact Omondi and tell him where she is staying. Whatever else needs to happen can happen tomorrow.

The next morning, there is a note from Omondi at the front desk. It says, "I will be here at checkout to receive the blessing."

This is happening, Sarah thinks. *This is really happening.* She eats a luxurious hotel breakfast: crumpets, tea, croissants. She packs. She waits.

Sarah likes Omondi from the moment he arrives. He is warm, cordial, decorous. Together they head into the city, all music, food stalls, and motorbikes driving in the wrong direction.

They soon arrive at the siblings' cinder block house. It is modest but well maintained. Shyly Sarah follows Omondi inside.

There she is. Ruth.

Soft face. Curly black hair. The bulging breasts of a new mother. Ruth appears slightly older than Sarah expected, older than Deborah described her.

The two women embrace. They sit down and begin talking—about the baby, about being a new mother.

A cry erupts from the back of the small house. Ruth gets up and disappears, returning with a tiny bundle at her chest. *Trinity.* That's the name Deborah has chosen for the child. She appears to be a few weeks old.

Ruth hands Sarah the baby. She is sweet and bubbly, with long fingers. Sarah wonders if she will be a violinist someday, perhaps a pianist.

Trinity seems happy, but her neck and torso are covered with tiny sores. Ruth says a doctor said to give her an herb bath, but Sarah suggests they go to a different clinic.

The two women spend the next several hours talking. When several family members stop by the house, they pose together for a picture. In the photo, a small boy sits in Sarah's lap. A woman next to Sarah gazes down at the baby in her arms: Trinity. Ruth wears a loose white blouse and a purple, lily-print skirt. Her face is impassive, difficult to read.

Sarah spends much of the next day confined to a room at Ruth and Omondi's house, sick with a stomach virus. When she feels better, she and Ruth go to a nearby medical clinic where they get an antibiotic cream for Trinity's skin. Sarah wonders if the infection is the reason Ruth has decided to go through with the "adoption," this after telling the Greens she wanted to keep the baby. Perhaps the prospect of a sickly child had been too much to bear.

They go to the facility, perhaps a hospital, where Ruth can get Trinity a birth certificate. The plan is for Ruth to go inside and identify herself as "Sarah Green." If anyone asks Ruth for ID, everything will fall apart, but Ruth doesn't seem worried. She walks inside with the baby. Sarah waits outside.

Eventually Ruth reemerges with a birth certificate that lists, as the mother, "SARAH JAMA GREEN, MIDWIFE, U.S.A." When Sarah sees that the father's name is on the form, too, she starts to panic. His name isn't supposed to be there. It may raise questions at the embassy.

Sarah, Ruth, and Trinity go back to the house. Sarah says she can look after Trinity while Ruth takes some time for herself.

Soon Sarah is alone with Trinity for the first time. She gives the baby a bath, dries her off, and applies the antibiotic ointment.

Sarah sits down on the bed and lifts Trinity's mouth to her breast. Ruth has given her permission to do this, to try nursing Trinity herself. The baby hesitates. Sarah has brought formula, if this doesn't work. But she needn't have bothered. The baby grabs the breast and starts sucking.

In this moment whatever love Sarah offers—freely, joyfully—is counterbalanced, if not outweighed, by the broader criminality of the plan, and the woman, Deborah Green, who has engineered it. Sarah, too, may be a victim to her mother's manipulations, but she is also complicit, blind to the warped intimacy of what she experiences as a more straightforwardly beautiful connection. Eyes locked, mouth on breast: The moment is underscored by two opposite and competing soundtracks, one warm and twinkly, the other bleak and chilling.

The final hurdle is the highest. A few days after getting the birth certificate, Sarah, Ruth, and Trinity go to the US embassy. Ruth stops a few blocks short. She will wait there until Sarah reemerges with the baby.

Sarah carries Trinity though a series of checkpoints. Inside, she tells a receptionist she has come to report the birth of her daughter. She is directed to a nondescript interview room with a table and chairs. Sarah sits. She holds Trinity tightly to her chest.

Two officials, a woman and a man, enter the room. They sit down across from Sarah and begin their interrogation.

"Are you traveling alone?" "Why did you choose to have the baby in Uganda?" "Where is the father?" "Why were you traveling so close to your due date?"

Sarah has come prepared for their questions. On an ACMTC mission trip years earlier, she'd met a white woman with several mixed-race children. Sarah now parrots a version of this woman's life story back to the officials. Her partner is a Ugandan coffee importer, she says; they'd been on their way to a coffee conference when she went into labor. After the birth, she says, the father flew back to America, where they both live. Sarah says she plans to follow him there as soon as she has gathered all the necessary paperwork for the baby.

This whole time Trinity has remained quiet. Now she begins to squirm, clearly hungry. Sarah feels a surge of optimism. If she feeds the baby in front of the officials, surely they will believe she is the baby's mother. She opens her shirt and begins nursing. When the baby is finished, Sarah burps her onto a small cloth. A bright earthy scent fills the room. Emboldened, Sarah says she needs to change the baby's diaper—can they wrap things up?

The officials excuse her to the bathroom. She cleans the baby and collects herself. When she reemerges, everything is in order. She can return for Trinity's documents tomorrow.

Sarah puts the baby on her lap to pose for a passport photo. Trinity stares good-naturedly at the camera, mouth open, hair thick and curly. She wears a onesie with the cartoon image of a sea creature. A whale, perhaps.

The next day, Sarah returns to the embassy, where she picks up Trinity's passport and a Consular Report of Birth Abroad. Trinity is officially a US citizen.

Sarah exits the embassy and goes to a travel agency storefront where she buys a plane ticket for a return flight the next day.

That evening, Trinity's father comes by Ruth and Omondi's house. He looks Sarah up and down, incredulous, but Ruth tries to assuage him. Sarah has two little boys at home, she says. She knows what she is doing. The father seems doubtful. Still, he does nothing to stop them.

The next day, Sarah, Ruth, and Trinity go to the airport. They say little. Outside the terminal, Sarah gives Ruth a stack of bills, maybe a thousand dollars' worth. The rest of the remaining money is plastic-wrapped to Sarah's inner thighs.

Crying, the two women embrace. Ruth takes a final moment with the baby—and then, so swiftly, she is gone.

Inside the airport, at the gate, Sarah requests help with her luggage. Two men, both Black, meet her on the tarmac. They needle Sarah meanly. What is she doing with a Black baby? they ask. She tells them it's none of their business.

The men keep hounding her as she walks toward the plane. There is no way a woman of Sarah's tan coloring could've produced such a dark-skinned child, they say, none.

Sarah clutches Trinity tightly. She is terrified, disbelieving that after everything, the plan may collapse here, when she is just feet from the plane.

We're almost there, she thinks, eyes trained forward. *Just fucking leave me alone.*

And then, at the plane, they do. A flight attendant takes Sarah's bag and directs her to her seat. Sarah fastens her seat belt and looks down at the child, her "daughter," in her lap.

"We did it," she whispers.

CHAPTER 21

The plot to smuggle Trinity out of Uganda might have seemed like a bizarre one-off. But international adoption was about to become a major force in the evangelical Christian church.

The boom arrived in the early 2000s, when superstar preachers like Rick Warren encouraged believers to take in orphans from poverty-stricken countries around the globe. Evangelicals embraced adoption as a matter of social justice—and a model for what a post-abortion America could look like. "Adoption is the new pregnant," quipped one observer, not without cause. As journalist Kathryn Joyce reports, in 2004, when the movement reached its peak, almost twenty-three thousand children were adopted into the United States.

Many if not most of these adoptions were legitimate, providing homes to children in need. But the international adoption market had a dark underbelly. The enthusiasm for adoption among evangelicals sometimes led to the creation of orphans who were nothing of the kind—so-called manufactured or paper orphans who still had living relatives. For families mired in poverty, there could be a financial incentive to give up a baby; some poor mothers even became pregnant "explicitly to relinquish" their children, according to Joyce. Joyce also notes that parents in the developing world didn't always "understand the concept of Western adoption," where birth parents give up all legal rights to a child. These and other issues led some countries to clamp down aggressively on the practice. In Guatemala, where for a time one out of every hundred children born was adopted into the United States, corruption was so rampant that the government halted all international adoption in 2008.

Deborah's child-trafficking scheme belonged in the most predatory and exploitative category of "adoption." Yes, Ruth appears to have consented to the plan. Yes, she'd helped forge Trinity's identity papers. But Ruth's responsibility in the conspiracy was far outweighed by Deborah's, and, to some extent, Sarah's. Ruth was vulnerable, and into this maw of confusion Deborah had extended a hand: an apparently God-given solution to her situation. Over the decades, dozens of men and women had been sucked into Deborah's dark orbit. Ruth—and now Trinity—were simply her latest victims.

When Sarah returned to Berino, group members fawned and cooed over Trinity, impressed and even awed that Deborah's prophecies had come to such impressive fruition. Deborah, too, was thrilled by Sarah's success. More children were sure to follow.

Sarah threw herself into Trinity's care, feeding her and Isaiah at the same time, each child nuzzled to a breast. Soon Trinity and the boys began to act like siblings, giggling together on the floor mats where they slept next to Sarah and Peter.

Sarah turned twenty-five a month after returning from Uganda. As 1997 became 1998, Deborah grew more unpredictable and creative in her mistreatments. She called herself Living Word. She put on a burlap robe and preached barefoot around El Paso. She made the group's half-dozen children press their faces up against a "nose wall" and hung cruel name tags around their necks: "Jane the Pain," "Bruce Daisy," "Demon Dark Face." One time she made people eat food off a cookie sheet on the ground, as if they were dogs.

These mistreatments didn't necessarily make people want to leave the group. Suffering, as framed by the Greens, was merely evidence of righteousness. "There are saints who have literally fed on the negative principle," writes William James, "on humiliation and privation, and the thought of suffering and death, —their souls growing in happiness just in proportion as their outward state grew more and more intolerable."

In the spring of 1998, about five months after Sarah's trip to Uganda, a young woman claiming to be Ruth's relative appears to have reached out to the group. Deborah flew into a panic, convinced Trinity was about to be taken away from them, and ordered everyone to pack their things. They were moving—where, no one seemed to know. Two members were assigned to stay behind to take care of the schoolhouse.

For several weeks the group lived out on the road, in campgrounds in Arizona, Colorado, and beyond. Eventually, having nowhere else to go, they made their way back to the Fence Lake property in central-western New Mexico.

Sarah's slow-building ambition to leave the group was growing unignorable. But how to escape? Would she return? What was she supposed to do with the kids? Out here, under an endlessly blue sky, the world felt more remote—more inaccessible—than ever.

Before the move, Jim and Deborah had acquired almost eight thousand acres across the highway from Cedars of the Sun. They'd paid $550,000 for the land, much of it up front—by far the largest transaction the Greens had ever engineered, and one that raised fresh questions about the group's hazy finances. The peddling business generated significant income (in addition to the food sales, Steve Schmierer and others made and sold highly profitable furniture), but was this enough to acquire a half-million-dollar property?

Deborah was extraordinarily tightfisted with money, refusing even to buy such "indulgences" as floss, bras, or tampons. The Greens' apparent invisibility to the IRS also meant the group paid no taxes (as it had back in Sacramento and in Klamath Falls), to say nothing of the strenuous, fourteen-hour days members regularly worked.

It was also possible, however, that the group was receiving financial help from someone on the outside. A lawyer with knowledge of the Fence Lake purchase later stated, "$305,000 came in a wire transfer from . . . the state of Washington." The *Albuquerque Journal*, too, later reported, "authorities say it's Peter Green who comes from a wealthy family and helped buy up land" for the group—though it is unclear whether or not Peter's family was behind this exact wire.

Sarah, Peter, Josiah, Isaiah, and Trinity moved into the old farmhouse on the original Fence Lake property. The others lived out in ACMTC vehicles or in the huge metal warehouse. Weeks passed, and still there was no sign of Ruth's relative.

Almost twenty years had passed since Jim and Lila Green had founded Free Love Ministries. What had once been a tiny ad hoc operation was now a bustling, if still relatively small, off-the-grid community. Members woke at 4:00 a.m. to worship in the warehouse. They gardened and took care of the property. They sold not just baked goods and furniture but also llama sweaters, soaps, and tiny crocheted socks to hold incense sticks. They wore long skirts, military uniforms, and purple work T-shirts emblazoned with the Lion of Judah. They ate a largely vegan diet of rice, tomatoes, okra, tofu, kimchi, peanut butter, brown rice, and sprouts, and drank teas made from alfalfa and red clover. There was still no orphanage, but by now the group had crossed a certain threshold of success. The group owed Maura more than $1.5 million (interest on the outstanding portion of the original judgment had been accumulating steadily), but there was no reason to believe she would ever manage to shut down the group, not when she'd failed, and failed to try, for so long.

It was around this time that the Greens began to embrace the word critics had hurled at them so relentlessly. "We count it a privilege to be called a cult," Jim wrote. "WE *ARE* A CULT OF THE LIVING GOD! . . . I obediently follow my 'cult' leader, Jesus Christ the Lord." Early Christians had been called cultists, Jim said. Why wouldn't ACMTC want to be any different?

Sarah, though, was approaching her limit. She wanted to go to school. She wanted to get a job. She wanted to be with a man whose touch didn't make her pull away.

In the summer of 1999, when Trinity was a year and a half old, Sarah told Deborah she was unhappy in her marriage. "You were put together by God," Deborah said. "You don't have a choice." Sarah asked to go to midwifery school, but Deborah was steadfast in her refusal. It was a pattern that had repeated itself for decades, Sarah asking for something, Deborah saying no. This time, however, things felt different. The intensity of Sarah's desire, her need, was now too strong to suppress.

* * *

It was in a café in Albuquerque that Julie Gudino noticed the scruffy young man. He was blondish, a backpacker type. He appeared to be in his early twenties.

Julie went up to him, introduced herself, and asked if he knew about the Lord Jesus Christ. The young man responded in a New Zealand accent. His name was Anthony, he said, and he was in America exploring. Julie gave him some tracts and invited him to come see the compound. He accepted the invitation and followed her back to Fence Lake.

Sarah was immediately attracted to Anthony—his accent, his sense of humor. He participated in meetings, meals, and chores, but his time in the group was limited. He had to leave the country in the next few months, before his visa ran out.

He and Sarah started taking surreptitious walks around the back of the compound. Sarah loved it out here among the trees, the stones, the sky. Sometimes she went looking for arrowheads or pottery shards: artifacts of a world far beyond her own. She asked Anthony about his travels. He said he'd been to Togo, Fiji, Indonesia. They started holding hands. They kissed.

Soon it was August. In several weeks' time, Anthony would head to Canada. Sarah thought about his departure, turned it over in her mind. Days went by. Slowly an idea developed, pearl-like, within her.

What if she left with him?

She wouldn't follow him all the way across the border. But she could accompany him to Seattle, where she could enroll in one of the schools she'd read about in *Midwifery Today*.

She proposed the idea to Anthony on a walk one day. He was hesitant. Sarah was the oracle's daughter, he said—she couldn't just *leave*. Sarah said it was worth a try.

The most difficult, most intractable question was what to do with Josiah, Isaiah, and Trinity, whom Sarah considered a daughter. Sneaking them off the compound undetected was all but impossible, Sarah told herself. And what was she supposed to do with them in Seattle? Establishing a new life there would be difficult enough on her own. No, they had to stay here, if only for a few months. She would come back for them later.

This was not a small decision, not for anyone, and certainly not for Sarah, whose very idea of herself was so tightly wrapped up in her identity as a mother. She told herself she wasn't really *leaving* the children; she was going away to build a new home for them. The separation was as temporary as it was necessary. But was this a delusion, a lie she told herself to justify her decision to escape the compound? Sarah was eager for a fresh start, for a chance to have the kind of young adulthood her mother had withheld from her. Perhaps some unspoken part of her actually *wanted* to have some time on her own to explore.

Excitedly, nervously, she started planning her escape and fantasizing about her new life. She stared at a *People* magazine she nabbed while grocery shopping, its contents bizarre and alluring. *The Blair Witch Project.* Ricky Martin. *Family Guy.* What did any of it mean?

There was another emotional hitch. As much as Sarah resented her parents, part of her still longed to please them: to be a good daughter. It was almost biological, this impulse, and contradictory to her more obvious ambition to get out. Sarah was desperate to experience the real world. But she also wanted to make her parents proud. To hear them say, "I love you."

I love you. Sarah couldn't remember the last time Jim or Deborah had said those words to her. Perhaps it didn't even matter. Theirs was a barbed love, a love that drew blood.

Sarah and Anthony decided to leave at midnight the Sunday before Labor Day, when the peddling teams wouldn't be out on the roads. They would hitchhike to Los Angeles and then catch a bus north. In preparation Sarah packed a small backpack with just the essentials. She wrote letters to her parents, her brother, and her kids. She wasn't happy at ACMTC, she said. She would be back in several months' time.

The day of the escape, Sarah could barely eat. She and Anthony went from breakfast to morning worship, from lunch to afternoon worship, from dinner to evening worship. Along with everything else, Sarah had packed a small stack of tracts—an alibi, she told herself, if she got caught.

"I wasn't running away," she would tell her parents. "I was looking for new recruits." But the multicolored booklets were also a memento, a set of alternate birth certificates she'd never asked for or wanted. The group was home, whether she liked it or not.

After the final service, she put the kids to bed. At around eight o'clock she and Peter got into their sleeping bags. She set the alarm clock for midnight, same as always. At her side lay Josiah, Isaiah, and Trinity.

Good-bye, she thought. *I love you.*

PART THREE

BORN AGAIN

CHAPTER 22

The dew is nearly dry, the heat of the day just starting to build. Sarah and Anthony are two specks, gnat-like against the broad, unfurling landscape. Around them the ground is matted with low trees, thick grasses, and tiny yellow flowers. There are lizards, too, and butterflies, and cacti almost vulgar in their proud, phallic majesty.

A passing driver offers them a ride to church. The irony of the situation is not lost on Sarah. Here she is, not eight hours into her new life, and already God is after her. She and Anthony hop in the car and go to the service. At a potluck afterward, Sarah surveys the offerings with a kind of frozen panic. Her diet has been restricted for decades; she has forgotten what regular food tastes like. She opts for macaroni and cheese, something simple.

She and Anthony wander the midsized town buzzed, dazed, and exhausted. Before they hitchhike any farther they need to sleep. They get a room at a pay-by-the-hour motel that smells of cigarettes and booze. The shower is dank with mold. Yellow curtains flutter in the breeze.

They rinse off and meet on the bed, naked. Hands, mouth, breast: They've been wanting to do this for weeks. They don't have sex as much as they fumble with and at each other, working off their fear and excitement. Sarah has never touched a man like this—has never been touched *by* a man like this.

Over the next two days they hitchhike west. Heat waves flicker and dance on the road.

When they get to Los Angeles, they buy cheese tacos from a food truck. Sarah says she wants to see the ocean, so they take an hour-long train south to Long Beach. Sunset is approaching. At the water she takes off her sandals and wades into the surf. She wiggles her toes in the sand, breathing in the fresh, briny air.

Is this what freedom feels like?

That night they try to sleep under a lifeguard stand, but the cops kick them out, so they spend the night walking around until the first train can take them back to the center city.

In downtown Los Angeles, they buy bus tickets to Sacramento, where they'll briefly stop on their way to Seattle. Sarah wants to see her old hometown, wants to show it to Anthony.

It takes all day, getting there by bus, so they spend the night at the Sacramento station. The next morning, they make their way through the city, toward what was once Fort Freedom. At X and 23rd Streets they stand across from the old Citadel, the still-familiar sound of freeway traffic whizzing behind them. Barracks 1 and 2 are still standing. Barracks 3 is a flat patch of nothing.

Sarah has changed in so many ways in the decade since she lived here, but she is also still a version of herself. The girl who threw pomegranates at her brother. The girl who collected antiques in her closet. The girl who swallowed a fistful of Tylenol and slashed a man with a razor.

Those old lives, old selves, are with her and not, indelible and still, somehow, gone.

Within a couple of days, they arrive in Seattle. They spend their first two nights under a bridge on a bed of cardboard. The next evening, they move to a local hostel with fresh white sheets and an expansive breakfast spread. Sarah and Anthony don't have enough money to stay there more than one night, however, so they soon head back into the streets.

In another day or so they come across a line of people outside a soup kitchen. A man there tells them he has room for one person at a church shelter—but only one. Sarah turns to Anthony. They have never intended to have a serious romantic relationship, and yet they've still been through something momentous together. They hug, say good-bye. Sarah wishes him well on his journey to Canada—and then watches him disappear into the city.

She is now overwhelmingly, almost inconceivably alone.

She spends her nights at the shelter, her days looking for work. When she applies for a job at a café, the manager asks why she has no résumé, no references. She says she has spent the past several years abroad working with her parents, both social workers. The manager hires her for a trial run.

She logs extra-long shifts at the café, hawking pastries and pulling espresso shots. She eats leftover cookies and cinnamon rolls at the end of the day, the zing of all that processed sugar keeping her up at night, on the floor of the shelter, turning over the same questions that have consumed her since her escape. *How do I make it all work? How can I get my kids back?* She has decided she will establish a financial base and find a place to live before she pursues her midwifery ambitions. School, she decides, will come in the spring.

She works long hours, not just for the money, not just to build a foundation for her children, but to distract herself from the guilt and shame that often consume her. She wonders about her kids. She wonders if she is headed to hell. Sometimes she places tracts out in public—at the bus station, on park benches. Who knows? Maybe they can help someone.

She doesn't drink. She doesn't date. She works. At night she takes the bus back to the shelter exhausted, drained, her tips collected in a little black pastry bag in her lap. She goes to a party with her coworkers; on Halloween she dresses up as Poison Ivy, the comic book character. One day a customer at the café asks her to be his wing woman at a gay bar. She says yes, startled but also intrigued by everything she sees there—all that leather!

She buys clothes at the thrift store. She sees *Riverdance*. She eats ramen and mini powdered doughnuts: the overprocessed, regret-inducing kind. It is exhilarating. It is overwhelming. Much of the time she hates herself for leaving behind Josiah, Isaiah, and Trinity. And yet the success of her escape is also inarguable. She has left ACMTC. She is building something new.

In December, three months after running away, she rents a room in West Seattle, across the bridge, near where the orcas like to swim. It's nothing special, just an empty bedroom at the top of an old Victorian, with an ugly brown carpet, white walls, and a pair of windows that look out across the street. But at $325 a month, it's perfect.

She buys a used sleeping bag and brings it back to the apartment. Alone there for the first time, she stands in silent awe, taking in the empty space. Then she lies down on the floor and cries.

CHAPTER 23

Abi Stewart was nineteen years old when she got a job at Seattle's Best Coffee. She quickly became fascinated by one of her new coworkers—a salty, strikingly attractive woman in her mid-twenties who'd been hired shortly before Abi. The woman was confident and funny. She didn't take shit from anyone, particularly not the male customers who always seemed to be asking her out. "Wasn't your girlfriend here last week?" she would taunt them wryly. "Unless you're buying everyone's coffee, you need to keep it moving." Abi was a large woman with wire-rim glasses and bangs. She enjoyed being around someone so charismatic and classically beautiful. But the new barista could be intimidating. Looking at her was like looking at the sun.

They'd both been working at the café for just a few weeks when the woman—Sarah was her name—got promoted to assistant manager. She seemed never to be still, joking with customers, moving boxes of vanilla syrup, or showing Abi how to make whipped cream. Abi, somewhat directionless, had never met anyone so competent, who had men falling over themselves or once even offering to buy her diamonds. *What the fuck is this life?* Abi asked herself watching the exchange unfold.

At twenty-six, Sarah was seven years older than Abi. But the two young women soon became friends, hanging out after work and cracking jokes about men who wore ugly "birth control glasses." At the café, Sarah taunted Abi ironically whenever Abi paused to catch her breath. "Are you dying?" Sarah asked. "Do you think you're going to make it?" Still, Abi loved being around her. She seemed like the coolest person Abi had ever met.

At the end of November, about two months after Sarah and Abi both started working at the coffee shop, the World Trade Organization descended on Seattle for a negotiating conference. About thirty-five thousand people turned out in protest, swarming the streets outside the café with bullhorns and placards. Sarah, thrilled by the excitement, told Abi they should close the café early to go see the action for themselves.

It was a wild scene—protesters throwing rocks and lying down in the streets and setting dumpsters on fire. Sarah and Abi both wore khaki pants and white polos, their work uniforms comically mismatched to the scene around them. Abi wanted to go home, but Sarah was clearly thrilled. She seemed like a child, eyes bulging, desperate to take it all in.

From time to time the two young women hung out at Sarah's apartment. To Abi it looked like an opium den inhabited by fairies—vintage lace curtains, a futon with a bamboo headboard. There were twinkly lights, too, and plants, and an earth-toned quilt made from scraps of taffeta, velvet, and satin. When Abi asked Sarah where she'd gotten the quilt, Sarah laughed.

"I made it myself," she said.

There were limits to the young women's intimacy. Sarah was never vulnerable, never open about anything deep or emotional. Sometimes she spoke in bracing absolutes. If a person wasn't busting their ass, they were lazy; if a woman showed too much skin, she had loose morals. Sarah could be cutting, too, even if she didn't mean to be; a few times she made Abi cry. Always, too, there lingered the question of Sarah's past. She said she'd come to Seattle from New Mexico on a Greyhound but revealed little more.

On New Year's Eve 1999—the dreaded Y2K—Sarah and Abi went to a warehouse rave along the Seattle waterfront. The space was dark but also colorful, flashing with lights that made people's skin look purple, their eyes green. It was clear who whitened their teeth and who didn't.

Sarah and Abi danced to the thumping, obliterating house music, the warehouse growing hotter as more and more people crammed inside. Every so often Sarah and Abi sat on the speakers to rest, the sound pulsing through their bodies. Mostly, though, they danced, the music unleashing a kind of looseness in Sarah she rarely displayed in her regular life.

She jumped, she writhed, she shimmied: an exorcism in sound.

Hours passed like this. Men kept trying to dance with Sarah, but she ignored them, closing her eyes or giving them a sharp, intimidating death stare.

It was 4:00 a.m. when she and Abi decided to leave. Sarah had danced virtually the entire time.

CHAPTER 24

Sarah wasn't lying when she presented herself as a capable, confident young woman. She *was* capable and confident, at least in certain contexts—at work, out with her friends. On the inside, however, she was often consumed with sadness and self-loathing. She loved going to the rave, loved feeling the music vibrate throughout her body. But that night at the warehouse also highlighted the extent of her rebellion from the group. Yes, she'd wanted to escape. But that didn't mean she wasn't haunted by the worry, marrow deep, that she was in error; that every step away from her former life was another step closer to the flickering blue flames of hell.

In this, Sarah was hardly alone. Since the cult boom of the late sixties and seventies, thousands of ex–cult members have embarked, voluntarily or not, on a version of the same transformative process Sarah was just beginning. In those early days, when the counterculture was still active, former cult members were often met with befuddlement or even scorn on their arrival back in society. People couldn't understand why anyone would join such obviously destructive communities, giving away their belongings, cutting off their families, and ceding their very souls to such hateful, authoritarian leaders. Ex-cultists often found little help from therapists or clergy members, either; unschooled in the ways of totalist groups, professionals often approached former cult members as if they were deranged, mentally ill, or even psychotic.

But the disorienting fact of the matter was that they usually *weren't* deranged or mentally ill. The majority were ordinary men and women whose desire for love, community, and meaning had led them to some of the darkest corners of society.

As public consciousness around cults grew in the 1970s and eighties, researchers developed more effective methods of helping people pass through these brackish, intermediary waters. Even in the best of circumstances, however, that process could be a grueling one.

There are the obvious difficulties, like depression, anxiety, self-doubt, guilt, and fear. Having spent years or even decades in the ideological grip of abusive, exclusionary communities, ex–cult members must face the complexity of life in the real world. Some respond by drinking too much. Others die by suicide. The success of a cult is in many ways reliant on the leader's ability to strip their followers of any sense of self; having shed their worldly identities, ex-members reenter society profoundly unmoored.

Practically, too, the challenges are daunting. Former cult members have often spent many years relying on others for food, shelter, and other material needs; on arriving in mainstream society, they must learn to provide for themselves. Few former cult members have any money. Some turn to old friends or family members for help, but these relationships may be frayed beyond all repair, at least in the mind of the ex-cultist. Former members may seek out government assistance, but the paperwork is often prohibitively daunting. Getting a job, too, comes with its own catalog of challenges. How to explain a years-long gap in a résumé? How to decide on an outfit for an interview?

Even if a former cult member manages to find employment, spending money can itself be an overwhelming experience. One former ACMTC member would recall wandering around the grocery store for hours at a time, paralyzed by the variety of choices available to him.

Many former cult members furthermore arrive in society beset by health problems. People who've been sexually abused may need treatment for sexually transmitted infections. Panic attacks are common, often the result of sensorial triggers that take ex-members back to their time in a cult: an old song, a familiar cologne. Some may even receive official diagnoses of post-traumatic stress disorder.

Former cult members must learn how to relate to others, how to "carry on casual conversations without turning them into recruiting sessions," per cult exit counselor Patrick L. Ryan. Dating can be immensely complicated, particularly for people who have spent time in groups that were especially punitive (or liberal) in their approaches to sex. It is embarrassing, too, being unfamiliar with the movies, books, and music that everyone else seems to know. Ex–cult members may also have to learn how to tell (and understand) a joke: Cult expert Margaret Thaler Singer writes, "lack of humor is almost universal" among people who have recently left cults.

Ex-cultists may feel overtaken by rage, regret, and sorrow for all the time they spent separated from the world—time they could've spent building relationships, families, careers, *lives*. They often feel distrustful of others and themselves, anxious they won't realize if they're being hoodwinked yet again. Sometimes ex–cult members dissociate, breaking off in the middle of a conversation, their minds pulled back to the world of the cult. (Cult experts refer to this phenomenon as floating.)

Former members may find it difficult to read, concentrate, or speak in anything but generalities. They often have "diminished abilities in the areas of perception, decision making, discrimination, judgment, and memory," writes scholar and psychotherapist Lorna Goldberg. "It [takes] time for them to collect their thoughts; speech [is] often colorless or halting." Until ex–cult members are able to find language for their experiences, until they can piece together a coherent narrative about who they were, who they are, and what they've experienced, they may remain mired in this emotional purgatory.

Loneliness is typically the most difficult challenge faced by ex–cult members, according to expert Madeleine Landau Tobias. Recalling her time in a cult, one former member told a researcher, "I had always had close friends or someone there that I could talk to." In her new life, "it was strange to come home after a night out with a bunch of friends and be sad by myself."

Of course, many ex-cultists do find healthier versions of the close-knit communities they have left behind. Maura developed meaningful relationships at church. Another former member found acceptance among the gay people he met in Santa Fe. Like them, he'd "come out" of a kind of closet. Those who remain isolated, however, may go back to their old lives, or else go cult hopping, as experts call it, jumping from one extremist group to the next.

Still, former members, "don't generally return to the cult," writes Michael D. Langone, editor of *Recovery from Cults*, a definitive work on the subject. "The suffering they experience after leaving the cult is more genuine than the 'happiness' they experienced while in it. A painful truth is better than a pleasant lie."

Paradoxically, moving on from a cult may require recognizing the good things that came with it. Former members often emerge from cults with an impressive work ethic. They know how to be part of a team, how to push themselves to their limits. To accept that the cult has given them these useful skills, while also acknowledging how it has hurt them, can help former members become comfortable with contradiction—with real life, in other words.

To many ex-cultists, it is in the spiritual realm where they must confront this complexity. Former members may recall experiences of "spiritual abuse" or even "spiritual rape" from their time in a cult. Others report having had profound religious experiences that can be hard to square with a cult's more obvious abuses and deprivations. One former ACMTC member would recall praying one morning while in the group and feeling overcome with love for humanity—a pinprick of adoration that quickly grew, spreading throughout her body with an emotional force she'd never experienced before.

Oh, she thought, kneeling on the floor. *This is how much God loves us.*

It was a revelation, a life-defining experience that far outlived the months she spent as a soldier in God's Army. What to make of that ten-second blast of God, a revelation that occurred in an environment so otherwise rife with difficulty? She would wonder for decades to come.

CHAPTER 25

At the end of 1999, Sarah turned twenty-seven. By now she'd been out of the group for three months. She still felt confused, lost, anxious, and guilty—even if no one around her knew it.

Some days she considered ditching everything and returning to ACMTC for good. Other times she worried that someone from the group might appear at the café and try to take her back to New Mexico. For weeks she resisted getting a bank account, afraid her parents would somehow find out about it and deduce where she was living.

She took an additional job at a gym, washing towels and cleaning the locker rooms. Except for bras, underwear, and socks, she bought almost nothing new. One day, however, she splurged on a brand-new pair of black Converse sneakers. They did little to keep her feet dry in the wet Seattle winter. But that hardly mattered: They looked amazing.

Weeks passed and she allowed herself a few further indulgences. She visited art galleries. She saw a Samuel L. Jackson movie. She went to a play called, appropriately enough, *Metamorphoses*. She remained steadfastly focused on building a new life so she could get her kids out of ACMTC, though there was an element of unreality, even delusion to her thinking. Was she *really* going to drag them off the compound? Was she *actually* going to raise them in Seattle as a single mother with practically no support?

At first, she maintained a hard barrier against all the men (so many men!) who asked her out at the café. Eventually, however, she agreed to get dinner with an architect who charmed her with exotic descriptions of Kilimanjaro. She went out with a German rower, too, a tall, lithe man with a hilarious accent and the tight, vigorously maintained body of a serious athlete. The first time they slept together, Sarah was self-conscious about her breasts, how they bore the wear of her years as a mother. As for the sex itself, it felt like—well, nothing, really. All the time Sarah had spent disassociated from her body, from the idea of pleasure as something to be enjoyed, was very much alive within her.

One day the German rower invited her back to his apartment, where he made her an arugula salad, her first. Sarah had never tasted anything of such bitter perfection—the spicy greens, the sunny tang of citrus. The rower took her on a biking trip in Vancouver, too, and helped her get an email address. Through everything Sarah remained evasive about her past. She'd grown up on an organic farm, she said. Her parents were social workers. When she found out the rower had a pregnant girlfriend back in Germany, she broke up with him on the spot.

Deborah had always denounced tattoos as markers of evil, but Sarah decided to get one anyway, in part precisely because of how fervently her mother had objected to them. A tattoo would mark her as permanently unacceptable to the group, would eliminate the low-simmering allegiance that still bubbled within her. She got a series of black Japanese characters that ran from her left shoulder down to her elbow. *Love is pain*, they said. *Endure it.*

By spring it was warmer outside, but the weather remained maddeningly damp. Soon the cherry trees burst into bloom, their feathery pink pom-poms cheering wetly in the breeze.

Sarah had initially planned to go back for her kids after six months in Seattle, but she was reluctant to return to Fence Lake before starting midwifery school—an arbitrary threshold, and one that suggested Sarah was more reluctant to go home than she might have admitted, even to herself. She was far more established than she'd been only a few months prior; and although three little kids would've been an enormous added strain, it was a strain that Sarah had originally seemed willing to bear. Giving them a better life had been one of the main reasons she'd left, after all.

It was also possible, however, that part of her wanted to remain on the outside for a bit longer, to be an adventurous, desirable twenty-seven-year-old trying ramen, yoga, and almond Hershey's for the first time.

When she missed the start of the semester at the midwifery program she'd been eyeing, she enrolled in a technical school and took doula classes on the side. Her new goal was to become a medical assistant and later parlay that experience into a job—any job—working with babies.

By this point she'd left Seattle's Best Coffee for a bakery closer to her apartment in West Seattle. She chatted easily with customers, among them a black-haired teddy bear of a man named Geoff who came in early every morning. He was part Korean, funny and disarming. Sarah asked him out when she ran into him along the beach one day.

For their first date they got pizza and hiked to a grassy outlook behind Alki Beach. They looked out across the bay, at the sunset and the flying saucer skyline of downtown Seattle. Sarah taught Geoff some yoga moves she'd learned, and he gamely (if awkwardly) attempted them, much to her cackling amusement.

That, really, was when she started falling for him.

Geoff had a daughter and a history with drugs and alcohol. He left town for months at a time to do refrigeration work on fishing boats and cruise ships. He had baggage, in other words—but so did Sarah. Weeks passed and they continued to hang out. Geoff made Sarah feel good. He made her feel safe.

Geoff, too, was taken by Sarah. He thought she was an amazing person—spirited, courageous, eager to explore the world. He liked that she didn't smoke or drink. Perhaps she could help keep him in line.

Soon it was summer. Sarah worked and studied, worked and studied. Only a few weeks after meeting Geoff she moved in with him; not long thereafter she missed her period. When she told Geoff she was pregnant, she said he could stick around or get lost. Geoff said he was all-in. He even raised the possibility of marriage.

In June 2000, Sarah's phone rang. It was Deborah.

At first, Sarah had worked hard to keep her parents from finding her.

Eventually, though, she started sending cards and gifts to the children. Then she gave Deborah her phone number.

Deborah was ecstatic when she heard Sarah's voice, emphatic that she come home immediately. Peter got on the line, too, and promised to take her back no questions asked. Sarah, unsettled, said a few vague words about returning to Fence Lake at some point. When she revealed she was pregnant, Deborah insisted the baby was Peter's.

Sarah hung up, heart pounding. The call had been so disorienting, so strange and confusing, that she immediately decided to get another tattoo: a red, twisty dragon beneath the Japanese characters on her left arm. Again, the tattoo served as a marker, to Sarah, of her new life, and a means of pinning herself *to* that new life. She sensed, from the call, how easy it would be to give up everything she'd built in Seattle. The tattoo, then, was a kind of armor against Deborah's exhortations, a way of buttressing the barrier of unacceptance Sarah had been building between them.

On June 16, 2000, Deborah sent Sarah an email. "Praise God, we are all glad to have had contact with you after so many months," it said.

> The children are glad and they of course now expect you home any day. So sweet, so trusting, so vulnerable. They have tried so hard to be brave throughout this period of their lives, they have prayed for you constantly . . . I had a dream several days ago and you were here, helping me to make soap, I am going to try my hand at it, we are completely out and have even used the scraps! I might try and call you to see if you can advise me.
>
> The weather here is beautiful today, trying to work itself into a rain, the air smells so beautiful. The sunrises and sunsets continue to be the most beautiful in the world.
>
> You are coming back, you are going to be delivered of the demons that have held you in captivity, and you are going to be restored with the fear of God in your heart! The idols in your life which led you into captivity will be broken and their hold over you

will be devastated. When God's word is finished in you, it is going to be beautiful and we hold to that!

Gone was the woman who'd retched and wailed on the floor of the sanctuary. This was a concerned Deborah, a Deborah who was curious to make soap. She was going to try her hand at it! Could Sarah show her how?

Sarah's response burned with shame: "i can not state it enough times that i am a horrible mother and that it is the lords mercy that [the children] have such a wonderful father and grandparents. only in his mercy are they kept." She signed the message "your worthless daughter who is finally starting to see herself."

Sarah wasn't being entirely sincere. She knew that coming back for her kids would require her parents to believe she was returning a chastened woman: There was no way they would allow her on the compound otherwise. But neither was the email a lie. Sarah *did* feel like a horrible mother and a worthless daughter. Life in Seattle was exciting, but it was also overwhelmingly, staggeringly difficult. Her awareness of what her freedom had cost was hardly diminished. If anything, it had only grown stronger. Physically leaving the group, it turned out, had been the easy part.

As for the ACMTC verbiage, perhaps she'd laid it on a little thick ("only in his mercy are they kept"), but there was more than a hint of honesty to her words. How many thousands of sermons had she heard her parents preach? Enough that in Seattle they continued to play in the background, a shouty, ominous reminder that damnation might well be in store. She didn't fully believe in the god of her mother. But neither did she *not* believe. She remained, instead, in a kind of spiritual no-man's-land, entrenched in one life but obligated to another. She still put out tracts occasionally, a decisive tell that she wasn't nearly as liberated as she might have seemed. Her words and her actions remained in jarring contradiction, as if even she didn't know what she really wanted—or perhaps she wanted everything, wanted somehow to blend the oil and water of her two opposing lives, even as that remained obviously, despairingly impossible.

In an email, Deborah said Trinity, not yet three, had been chanting and praying for Sarah's return. The boys, too, had "one continuing message: Tell our Mom to get home!

> They pray for you everyday, they are so relieved to know that you are alive, you cannot believe how much of a weight it was on them to think that you were dead or in prison or in hell. Which we will pray that none of those things occur. Of course Josiah has a very clear understanding of spiritual matters and he has known for a long time that your heart had turned away from God and he even at times manifested some of the spirits that were trying to take control of your life. But he is very profound for his age and he readily admits when he has been tricked or duped by the devil, then he rebukes the devil, repents, says sorry and goes onward.

In her own messages Sarah sometimes performed the part of the devoted, repentant wife, a role she had virtually never played while in the group. Then again, perhaps it *wasn't* a role, or wasn't *fully* a role—was, instead, yet another expression of the very real pain and confusion that had come from exploding her life. "You are a good man & a wonderful father to our children," she wrote Peter, in jarring contradiction to how she'd thought of him while in the group.

> Me on the other hand am extremely selfish only thinking of myself and how I felt. I just wanted to take this time to thank you for your enduring love toward the children & most of all Christ. Something I have completely failed at and hate myself everyday for leaving the children like that. Even though it was completely wrong of me to do I knew that it was wrong for me to drag them along on my little sinfull binge.

Was Sarah about to bail on her new life and return to Fence Lake, not just to get the children, but to stay? It certainly seemed like it. But Sarah also reminded her family—reminded herself—why she had left. She told

Peter their marriage had died years earlier, that she hadn't wanted the "bad vibes" of their relationship to affect the kids. She even framed her decision to leave behind the kids as an act of magnanimity: "maybe I am selfish but not so selfish that I tore the kids away from you or every one else," she wrote. Sarah was accepting responsibility but also deflecting it: yet another example of the competing emotional vectors at play within her.

She was more contrite, more yearning, in other messages:

JUST A SHORT NOTE TO SAY THAT I LOVE YOU VERY MUCH. . . . I WANT TO COME HOME THIS FALL TO VISIT AND PROBEBLY TO STAY. I AM A TOTAL FAILURE AS A MOM, WIFE, AND DAUGHTER. . . . WHEN YOU TRULY LOVE SOMETHING, AND LET IT GO, IF ITS TRUE LOVE IT WILL RETURN TO YOU.

If it's true love it will return to you. Leaving ACMTC had given Sarah a kind of retroactive loyalty to it. She knew she had to play the game when communicating with her family. But her words still held an element of truth, though it was also unclear, perhaps even to Sarah herself, where sincerity bled into pretense.

Sarah's actions, however, told a far less ambiguous story. September arrived and she made no plans to return home. For now, the story she'd told herself and her family about going back to Fence Lake remained just that: a story.

Her life in Seattle was full, busy, crammed with classes, shifts, hikes around Alki Beach. But beneath this productive, confident exterior, Sarah remained in anguish. "If you only knew the torment i live with every day that i have failed every one that was so true to me," she emailed Julie's husband, Bernie. "many days i wake up hating my whole existence of every thing that i have ever done. . . . i turned 28 yesterday and i feel alot older than that."

Soon the cherry trees were blooming again: her second spring in Seattle. Her belly grew as she kept working, kept taking classes. Unlike Sarah's previous pregnancies, she could eat whatever she wanted—soy ice cream, spicy potato chips. She gave birth in May 2001, in a hospital room an entire world away from the Berino schoolhouse where she'd had Josiah. When the baby—a girl—was born, Sarah named her Ellexis. It was the first time she'd ever named one of her children herself.

Ellexis was an easy baby, but the added stress of a newborn was still an enormous strain. By this point Geoff's struggles with substances had resurfaced. Sarah hoped she could help him kick his destructive habits, in effect to "convert" him to sobriety.

She was up early nursing Ellexis and watching television on the morning of September 11, 2001. For Sarah, it was especially shocking and bizarre to watch as the crisis unfolded; current events had always felt so remote at ACMTC. Once a member of a self-proclaimed Holy Tribal Nation, Sarah was now part of the *American* nation. 9/11 only underscored that shift in citizenship.

In early 2002, almost two and a half years after fleeing the group, Sarah finally decided it was time to go back to the compound for her kids. Geoff was alarmed, not because he thought Sarah was going to stay—he felt confident Sarah's allegiance was to her life in Seattle—but because it seemed like such an obviously futile and painful endeavor. He and Sarah went to counseling to discuss the matter. Over Geoff's objections, Sarah made a plan to return to Fence Lake with Ellexis, now eleven months old.

"Maybe I'm coming to get my judgement or get a renewal in Christ which I need desperately," she wrote Deborah. "I have changed so much I highly doubt you want me around. What ever the case, I will be there to receive a blessing or a curse."

It was April 22, 2002.

CHAPTER 26

Sarah stares out the van window, Ellexis held tightly to her chest. The desert is dry, tree speckled. They pass cows, sign for elk, little white crosses at the side of the road. The baby cries, nurses, cries again. She can tell, clearly, Sarah is anxious.

A pack of dogs announces their arrival at the compound. The property is much as Sarah remembers, if somewhat shabbier, with rusty farm equipment scattered across the ground like so much driftwood. Sarah gets out of the van and breathes in the earthy air.

Jim emerges from the main house, walks up to Sarah, and hugs her. He has a long white beard. "Welcome back, Sis," he says, a nod to her old nickname, Sissy Bug.

Sarah feels alert, nervous, highly conscious of her body. A new nose piercing is covered with a Band-Aid. Her tattoos are hidden with a sweatshirt.

Deborah emerges from the house. She stands at a distance, regal, mute, aloof. She has always been skinny, but now she is *whittled*.

Peter comes out, too. He remains silent.

Sarah carries Ellexis to the main house, walking gingerly, as if stepping around broken glass. Inside, everything is familiar—the desk, the computer, the clock with a different bird for every hour.

Then the children appear. The boys are five and seven, their hair blond as hay. Isaiah's face is bright and chunky, full of delight. He runs to Sarah and hugs her. Josiah holds back, clearly resentful. He stares accusingly, as if to say, *You abandoned me.*

Trinity is also there, a wide grin stretching across her face. She is four years old, fully a girl now, not the toddler Sarah once knew. She steps forward and grabs Sarah's legs. Sarah sits down, takes Trinity in her lap, and runs her fingers through the girl's curly black hair.

"I'm going to take you with me," Sarah whispers when no one is listening. "Would you like that?"

"Yes, please," Trinity says, smiling.

Sarah sees the rest of the group at lunch in the warehouse. Here they are, many of the old faces—Stephanos and David, Jochebed and Amos, David, Johanna, Julie, Sabbath, and the others. The women wear T-shirts and jumpers. The men wear pants and suspenders; most of them have beards. Deborah has arranged the meal as a feast in honor of Sarah's return, in spite of her ongoing coldness. There are about thirty people here, everyone packed together at the cafeteria tables near the kitchen. Sarah says little and eats almost nothing.

After lunch, Sarah carries Ellexis around the grounds. She sees, now, the growth of the group's infrastructure. There are new (used) trailers, new (used) equipment parts. New orchards and vegetable gardens, too, with tomatoes, beans, carrots, and cabbages, their teal fronds raised to the sun in worshipful supplication. Things seem to be going well at ACMTC, though the possibility lingers that everything is all a show. That certain things are being hidden from her.

Sarah takes pictures with an old camera she has brought from Seattle. She looks for her kids but cannot find them. This has been one of her worries from the beginning, that her parents won't allow her to be alone with them.

In the evening Sarah takes Ellexis back to the warehouse. Deborah barks from behind a wooden lectern, ranting about "backsliders," a message clearly targeted at Sarah. The lighting is harsh and fluorescent. Around Sarah the members sit listening, their faces rapt and empty. Sarah has barely spoken with any of them since her return.

Deborah steps forward from behind the wooden podium. She places her hands on Sarah and starts performing deliverance, summoning forth her daughter's demons *in the name of Jesus Christ*. Then Deborah collapses onto the floor and launches into one of her spiritual birthing ceremonies, screaming, moaning, panting as if a baby is clawing its way out of her. But of course there is no baby. There is only Deborah, fifty-five years old, her once resplendent face gaunt and wrinkled.

The whole point of this visit, as Sarah has explained it to herself, is to get Josiah, Isaiah, and Trinity off the compound. But the particulars of how she will do so remain hazy, all the more so because Deborah is clearly keeping the children away from her. In Sarah's comings and goings, in her visits to the warehouse, the main house, and the gardens, she hardly ever sees them.

Sarah and Ellexis spend their first night in the hallway of her parents' house. The next morning, after prayers and breakfast, Sarah goes for a walk with Josh. Her brother is twenty-seven, as effortlessly handsome as Sarah is beautiful, with dark hair and a mole on his left cheek. He points out the changes and upgrades that have been implemented since Sarah's departure. Eventually he asks Sarah if she has come to stay.

"No," Sarah replies, dispensing with all deception. She says she wants to take Trinity and the boys back to Seattle.

Josh asks if Sarah has told their mother. Sarah says she hasn't.

That afternoon, Sarah finally finds Trinity outside with the other girls. Together they walk among the flowers that will soon bloom: African daisies, purple coneflowers. Sarah notices a strange inward bend in Trinity's right knee. The girl remains as sweet and cheerful as ever. But still, Sarah is worried.

After the walk, Deborah stops Sarah at the top of the driveway. When Deborah speaks, her words are bent, contorted by the snarling fury she still feels for her daughter's decision to run away. Gone is the caring mother of her emails.

Sarah mentions Trinity's leg: The girl needs real medical care, she says. Deborah swats away Sarah's concern, dismissing the condition as a side effect of Trinity's skin problems back in Uganda. She says she is going to take Trinity to an orthopedic surgeon, though this hardly seems likely.

Deborah is more interested in talking about Ellexis, still nestled in a carrier at Sarah's breast. Again, Deborah insists the child is Peter's, an assertion Sarah dismisses out of hand. Glowering, Deborah concedes that Sarah may be right. She says she will allow Sarah and Ellexis back into the fold, even if the child is a bastard. She will grant them that one mercy.

It is at this point Sarah tells Deborah she has no intention of staying. Trinity should come live with her in Seattle, she says, where she can see a doctor. The boys, too. But Sarah has barely started speaking before Deborah explodes, her warrish screams audible from across the compound.

No, Deborah shrieks, *absolutely not!*

Sarah tries to push back, but Deborah merely continues her caterwauling, excoriating the daughter who has whored herself out to the world.

A ringing sound fills Sarah's ears. She runs back to the house, her mother's wails chasing angrily behind her.

Inside, Sarah finds Peter ripping the film from her camera.

"What are you doing?" she asks.

"You're not taking any of this with you," he replies, his voice full of contempt.

Sarah retreats into the hallway. The idiocy of her plan is now so obvious. *Of course* she was never going to get the kids away from the group. She feels dizzy, almost frantic.

That night she goes to dinner and evening worship. Again, the children are nowhere to be seen. Sarah wonders if Deborah has sent them to some remote corner of the compound or to the Berino schoolhouse, as she often does with disobedient group members.

The next morning, Sarah takes Ellexis back to prayers and breakfast.

No Josiah. No Isaiah. No Trinity.

After the meal, Sarah carries Ellexis back outside. Deborah appears suddenly before them and hurls Sarah's packed bag at her feet. It is time for Sarah and the baby to leave, she says. If Sarah won't submit—to Deborah, to God—she is no longer welcome here.

Behind Deborah, Jim stands shaking his head.

Ellexis wails at Sarah's chest. The trees go glassy.

An ACMTC van suddenly pulls up in front of her. Dazed, Sarah gets inside with Ellexis. Julie Gudino and her husband, Bernie, sit crying in the front.

The car starts down the driveway, through a corridor of trees, and turns onto the main road. The compound disappears quickly behind them.

Sarah keeps crying.

She will never see Josiah or Isaiah again.

CHAPTER 27

In the 1990s, the number of private militia groups—gun cults, really—exploded. Figures vary according to source, but by the middle of the decade, an estimated nine hundred groups could claim more than forty thousand followers. Like Jim and Deborah Green, members of these militias were highly suspicious of government power, and paranoid that state actors were out to get them. The only way to defend themselves, they believed, was to form independent pockets of resistance.

In the lead-up to the 1992 presidential election, the National Rifle Association warned gun-owning Americans about the grave threat posed by a Democratic presidency. If Bill Clinton won the White House, the NRA insisted, the Second Amendment was effectively gone. So, too, did the impending millennium cultivate a climate of conspiracism: Who knew what would happen when the year 2000 arrived? Better to have guns at the ready, to be allied with others who were similarly prepared in case something happened.

But perhaps the most decisive factor in the proliferation of private militias came in 1993, on a tree-shorn rise of earth called Mount Carmel, about twelve miles northeast of Waco, Texas.

Since the 1930s, a group of fringe religious dissidents had lived together outside Waco. These were the Branch Davidians, members of a pseudo-Christian community that followed the teachings of a charismatic, Jesus-handsome leader named David Koresh. Koresh foretold a day when his followers would face off against the secular world ("Babylon"). The resulting conflagration would take their lives, he said, delivering them into eternal glory.

Like ACMTC—like many cults—the Branch Davidians had emerged out of a more recognizable faith tradition. In the 1840s, near the end of the Second Great Awakening, a Baptist minister named William Miller announced he'd figured out the fast-approaching date of Jesus's return to earth. As the hour approached, hundreds of thousands of Americans donned white "ascension robes" and prepared to rise up to heaven, congregating on hills, rooftops, and in graveyards. One woman became "quite hysterical" when she realized she'd forgotten her dentures: "What do you think the Lord would have said to appear before him without teeth?"

She needn't have worried. Christ didn't appear, and many of Miller's followers returned glumly to their lives. Some people, however, came to believe Jesus had made a kind of spiritual return rather than a physical one. These holdouts worshiped on Saturdays, the seventh day of the week, and thus became known as the Seventh-day Adventists.

By 1929, the denomination could boast about 300,000 members, among them a washing machine salesman named Victor Houteff who said the church had gone slack in its commitment to Christ. Houteff decided to build a community apart from mainstream culture, on a plot of land large enough to contain the 144,000 souls he believed would be among the elect. Houteff ultimately settled on a large property outside Waco, Texas.

For decades the group operated without incident, evangelizing and building a contained community around Waco. Eventually members became known as the Branch Davidians, a nod to King David of the Old Testament, and a verse in the New Testament where Jesus calls his followers the "branches" to his "vine."

In 1955, when Houteff died, the group entered a period of intense leadership squabbling; for a time, it was even led by a woman. In the early eighties, a young man named Vernon Howell joined and ultimately took over the group, claiming to be one in a line of messiahs, a "Lamb of Revelation" who would lead the faithful in an end-time battle with the secular world. Howell was also given a new name that referenced two key figures from the Old Testament—King David, and the prophet Cyrus

("Koresh" in English). From then on, Vernon Howell would be called David Koresh.

Under Koresh's leadership, life at Mount Carmel took on a new intensity. In 1989, Koresh announced the dissolution of all marriages except his own: It was his job, and his alone, to sire children. He allegedly had sexual contact with girls as young as ten and fathered seventeen children with eleven different women in the group. "My lot is to procreate," he told the men. "Yours is to tolerate." Many male members complied when Koresh instructed them to abstain from sex and masturbation; as journalist Jeff Guinn writes, "If [Koresh] was wrong about this, then perhaps he was wrong about everything else, and this was something most of his followers would not even consider."

Allegations about Koresh's sexual activity with children prompted a 1992 investigation by Child Protective Services. But when a key witness declined to formally testify, the case was closed. The FBI also interviewed Koresh, but that case, too, went nowhere.

The trouble for David Koresh, however, was only just beginning. The Bureau of Alcohol, Tobacco, and Firearms began its own investigation of the group when a deliveryperson discovered hand grenade casings in a box sent to the Branch Davidians. There were allegations, too, that the group was purchasing semi-automatic rifles and then converting them, illegally, into automatic weapons they sold and stockpiled.

It was a moment of extreme sensitivity for ATF. The previous August, the agency had been involved in a disastrous standoff with former Green Beret and white supremacist Randy Weaver, who lived with his family in a remote cabin in far northern Idaho. In late 1990, Weaver was arrested for selling sawed-off shotguns to an undercover ATF informant, and released on bail in 1991. Weaver refused to negotiate and didn't show up for a court hearing, so in August 1992 US marshals arrived at his rustic property to scope out a raid. Their appearance triggered an exchange of shots that left Weaver's son and a US marshal dead. For several days Weaver held off additional state law enforcement, as well as FBI and ATF operators who arrived to help quell the situation. Weaver's efforts were ultimately unsuccessful, however, and on August 31 he surrendered to the authorities.

"Ruby Ridge," as this episode became known, only legitimized the paranoia of many in the then-burgeoning militia movement. As Weaver's sympathizers saw it, the government had brazenly murdered Weaver's son and taken Weaver into custody, all for the simple exercise of his Second Amendment rights. If anyone needed proof the feds were out to get people, this was it. Mainstream news coverage, too, was critical of the government, such that by February 26, 1993, when ATF secured search and arrest warrants for a raid on Mount Carmel, the pressure to redeem the agency's reputation was intense. Everything had to go right.

On the morning of Sunday, February 28, seventy-six ATF agents arrived at the compound hidden in a pair of cattle trailers, prepared for and expecting a quick, nonviolent search-and-arrest mission. One agent had even made golf plans for later that afternoon. But the agents were stepping into a powder keg. Shots rang out across Mount Carmel as agents arrived at the large, rambling complex; four agents were quickly killed, as were (reportedly) six Branch Davidians. What ATF didn't understand was that in storming the compound, they were effectively fulfilling Koresh's apocalyptic predictions. Here it was, the battle he had long predicted, the confrontation with "Babylon" that would usher in the end of the world.

"They didn't fear an assault," Guinn writes. "They welcomed it."

The FBI quickly took over from ATF, but the standoff persisted. Days passed, then weeks. Hostage negotiators successfully managed to arrange the removal of more than thirty people from the compound, but the rest of the group remained either dead or huddled inside, the conditions growing more apocalyptic with every passing hour.

By the morning of April 19, 1993, negotiations had ceased. Tanks rolled toward the compound, hurling "ferrets" of tear gas intended to force the Branch Davidians outside. But even here the Branch Davidians held strong.

It was never fully clear, in the end, who started the blaze. Perhaps it was simply an accident. Whatever the case, at around noon, roaring flames were visible outside. Hordes of onlookers waited, convinced the remaining Branch Davidians might finally flee the building. Except for a few isolated souls, however, no one emerged, David Koresh included. He was thirty-three years old—the same age as Jesus when he, too, was executed by the state.

So this was Waco—not just a city but also an idea, a rallying cry against what critics saw as the oppressive, murderous forces of government power. The disastrous handling of the raid validated otherwise fringe voices who told wild jeremiads about the state's real intentions. According to the Southern Poverty Law Center, "while before the siege there were only a few dozen scattered militia groups, by 1995 the number had increased to 441."

Waco took on an almost mythic quality for militia groups that proliferated in the nineties. The events at Mount Carmel were "constantly referenced" by members of these groups in interviews with journalists, Guinn writes. Anti-government terrorist Timothy McVeigh was among those who made the pilgrimage to Waco as the siege unfolded, blowing up the Oklahoma City federal building on the two-year anniversary of the blaze. ("It's because of Waco," his father told the media.) In 2000, talk-radio fanatic Alex Jones spoke at a memorial in a church that had been built on Mount Carmel. Jones also made his own conspiratorial documentary—*America: Wake Up or Waco*—that foreshadowed the most deranged, most destructive lies he would tell about the 2012 Sandy Hook Elementary School mass shooting.

Among those affected by the siege were Jim and Deborah Green. The couple had no cable subscription, no daily newspaper delivery. But they still managed to keep up with the news, reading magazines and other media while running errands. What they learned about the disaster enraged them and added to their already formidable paranoia. Despite Deborah's significant theological differences with the Branch Davidians, she clearly saw them as martyrs. They'd been "persecuted for righteousness's sake," she said, just as ACMTC had been persecuted by Maura Schmierer and the rest. Even decades later Deborah was still denouncing the events at Waco, and the way (she claimed) the government had used the "cult" label as an excuse to exterminate the Branch Davidians. "You can go to Waco and you can burn alive a bunch of people because they're a 'cult,'" she raged. "Not because they're doing evil, not because they're doing wrong, not because they're violating the laws of the land, but because they are a cult."

Here it was, yet again—another moment of burgeoning American extremism that both reflected and inspired the Greens' own spiritual evolution. ACMTC didn't stockpile weapons (Jim and Deborah sometimes referred to the group as "The Army That Sheds No Blood"), but it was just as conspiratorial, as isolationist, as anti-establishment as those that *were* obsessed with firearms.

The Greens had been largely apolitical for most of their lives, contemptuous of Democrats and Republicans alike. But now, post-Waco, they, like others of their ilk, were increasingly allied with the far right.

CHAPTER 28

Johanna was the first person to discover Sarah was missing.

It was September 1999, barely an hour after Sarah and Anthony's escape from the compound. The sky was still dark as Johanna trudged to the warehouse kitchen, same as she always did. But on this particular morning, the kitchen was empty. Sarah was nowhere to be found.

That's odd, Johanna thought. It wasn't like Sarah not to show up. Disconcerted, Johanna got to work on her own. Another hour passed, then two—and still there was no sign of Sarah.

At around sunrise Johanna left the kitchen and headed to the main house, where Josh gave her the shocking news: Sarah and Anthony had run away.

Johanna couldn't believe it. She knew about the tension between Sarah and Deborah: Everyone knew about that. And something had certainly seemed off about Sarah in the days preceding her departure. But to flee in the middle of the night? To desert her family, her kids? It was unthinkable.

Deborah said nothing about Sarah's absence at morning prayer. In the days that followed, when, eventually, Deborah acknowledged Sarah was gone, she referred to her by a single letter, "S." Sarah had been overtaken by the devil, Deborah said; everyone should pray for God to make her life miserable so she would return to them. She told Josiah, Isaiah, and Trinity they should think of her as a dead person.

Peter seemed forlorn. Josh, too, was upset, as were many others. Sarah had always brought a welcome lightness to the group, cracking jokes and marking birthdays with little gifts—say, a bag of pistachios left on a member's pillow. She'd pushed Deborah to buy new underwear when members needed it. Now all that stopped completely.

One day Deborah got down on her hands and knees and dragged herself down the gravel driveway, "bleeding, crying, and praying all the way FOR YOU!" as Jim put it in a letter to Sarah. Halfway down the driveway Jim joined his wife. "Can't begin to describe the pain."

Deborah fasted for days at a time. She sat alone for hours in the main house, or at a particular spot out in the sun. One day she banished Julie Gudino; her husband, Bernie; and their son, Zechariah, to Berino. The schoolhouse was a mess, filled with dirt that had blown in from the desert. When Deborah learned Julie had cleaned the building, even venturing into Sarah and Peter's old room, she became apoplectic. No one was to go there, or to touch any of Sarah's old belongings. *No one.*

In Fence Lake, a kind of altar in Sarah's memory was built behind the compound—nothing grand, just a small circle of stones. One day a billow of smoke arose from among the trees. It was Sarah's belongings, being burned.

Over the years, the group had (mostly) succeeded in evading meaningful consequences for its abusive activities. In 1999, however, a former member threatened that equilibrium.

Ja'el Phalen had joined ACMTC in the summer of 1999, two months prior to Sarah's escape. She was fifty-four years old, Haitian, a former employee at Shell Oil. She first heard about the group from a tract she found at a post office. When she wrote to the Greens to request more literature (an "ammo pack," in ACMTC parlance), Deborah invited her to lunch at the compound. Ja'el and her two cats moved to Fence Lake shortly thereafter.

Sarah disappeared in September. Then, in November, Deborah told Ja'el to investigate how ACMTC might "adopt" a group of orphans from Haiti. Ja'el went to Albuquerque to conduct research at the library, deducing it might be possible to traffic a child through Florida, where regulation appeared lax. When Ja'el returned to Fence Lake to tell Deborah of her findings, Deborah was furious, perhaps because Ja'el had spoken with her son while away. Deborah said Ja'el was too attached to her race, too close to her family. She was "doing the work of the devil."

Ja'el was a devoted Christian, and sincerely believed Deborah to be a prophet. But Deborah had changed in the months Ja'el had known her. "She got inflated with her own goals and her own feelings for herself," Ja'el later explained.

"General, the glory of God has departed from you," she said.

Soon thereafter Ja'el visited a mechanic shop, where she contacted a local church to ask for help leaving the group; the church, in turn, contacted the state police. Officers came and picked up Ja'el and her cats, and took them to a women's shelter in Grants, population nine thousand, midway between Fence Lake and Albuquerque.

While a member of the group, Ja'el had seen things that disturbed her, so she decided to speak with law enforcement. On the morning of December 7, 1999, about a week after leaving ACMTC, she sat for an interview with a state police officer and two special agents.

Ja'el gave an overview of daily life on the compound. "[Deborah] wants to have a people raised after her," Ja'el said, according to a transcript of the conversation. "She's a revolutionary."

After more than an hour, Agent Pete Baca addressed the allegations that had prompted Ja'el to reach out.

"Have you seen anyone mistreated, locked up, disciplined?" Baca asked.

"No," Ja'el said.

"Have you ever seen bruises on people?"

"No."

"How about bruises on children?"

"Um."

"Have you ever seen the children disciplined?"

"The children are disciplined by—they don't feed them okay."

Ja'el told Agent Baca one of the children had fasted "for two days straight with nothing but water." She said she'd heard about times when they'd consumed only broth for approximately twenty days straight.

But this was the least of it, really.

"Have you ever seen any sexual abuse of the children?" Baca asked. Ja'el said she had.

"What have you seen?"

Ja'el said she'd seen an eleven- or twelve-year-old girl seated on her father's lap on a bed in the print room. Ja'el said the man's hand had been under the girl's dress.

"When they saw me they jumped out," Ja'el said.

Ja'el also said she'd seen the girl follow her father into the bathroom. "I don't know if they take showers together," Ja'el said. "But when he goes and takes a shower, she goes in there with him and holds his towels and things like that."

Ja'el said she'd told the girl's mother what she'd seen. "Whatever community it is, whatever style of living it is," Ja'el had said, "this is an absolute no-no."

The father was subsequently "pulled out of the print room," presumably his workplace, and "put on construction of the orphanage." His daughter was "not together with [him] anymore," Ja'el said, "and I did not see them again going up in the shower together. So, I guess he must have stopped."

Still, Ja'el was concerned.

Ja'el also said Trinity was experiencing physical abuse. "Peter is very hard with [her]," she said. "He'll pull her hair to make her sit straight; he'll squeeze her shoulder until she's—she won't scream, but she's, you know . . ." Ja'el didn't finish the thought.

Ja'el also said she'd witnessed Trinity getting "burned right in front of me" while making crafts with a woman named Rachel. "Rachel was using a hot glue gun," Ja'el said, "and I heard Rachel say, 'Touch this, touch this.' So, [Trinity] being a baby, [she] touched the hot glue gun, and I heard a scream. When I turned around, the whole body of that girl was shaking." According to Ja'el, when she told Deborah what had happened, Deborah wasn't concerned. Deborah said she "couldn't see anything [on Trinity's skin], and that [Trinity] being Black anyway, [a scar] wouldn't show."

Ja'el also told the investigators she suspected Deborah was mixing a poisonous, hallucinogenic plant called jimsonweed into members' coffee. Ja'el said she'd felt like she was hallucinating on several occasions, though also noted she had a "mental condition" she hadn't been treating while at ACMTC. Still, she said she'd seen jimsonweed on the compound. She believed others were being drugged, too.

At the end of the interview, Ja'el implored the officials to do something. "I don't care about the adults because they have chosen it," she said. "They have the choice of leaving. The children do not." Ja'el expressed particular concern for Trinity, who, without Sarah, had no one there to protect her.

ACMTC was no stranger to what Jim and Deborah described as "persecution." Child Protective Services had apparently visited Fort Freedom in Sacramento, and authorities had looked into training exercises the group had caried out in the California countryside. Investigators had interviewed Julie Gudino in Oregon, too, and kept an eye on the group in New Mexico. Through everything, however, officials had largely identified ACMTC as merely odd rather than criminal—"just another religious group," as the Butte County Sheriff's Department put it to a journalist in 1989, in a sentiment other officials echoed time and again.

This was something different. Ja'el Phalen was alleging physical abuse of a child and sexual contact between a father and his preteen daughter. Religion was obviously not a defense against claims like these, as it had been against some of the allegations that had arisen over the years. Maura Schmierer's lawsuit remained technically active, but unless she managed to transfer the judgment to New Mexico—a tall order—nothing further was ever likely to come of it. To a significant extent, the Greens had successfully impeded her efforts to shut down the group.

Evading Ja'el's allegations, however, was likely to prove more difficult, given the seriousness of the claims and the apparent credibility of the accuser. Ja'el wasn't a concerned neighbor or an angry relative. She was a former member, someone who'd lived with the group for several months and witnessed specific alleged crimes with her own eyes.

Officials from state and local agencies discussed the situation in the weeks following Ja'el's interview. Journalist Darren White received a tip-off about the case and interviewed Ja'el for an explosive report that ran on local television. In the interview, Ja'el said ACMTC children "were being forced to kill animals, a ritual to prevent them from idolizing things other than God." The kids put cats and dogs at the "bottom of a pail and pour water [on them] until they drown."

Ja'el also suggested Jim was abusing Trinity, perhaps sexually—a horrifying allegation, but also a perplexing one. In her earlier interview with law enforcement, Ja'el had been given ample opportunity to say Jim was molesting Trinity. But according to a transcript of the interview, she'd said nothing of the kind. The only claim of sexual abuse she'd initially made had been directed at the man who'd allegedly put a hand up his daughter's dress. It was certainly possible that both men were abusing children on the compound. But the discrepancy between the two accounts raised questions about Ja'el's reliability as a witness.

Those questions grew stronger on January 5, when two investigators visited Ja'el at the women's shelter. She refused to speak with them. "I want to heal," she said, clearly frustrated that officials wanted her to recount her story again. "I'm under medication. I'm praying and I have to get back to it."

Perhaps Ja'el was correct about what was happening at the compound. But she was also stressed, volatile. It also came out that she'd been involved in at least one other local case that had "turned out to be nothing," according to the county undersheriff.

Over the course of January, an alphabet soup of state agencies and departments got involved: CPS, COM, CYFD, the DEA, SID, CCA, DPS. The FBI, too, was aware of the case.

On January 26, a judge signed an order authorizing law enforcement to take Trinity and the other alleged abuse victim into custody. The judge also issued an order requiring ACMTC to bring the dozen or so other children living on the compound in for evaluation a week and a half later, on February 7. Officials would interview the kids, test them for jimsonweed—and, if necessary, place them in foster homes.

Then, on the afternoon of Friday, January 28, almost two months after Ja'el's initial interview with Pete Baca, approximately ten officials arrived at the ACMTC compound. But the children were gone—all of them.

The officials poked around the property, searching among the trailers and the gardening equipment, under the speckled shade of the pinyon pines. A handful of adult ACMTC members were present for the search, including Deborah, who said the kids were on vacation in Arizona. Deborah and the others "agreed readily to bring the children to court" several days thereafter, according to the *Cibola County Beacon*. "Members invited officers to visit at any time, and even handed out copies of their religious literature."

"We had no trouble," the sheriff told the newspaper.

But they did have trouble, even if they didn't realize it. Several days passed, and officials prepared to give the ACMTC children blood tests, as well as physical and psychological evaluations, when they were brought in. Ja'el meanwhile grew more and more agitated. "My job is not to do your job for you," she insisted to an official in a voicemail. "My job is to spread the word of the Lord. I am not being a pound [*sic*] in your problems with the justice system, or whatever you people have in mind, okay. The Lord says revenge is mine."

February 7 arrived, and again no one from the group came to Grants.

That afternoon, two officials drove out to the compound. "We saw a lady with a white dress waving at us," they later recounted in an internal law enforcement report. It was Deborah. Inside the house, Jim and Steve Schmierer joined them in the sitting room. The men wore purple T-shirts with a logo for "Christ's Royal Regiment," as the group sometimes referred to itself. "Deborah did most of the talking. Periodically [the men] would say 'amen' to things that Deborah would say."

The conversation soon turned to Ja'el Phalen, whom Deborah described as "a kid hater" with "forty-five different personalities." Deborah said Ja'el "had a sexual fascination" and talked about "how to have sex with Frenchmen." Ja'el "calls the young girls 'bitchy,'" and expressed a desire "to dress and undress the children." She'd even tried to shoot "a raving homosexual," Deborah said, which had made Deborah worried Ja'el "might go wacky." ("Her gun was her lover, her baby, her companion, her guardian.")

Deborah also said Ja'el "hates blacks," though Deborah "thought the blacks were exquisite people."

Deborah raised and dropped her voice as she spoke. She grew tearful. Addressing the most recent investigation, she confirmed there were no children on the property. ("In time of war, [ACMTC members] hide their children," per the report.)

In the course of the conversation, Deborah, Jim, and Steve all denied the allegations of physical and sexual abuse. Tellingly, Jim brought up Waco to explain why the children had been sent away. He said he'd wanted to avoid a repeat of the siege that had killed dozens of Branch Davidians, many of them children. "Nobody comes back [to Fence Lake] until everything is cleared."

The next day, February 8, officials decided to file a contempt order. They also considered using the Child Protective Services Unit to search for the children.

Then, on February 9, the sheriff's department served papers ordering Deborah and several others to appear in District Court on the sixteenth—but the date arrived, and again, no one appeared.

By this point, several officials had begun to sour on the investigation. It was "based on statements of a single witness who has had a history of making unfounded allegations to the police," reported the *Albuquerque Journal*, citing local law enforcement. Undersheriff Johnny Valdez told the paper, "Our department has had one or two cases involving [Ja'el Phalen] that turned out to be nothing. . . . I think it's the department's opinion that the case should probably have been investigated further [before executing the court order]. . . . In a nutshell, there is no situation."

No situation? Even if Ja'el's allegations were false, the circumstances surrounding the children's disappearance remained highly suspicious. District Attorney Mike Runnels gave a revealing explanation when he said, "I think you have to take what happened at Waco and Ruby Ridge and several other places into consideration. . . . These people are already normally paranoid. If you trigger somebody's paranoia, obviously they're going to respond in a typical paranoid fashion."

Here it was, further indication of Waco's long, destructive tail. People across the world had seen how the FBI and ATF had bungled the operation at Mount Carmel; how all those men, women, and children had burned to death. Those events, and the Oklahoma City bombing that followed, had prompted the federal government to crack down on militia groups across the country. Officials from ATF and the FBI had been excoriated in the press, berated in Congress. This wasn't the only reason the ACMTC case had encountered difficulty—there were glaring legal issues at play, namely officials' failure to locate the children—but the District Attorney's statements to the press spoke to the ongoing pressures exerted by Waco. Absent that skittishness, it's certainly possible that officials would have made a halfway decent effort to find the kids, or to ask Arizona law enforcement for help locating the children.

"Hey, this is America," District Attorney Mike Runnels said. "If they want to be by themselves, they have a right to do so."

On February 28 the legal case was dismissed.

CHAPTER 29

Cults weren't just an American issue. In the 1990s, a growing number of fringe religious groups sprouted across Europe, prompting a rush of reports, resolutions, and laws. In 2001, French legislators passed a bill to address the problem. "France has become the first country in the world to introduce specific legislation aimed at controlling the activities of cults," announced *The Guardian*. "The objective is to combat the 175-odd movements of a quasi-religious nature considered a danger to society." Cult leaders found guilty under the new legislation could face up to five years in prison and a fine of up to €750,000.

The new law was the culmination of years of study and debate. Following preliminary investigations into "sects and new religious movements" in the 1980s and early 1990s, the European Parliament had passed a Resolution on Cults in Europe, calling for communication and vigilance among member countries. A 1997 Report on Cults in the European Union took the investigation further, urging member states to pursue legal action when crimes were committed, while also "fully respecting fundamental civil rights," the difficulty of this maneuver reflected in the often-tortured tone of this and other similar reports.

France took a particularly strong interest in cults, or *sectes*. In 1995, sixteen members of the Order of the Solar Temple cult were discovered dead in the French Alps; most of their bodies were "charred" and "arranged in a star formation around a campfire, in an apparent mass suicide," per the *Los Angeles Times*. French leaders established the Parliamentary Commission on Cults, and, later, an agency for Monitoring and Combatting Cultic Deviances. In 1996, a subset of the commission released a list of 173 allegedly dangerous cults with a presence in France. These developments culminated in 2001, with the passage of the watershed anti-cult law, and, in 2002, the creation of a government agency known as the Interministerial Mission for Vigilance and Action against Sectarian Deviances.

The law allowed for the dissolution of cults whose members engaged in a range of harmful behaviors, from endangering children, to illegally practicing medicine, to advertising falsely or committing fraud. The law's supporters maintained they weren't legislating against belief; they were legislating against behavior. The new law merely allowed them to hold a group (and its leaders) responsible for illegal activities. But the law also raised complicated questions. The Universal Declaration on Human Rights guaranteed all peoples "the right of freedom of thought, conscience and religion." How, then, to distinguish between a cult and a religion? And who got to make that call?

The law also made it a misdemeanor to abuse a vulnerable person's "ignorance or weakness," even listing categories of vulnerability like age, pregnancy, disability, and psychological subjugation. In theory, there was no problem here: Exploiting a child or an elderly person was obviously objectionable. The broader implications, however, were more complicated. It wasn't illegal to recruit people into an officially registered faith, like Catholicism. But what about Mormonism, Scientology, or Seventh-day Adventism, all of them *sectes*, according to early versions of the government's 1995 report? Were they to be treated with greater malice than more established religions that had once fit the criteria of a cult?

Members of minority religions (or were they cults?) protested the legislation aggressively; as a prominent Scientologist put it, the law was "the work of a handful of extremists wanting to impose state atheism." The United States, too, opposed the law, pressuring French officials to express more tolerance toward fringe religious groups. The French president was not pleased. According to *The Guardian*, President Jacques Chirac "has told Mr. Clinton that religious freedom will no longer be a subject for bilateral presidential talks, in the light of what has been officially described as 'shocking' White House support for Scientologists and Moonies."

But it wasn't Scientologists or "Moonies" per se the US government was trying to support. It was a distinctly American idea of freedom of religion: an expansive right to pray and worship however a person liked. European countries approached the matter differently, as in France, where the principle of *laïcité*, or secularism, is enshrined in the constitution. As many a political scientist has put it, if America generally values freedom *of* religion, France values freedom *from* religion.

The anti-cult law got its first real test in 2004, when self-proclaimed prophet Arnaud Mussy stood trial for his leadership of a *secte apocalyptique* in Nantes. Two years earlier, Mussy had said the world was going to end by Christmas, prompting three of his followers to attempt suicide, one of them successfully. This was precisely the kind of "abuse of weakness" the law had been designed to combat, and Mussy was prosecuted accordingly. He was ultimately found guilty, fined €115,000, and given a suspended three-year prison sentence.

By now other countries in Europe and around the world had begun developing or at least thinking about ways to combat cults. But little corresponding action took place in the United States, where fringe groups were in large part protected by the First Amendment. Notwithstanding prosecution of individual bad actors—or, in the case of the militia movement, a crackdown on firearms offenses—elected officials appeared to have less appetite for the kinds of hearings or reports that had become almost commonplace in Europe. If anything, American officials were seen to be *defending* groups rather than prosecuting them. To onlookers abroad, this inaction was mystifying. As a French anti-cult official told a journalist in 2000, "The United States [*sic*] position is less and less understood in Europe."

What this meant for ACMTC was that things largely went back to normal when the Ja'el Phalen investigation concluded and the children returned to the compound. Group members coaxed apples, cabbages, tomatoes, and spinach from the gardens. They made and sold a range of baked goods. The children took homeschooling classes and helped with chores around the property, peeling bananas and shelling pistachios. In one sense, this was classic off-the-grid living. ACMTC had left the dominant culture in search of something better.

But ACMTC wasn't something better, not at all—and especially not now, in the wake of Ja'el Phalen investigation. Sarah's escape six months earlier had unleashed, in Deborah, a level of unbridled extremism that shocked even some of her most stalwart followers. "I literally watched that lady go crazy in front of my face," Julie Gudino later recalled.

Everyone at ACMTC suffered under Deborah's leadership, but no one bore the brunt of her alleged barbarity more intensely than Trinity. As the girl grew older—as she turned three, then four, then five—Deborah allegedly forced her to work harder, and to much more humiliating effect, than any of the other children on the compound. Trinity vacuumed and swept the floors. She picked weeds, carried heavy objects, and chopped vegetables for six to eight hours a day. Deborah called her lazy, evil, and cursed and made her run up and down the driveway for no reason. She shaved Trinity's hair because it had become a "source of pride."

Even by the group's punishing standards, the girl's treatment was noteworthy. Trinity received only one meal a day, and was forced to eat spoiled leftovers on the floor or at her own fold-up table, where she sat facing the wall. When she threw up at a meal one day, some of the vomit got in her food, but Deborah made her keep eating, anyway.

Which is to say, Deborah made Trinity eat her own vomit.

When Trinity was around four years old, Deborah allegedly started scratching, slapping, beating, and flogging her with a whip. "I can remember there being like round welts left from where it had landed on me," Trinity later recalled in open court. According to Julie Gudino, Deborah hit Trinity with an oak stick if Trinity didn't walk or work fast enough: "It usually left a bruise or a welt." When Julie talked to Deborah about Trinity's treatment, Deborah told her "to shut up and to keep my nose to myself."

Deborah justified her abuse by pointing to Trinity's race: The girl needed to be tough in case God wanted to take her back to Africa. (Deborah also said Trinity's skin was black because she was cursed.) Johanna later recalled seeing Trinity get "yelled at or whipped and humiliated by Deborah, who sometimes chased her, and called her names like 'lazy' and 'witch.'" Trinity frequently wondered "why this was happening to me, why I was seen as so evil."

"I can't believe we let this go on," observed Johanna, who left the group in 2003, before the alleged abuse reached its nadir. "It makes my stomach hurt to think about that. I think you become numb to it."

The alleged abuse temporarily stopped in the spring of 2002, when Sarah came to visit. Trinity, now age four, later said she didn't tell Sarah what was happening, though Sarah did notice that one of Trinity's legs had started to turn inward.

The alleged abuse resumed when Sarah returned to Seattle. By the summer, Trinity's right leg had begun to torque even more dramatically inward, "like a boomerang," as Trinity later put it. The pain became so intense she started crawling rather than walking, which allegedly only made Deborah angrier and more abusive. Trinity said Deborah claimed she was beating Trinity "because God told her to. That it wasn't her beating me; it was God."

According to testimony Trinity later gave in court, when Trinity was around five years old, Deborah started abusing her sexually, too.

Years later, when former ACMTC members learned of Trinity's claims, some were shocked. Deborah could be sadistic, yes, but she'd hardly seemed like a child molester to them. And yet, had she seemed like someone who might seek to dominate and violate the group's most vulnerable member? Perhaps.

Peter, Sarah's cult husband, allegedly started sexually abusing Trinity, too.

In 2004, in the midst of the alleged sexual abuse, Trinity turned seven. About two years had passed since Sarah's return visit to the compound. By this point the condition of the girl's leg had become so indisputably dire that even Deborah could admit she needed medical attention. Rather than investigating the underlying condition, however, Julie Gudino says Deborah approached the matter as a cosmetic issue. Deborah took the girl to a surgeon in Mexico, where care was cheaper and the group could evade the attention of American authorities. A doctor there allegedly broke Trinity's legs to reset them straight. According to Trinity, Deborah refused to give her any pain medication following the surgery. To take pills was to rely on man's power rather than God's.

Back in Fence Lake, Julie Gudino tried to give Trinity a get-well-soon card. But according to Julie, Deborah swatted the card away from Trinity. "You don't need any special attention," Deborah snarled. "Nobody wants to hear your whining and your crying."

Trinity's legs appeared more or less straight. But something—everything—was still wrong.

A few ACMTC members would later contest Trinity's claims of abuse and mistreatment. Trinity was "a really happy kid," a woman named Victoria River said years later while under oath. "She had a lively imagination." When asked if she'd ever seen Deborah hit, beat, or whip Trinity, or if Trinity had ever expressed pain or distress, Victoria repeatedly said no. Josh Green also disputed Trinity's allegations of child labor. Trinity did work around the compound, he said, but only "little chores. Stuff to make a kid think she's helping by [giving] her a zucchini and [giving] her a plastic knife, and she gets to chop it up thinking that she's helping cook dinner." Josh said Trinity took painkillers after the operation in Mexico, and dismissed all accusations of racism against his mother. "Deborah loves all races," he said, "all people."

Whatever the truth, the situation at ACMTC was clearly devolving, enough that even Julie Gudino, one of Deborah's most loyal, long-standing disciples, began to think about leaving. In 2004, the year of Trinity's surgery, Julie's son Zechariah started pushing back against the Greens. Julie says Deborah and Jim told her to "get rid of" Zechariah by leaving him "on the side of the road somewhere. . . . If he can't submit himself, he needs to learn the hard way." This and other developments were ultimately too much for Julie to bear, so Julie and her husband Bernie packed their bags and left—though, remarkably, they left Zechariah at the compound so he wouldn't go with them to hell.

Even Jim was growing frustrated. In October 2005, he and Deborah argued about a former member who'd come back to visit the group. Jim got physical with Peter Green and Steve Schmierer, threatening to kill them and Deborah with "a curved blade at the end of a pole," according to the *Gallup Independent*. When Peter and Steve threatened to beat Jim with walking sticks, the police were summoned and Jim was arrested. He received forty staples in his head at the hospital, and was taken to the Cibola County Detention Center, where he remained for four days. Perhaps sensing that further attention wasn't going to serve either of them well, the Greens only took a few days to make peace. According to the *Albuquerque Journal*, they "apologized to each other and were trying for a reconciliation. In addition, Deborah Green said she was retracting her earlier report to police that her husband threatened her with murder." Jim said he'd "been trying to get [the group] to introduce reforms, especially opening up communications.

"It turned into a shouting match and got out of hand," he added. "It was kind of a family feud."

Jim was released from jail, and nothing ultimately came of the encounter. But things were spinning more and more noticeably out of control.

In 2006, less than a year later, Trinity, eight, went outside to play with Isaiah, nine. A swing set had been installed at the compound—one of Deborah's few concessions to childhood. Trinity was swinging when Isaiah suddenly stepped in front of her. Trinity said she was going to hit him—but he didn't move in time, and when Trinity crashed into him, they both fell to the ground.

Pain shot through one of her legs. There was no cut, no blood. But something was clearly wrong.

Isaiah and several other children ran to the house for help. Jim and Josh rushed outside, duct-taped Trinity's leg to a board, and carried her into the house, where she passed out soon thereafter.

She woke up several hours later, when the day was almost over. By this point the swelling was so bad the Greens decided to go to the hospital. They placed her in the back of a Grand Caravan and drove her to a health center in Zuni, forty miles north. But "the condition of my break was too severe" for them to handle, Trinity later recalled in court. The staff told Jim and Deborah they needed to go to the hospital in Albuquerque; when Trinity was offered pain medication, "Deborah admonished them and said they could not give me anything." Trinity was loaded back into the van. The pain was now at its peak.

According to Trinity, at the hospital in Albuquerque a nurse tried to administer an IV to help with the pain, but again Deborah held her off. Trinity had broken her femur, the largest bone in the body, and one that should've never broken in a simple swing-set accident. She needed surgery. But the staff said it was too late for the operation. Trinity would have to wait until morning.

It was at this point that Trinity was taken away from the Greens. Someone brought her into a room where she was given pain medication—finally—that allowed her to sleep.

The days that followed were hazy. After surgery, Trinity went in and out of consciousness. Doctors and nurses came in and out of her room. They explained she was severely underweight and malnourished.

About three or four days after the surgery, a woman from the state asked Trinity if anyone on the compound ever hit her.

Trinity said yes.

The woman asked how many times a week.

Trinity said more than four.

The woman asked if Trinity was being fed.

Trinity said yes.

The woman left. It was a short conversation.

Deborah and Josh entered the room.

"Did she ask you if you were hit?" Deborah asked.

"Yes," Trinity said.

Deborah asked Trinity how many times she'd told the woman she'd been hit. Trinity said more than four.

Deborah became angry. "You should have said you only got hit twice," she said, according to Trinity. "You should have said less. You shouldn't have said that many times." Deborah told Trinity not to reveal anything further.

Maybe a day or two later, Trinity woke up to the sound of the phone ringing. It was Deborah.

"You have to stay there," Deborah said. "They're not letting me take you with me. So we're leaving. But you have to stay."

"Okay," Trinity said. She hung up.

It might not have seemed like a particularly noteworthy conversation. But this was it—the start of Trinity's new life.

In the days following their arrival at the hospital, Jim and Deborah were interviewed repeatedly about Trinity's treatment. The couple claimed to be missionaries on the Navajo Reservation, and stated through a lawyer that Trinity was from "a Native American Tribe in Kansas." The Greens evidently mentioned Uganda, too, given that state officials called the Ugandan embassy on several occasions. A social worker also communicated with the FBI's Special Investigations Unit about the case.

At the time, Trinity "failed to disclose abuse, and in fact denied abuse," according to a court ruling years later, though Trinity would state under oath that she made no such disclosure because "I was in fear that I would be sent back with [Deborah]." Although the case was to be "documented as substantiated for physical neglect involving malnutrition . . . as well as other neglect," all by Jim and Deborah, further investigation appears to have concluded by the end of the summer for reasons that remain unclear.

Officials did, however, open an inquiry into Josiah and Isaiah's treatment in the group. When three officials arrived at the compound to investigate, the driveway was blocked with a white van. Deborah forbade the officials from entering the property. The case was subsequently "closed as unsubstantiated for physical neglect involving emotional neglect due to having no sufficient contact with the Greens," according to official records.

Trinity entered foster care. Months passed. Then, in 2007 and again in 2008, Trinity alleged that both Deborah and Peter had abused her sexually. At this point officials conducted a more thorough investigation, interviewing Julie, Maura, and other former ACMTC members in Sacramento. A special agent from the FBI also indicated that the Bureau had been looking into the group for several years, according to official records.

But even this latest investigation came to nothing: According to a contemporaneous internal report, the office of a senior trial attorney determined there was insufficient evidence to prosecute the case. Now that Trinity was in a "loving home," the senior attorney didn't want "to continue to have victim remember [the] incident."

It was a tale as old as ACMTC. Yet again, the Greens had evaded accountability. And yet again, the justice system's failure to stop them would have devastating—even deadly—consequences in years to come.

CHAPTER 30

*M*eanwhile, Maura.

It was the late 2000s, around the time Trinity came forward with her allegations of sexual abuse, and almost twenty years since Maura's expulsion from the group. She was around sixty, with hair she wore in bangs and an elegant, welcoming face that had been weathered, slightly, by time and experience. By now all five of her children were out of the group, even Nathaniel, who'd run away from ACMTC in the middle of the night when he was eighteen. He, Rebekah, Sarah Chelew, and Lilly all had their struggles, but they were making their way in the world. Only Steven, the youngest, displayed signs of serious psychological distress.

Maura was certified as a registered nurse by now and worked at the medical center-turned-hospital where she'd met Lila Carter back in 1969. One day she wandered over to Camellia Cottage, the hospice unit where doomed, alluring Carlo had died. From the outside, it was still a charming, peaceful spot surrounded by flower bushes and palm trees. When a passing custodian noticed Maura peeking through the door, he let her inside. The space was white, linoleum floored, and largely empty. Being there wasn't poignant so much as it was strange.

The moment passed and Maura walked back outside.

Maura's life had been marked by several important transformations—from hippie to Christian, from Christian to cultist, from cultist back to Christian again—and now, more than twenty years into her new life, she experienced another significant shift. On a drive out to her parents' house one day, she heard a radio interview with religious scholar Bart

Ehrman, whose books questioned the inerrancy of the Bible. "Not only do we not have the originals," Ehrman wrote of the New Testament, "we don't have the first copies of the originals. We don't even have the copies of the copies of the originals, or copies of the copies of the copies of the originals."

Maura was fascinated. The Bible was "a very human book," Ehrman insisted, susceptible to the same errors and alterations that any text might experience when copied, over the course of many hundreds of years, by fallible human beings.

Maura began reading Ehrman's books, increasingly convinced by his claims. Rather than upsetting or destabilizing her, these new insights filled Maura with relief. For years she'd worried that her lapsed-Catholic parents were headed to hell. Ehrman's books effectively snuffed out her concerns.

For some time now Maura had been experiencing misgivings about her faith. At New Hope, members had been encouraged to sign loyalty pledges, which had brought unwanted associations with ACMTC. Then, when one of Maura's best friends was effectively excommunicated from the congregation, Maura had decided to move to another church. In an earlier life she might have stayed at New Hope, where she'd been a member for almost two decades. But Maura had changed—enough, at least, to discern whom she really wanted to follow.

Then came Bart Ehrman. His teachings, combined with her own personal frustrations, helped prompt her to leave behind her Christian faith once and for all. She felt liberated. She was free now, free *not* to believe in the smoldering underworld she'd feared since her teenage years. Yet again, Maura had dropped everything to start over.

It was a time of change, not just for Maura but also for Sarah.

After failing to retrieve Josiah, Isaiah, and Trinity in 2002, Sarah returned to Seattle full of self-recrimination. For two and a half years she'd operated under the hope, or the delusion, that she was going to get her kids back. Now that hope had evaporated; she told herself she simply had to accept the brutal truth.

But this, too, was a sustaining delusion. She could have contacted law enforcement or pursued legal custody of the children. She did neither.

In the past, whenever former ACMTC members with children had come back in an effort to retrieve their kids from the group, Deborah had banished them to Berino, or to a wandering caravan. Sarah figured the same thing would happen to Josiah, Isaiah, and Trinity if she got the authorities involved. It also seemed possible to her that the kids might get shipped off to Africa, in which case it would be that much harder for them to get up and leave of their own accord one day, as she herself had done.

But there was another reason, too, that kept Sarah from contacting the authorities. She knew that doing so might raise questions about her role in the plot to bring Trinity to America.

Sarah dealt with her ongoing guilt as she always did. She worked. She was full to the brim with her medical assistant studies, her job at the café, and a baby back home. One day Geoff proposed to her with a ring on a mushroom pizza, Sarah's favorite kind. In the moment she felt a surge of joy, love, and optimism. Maybe things were going to work out between them.

Overwhelmed with the difficulty of work and family life, Sarah asked her old friend Abi Stewart, from Seattle's Best Coffee, to come live with them. By now Sarah and Geoff had moved to a larger house where Sarah spent her scant free time fixing up the garden, pruning the rosebushes, and planting herbs.

About a year after Sarah's failed mission to Fence Lake, Abi found her crying in the garden. Abi asked Sarah what was wrong.

"I'm just so sad," Sarah said. "I'm so tired."

Abi, suspicious, asked if she was pregnant.

"No," Sarah said. "No way."

But she was. As with her three previous pregnancies, Sarah was excited but also anxious. She worried about what it would mean to raise another child around a father who seemed to be pulling away from her.

Geoff was on a work trip when Sarah gave birth to their second child, a son she named Jeremiyah. The baby was a delight, but Sarah was done having children, at least for now, and decided to get an IUD.

About a month after giving birth, Sarah received a startling phone call from Johanna, her old baking buddy at ACMTC. Johanna said she'd left the group and needed a place to stay. She asked if she could come live with Sarah in Seattle, at least temporarily.

The circumstances of Johanna's departure were shocking even by ACMTC standards. For years she and Sarah's brother Josh had been attracted to each other; when Deborah found out her son had kissed a woman who'd once been married, and in fact had two children, Deborah had made Johanna call her parents to tell them she was a whore.

But the attraction between Josh and Johanna kept building, and several years after Sarah's escape, they started having sex: in the bathroom, in the silver Airstream trailer, in a tent in the middle of the night.

The situation was untenable. In a fit of confusion, Johanna volunteered to get married to another member she didn't actually love. Deborah, in turn, ordered Josh to get married *to Johanna's own daughter*, now almost eighteen years old.

The night before Johanna's wedding, she sneaked into the craft room to have sex with Josh. The next evening, she slept with her new husband, John. It was thus with no small amount of horror that she realized, several weeks later, that she was pregnant. She had no idea who the father was.

It was an absurd situation, Greek tragedy by way of rural New Mexico. It was also motivation, finally, for Johanna to get out. Like several other women who'd left ACMTC before her, she couldn't imagine raising another child around the group's madnesses. She tried to get Josh to run away with her, but he refused. (Later, in Seattle, when Johanna learned how to use a computer, Josh emailed her the music video for a Puff Daddy song, "I'll Be Missing You.") Johanna's kids, eighteen and sixteen, would remain behind on the compound. Johanna was sorry to leave them behind but figured they were too old for her to tell them what to do anymore.

In Seattle she moved into Sarah's basement-level bedroom, the newest member of what was turning into another kind of matriarchal commune. Abi could tell how much Sarah liked having the whole klatch of them under one roof. In that respect, at least, mother and daughter were alike.

From here the months and years moved quickly. When Jeremiyah was still an infant, Sarah, Geoff, Johanna, and the kids relocated to Portland, where Geoff's behavior only got worse. Sarah says she found a $1,000 sushi charge from a strip club on their credit card statement. (Geoff later said, "I couldn't shake the drugging.")

Geoff was off working a job on the East Coast when he told Sarah he'd cheated on her. Sarah flew across the country to give him an ultimatum: He could pick Sarah and the kids or this other woman, but not both. Geoff, tearful, said he wanted to be with Sarah but also said she could be too rigid, too uptight. Figuring physical proximity was the only way to prevent future infidelity, Sarah moved the family east to be closer to where Geoff was then stationed, ultimately landing in New York City. They still weren't married, but maybe that could happen when they got settled. Maybe.

This was how Sarah would deal with her past: by rushing headlong into her future. As she saw it, there was no point wallowing in bygones.

Maura approached things differently. Through all stages of her post-ACMTC life, the group had remained steadfastly front of mind, a bee buzzing between her eyes. She stayed in touch with a handful of mothers and other relatives with loved ones in the group. She drafted the beginnings of a book. She started a blog.

By this point Jim and Deborah had created a manic, crazy-fonted website featuring their greatest-hits accusations against Maura—that she was a whore, a child pornographer, an orgy-loving drug user who enjoyed "showing off her vaginal area whenever she could." The unpaid portion of the judgment had accumulated substantial interest over the years, such that the Greens now owed Maura over $1.5 million. Years earlier, Maura had more or less given up on trying to get the money—the Greens' games had reduced her appetite for the fight—but the website made her angry, and she decided to try moving the judgment from California to New Mexico (as was required by law, if she wanted to collect the money). She successfully renewed the judgment and got a lawyer in Albuquerque who transferred the case to New Mexico. The lawyer discovered evidence that the Greens appeared to have engaged in extensive fraud, allegedly hiding their assets in a handful of shady trusts to keep them inaccessible to Maura.

The Greens were notified of the lawyer's allegations, but they refused—as ever—to cooperate. A year passed, and then another, and still a trial hadn't been scheduled. Jim and Deborah appeared to have slipped free yet again.

Maura also tried to go after the Greens in the media. In 2006—the year Sarah moved to the East Coast and Trinity entered state custody—Maura and the mother of a then-active ACMTC member appeared on the *Dr. Phil* show to talk about the group. In years to come Maura would also participate in a handful of TV programs about the group, most of which portrayed Maura as an exotic, behind-the-glass zoo creature victimized by Deborah and Maura's own disordered thinking. Maura's acceptance of her own mistreatment while in the group was, of course, astonishing. And yet that acceptance had been the product of wholly unremarkable desires and ambitions. Maura had wanted to do right by her kids, her husband, her god. She'd wanted to make a difference: to really live.

Sarah had spent much of her life in rural settings, among blackberry bushes, crawdad gullies, and bird-pecked roadkill. Now she lived in Hell's Kitchen, New York City, surrounded by gay bars, Thai joints, coffee trucks, and sex shops.

Geoff remained as volatile as ever, and within three months of the move to New York, Sarah knew the relationship was over. She kicked him out and got sole custody of the kids. (Their story would come to a strange coda when Geoff moved back to Seattle and entered a long-term relationship with Johanna.)

Sarah got a job as an office manager, picked up shifts at a café, and worked as an extra on TV shows like *CSI: NY*. She did some modeling, too, even appearing on a Times Square billboard as a jaunty, stylish publicist. The image she presented in the ad—affluent, urbane, with black-and-white stilettos—stood in marked contrast to her difficult, strained reality. She could barely afford to pay for childcare for the kids, now around five and six. When they moved to an apartment in Harlem, they slept together on a futon, Sarah sandwiched in the middle.

Eventually Abi moved east to help out. Deborah remained in contact ("IF YOU WERE TO FACE DEATH ARE YOU RIGHT WITH GOD???") and sent stacks of tracts. Even now, years after leaving the group, Sarah still occasionally put them out around the city. Mystified, Abi asked Sarah why she was promoting a world she'd upended her entire life to escape.

"I don't know," Sarah said. "People can read it if they want." It was shocking behavior—shocking but also typical of ex–cult members, who often struggle to shake their proselytizing impulses.

Sometimes Abi even caught Sarah reading the tracts herself.

When the kids were old enough, Sarah enrolled them in a Catholic school not far from the engineering firm where she worked. She said she didn't care about the school's religious affiliation, but Abi also wondered if some vestigial guilt or even faithfulness was still at play. One day Sarah bought Jeremiyah a bendy Jesus figurine—because she thought it looked funny, yes, but was there another reason?

As for her other children—as for Josiah, Isaiah, and Trinity—Sarah decided there was nothing further to be done. In 2006, Deborah told her that Trinity had been taken into state custody, but Sarah remained unclear about the broader circumstances of the girl's removal. She was concerned but also relieved: At least one of her children had gotten out. She reached out to the state in an effort to get in touch with Trinity but made no progress. She still sent the boys cards on their birthdays, though she figured they'd been indoctrinated too deeply for her messages to mean anything.

In 2007, Sarah met a funny, hardworking Frenchman named Xavier. They started dating and soon got married.

By this point Sarah had picked up running as a hobby. She went jogging around Central Park and started running races. In 2009, she ran the New York City Marathon. When she crossed the finish line, she felt broken, half-dead. And yet the marathon was to be a pivotal accomplishment—a reminder of her capacity to endure, to make it all the way to the end. The hard stuff was part of the good stuff: the price she paid to get here, foil cape wrapped around her shoulders, the sun shining dimly on her salty, upturned cheeks.

PART FOUR

DELIVERANCE

CHAPTER 31

In 2008, Republican presidential nominee John McCain selected Alaska governor Sarah Palin as his running mate. It was a "Hail Mary" pick, writes journalist Tim Alberta, an out-of-left-field choice that shook up the race in precisely the ways McCain aides had hoped it would. White evangelicals were largely thrilled by the selection, given that Palin was an anti-abortion, anti–gay marriage, self-described "Bible-believing Christian" who'd worshiped at several different evangelical churches over the course of her life.

Palin's selection was a surprising one for McCain, who'd grown up outside the evangelical church, and who'd previously denounced evangelical heavyweights Jerry Falwell and Pat Robertson as "extremists" and "agents of intolerance." By 2008, however, McCain's tune had changed, enough that evangelicals who'd once viewed him with suspicion came to embrace his and Palin's candidacy with rapturous excitement. Describing the perspective of many commentators at the time, *Time* magazine said Palin had "supposedly erased McCain's Evangelical problem and united the base that proved so key to George W. Bush's victory in 2004." Palin's selection was a counterpunch to commentators who had claimed: "The Religious Right's Era Is Over," as *Time* put it in a 2007 headline.

Still, it had been a tumultuous few decades for the movement.

Evangelicals' political and social influence had declined since the height of Falwell's Moral Majority in the 1980s. In 1998, President Bill Clinton was impeached for perjury and obstruction of justice related to an affair with a White House intern, but Clinton remained immensely popular through the investigation, with an approval of 71 percent in the immediate wake of the impeachment, according to Pew Research Center. Evangelical leaders were horrified. "I am left to conclude that our greatest problem is not the Oval Office," wrote prominent activist James Dobson. "It's with the people of this land." As another commentator put it, "I believe we have probably lost the culture war."

That didn't mean they weren't going to fight back. In the 2000 presidential election, Republican nominee George W. Bush enjoyed only nominal support from the Christian right; turnout had fallen since 1996, when Bill Clinton served as a galvanizing boogeyman. But movement leaders hardly needed to worry. George Bush courted evangelicals aggressively in his 2004 reelection campaign, granting them considerable access to the White House. This resurgent influence coincided with evangelicals' growing prominence in mainstream culture. In 2004, Mel Gibson's crucifixion epic, *The Passion of the Christ*, grossed an astonishing $125 million in just five days. The *Left Behind* books, which imagined life in the Christian end times, ultimately sold almost 80 million copies. No less impressive was adoption advocate Rick Warren's *The Purpose Driven Life*, "the fastest-selling book of all time, and the best-selling hardback in American history," as *Publishers Weekly* announced in 2004.

Evangelicals used their considerable cultural muscle to fight gay marriage, an issue of particularly urgent importance to the movement. "Unless we act quickly," James Dobson warned, "the family as we have known it for 5,000 years will be gone. With its demise will come such chaos as the world has never seen."

After years in the wilderness, the Christian right appeared to be back on top. And yet 2004 was to prove a high-water mark for the movement. During the 2008 presidential campaign, Democratic nominee Barack Obama worked hard to bridge the "God gap" between the parties, with some success. But his priorities were not the priorities of white evangelicals, and when he won, the impressive margin of his victory suggested conservative Christian voters had lost the ability to swing an election.

In 2015, the movement suffered an even more significant setback when the US Supreme Court granted same-sex couples nationwide the right to marry. For the Christian right, this was a catastrophe of biblical proportions, "the worst defeat they had ever suffered," according to historian Frances FitzGerald.

Opposition to gay marriage was hardly unanimous among churchgoers: According to a Pew Research poll conducted at the time, 27 percent of white evangelicals supported same-sex marriage. Among the sizable majority that didn't, however, the anger and despair was raw. "We're prepared to go to prison," one pastor told a reporter. The war would continue on.

The Greens stayed up-to-date on current events all through the Bush and Obama administrations. Jim even assigned one member, a former UPS driver, to gather news clips about the latest cultural abominations, particularly those concerning President Obama, a.k.a., the "sodomite captain" of the "Pink House."

"The United Nations is full of demons in human bodies," Jim wrote. "This land is run by Freemason, Socialist, Zionist Jews (crypto-Jew revolutionaries) . . . all persecutors of the Christian religion." Tracts and sermons were filled with rants against the "FBI, KGB, CIA, DIA, NSA, IRS, EPA, NCIC, USDA, FDA, NRO, BATF, FINCEN, INS, DOJ, DOD, WTO, Europol, Interpol, M16, M6, Mossad, MAB, etc., etc." Tracts were a frenzied splatter of exclamation points, bold, underlined type, and multicolored headlines. In one essay, the Greens promoted a videotape sermon series called *The Solution to Pollution Is Bloody Revolution*. It was eight hours long.

9/11 was a particular fixation for the couple. "WRITE FOR OUR (free) DVD CALLED '911 Deception' if you have any doubts about America or Israel's involvement in that ACT OF BRUTAL TERRORISM," Jim wrote. "WAKE UP! These same people who planted the bombs in those NYC towers have another plan called 'The Samson Option'—something BIGGER than 911 (this is nuclear dear ones, nuclear)." The statement echoed a speech Jerry Falwell himself had given on television in the days following the terrorist attacks. "The abortionists have got to bear some burden for this because God will not be mocked," Falwell said. "I really believe that the pagans, and the abortionists, and the feminists, and the gays and the lesbians . . . the ACLU, People for the American Way, all of them have tried to secularize America. I point the finger in their face and I say, 'You helped this happen.'"

Falwell's status in the church had fallen since the 1980s, but he was still *Jerry Falwell*, the father of the right-wing conservative Christian movement. Though the Bush White House and others condemned Falwell's comments, Falwell was keying into an intense, *God-is-judging-us* ethos that had long been present in the evangelical church.

Like the evangelical church more broadly, there was no issue that enraged the Greens as much as gay rights. After the Supreme Court legalized same-sex marriage nationwide in 2015, Jim and Deborah unleashed a rampage of rhetoric against this "Pink Stink," this "Pink Osmosis," this "Pink Death Culture."

"These 5 PAGANS in black robes are an ABOMINATION themselves," Jim wrote of the majority justices. "We refuse to bow to this very sick government, refuse to fear the queer."

Jim and Deborah remained fringe figures with only the thinnest, most frayed tether to reality. But the marriage issue had brought them closer to the conservative Christian mainstream than ever before.

On June 16, 2015, when Donald J. Trump announced his candidacy for president of the United States, white American evangelicals had little reason to think of him as their political savior. Here was a man who'd spent his entire life in the church of secularism, a profane money-grubber who'd allegedly cheated on his third wife with a porn star and mused about what it would be like to date his adult daughter. "Blessed are the meek," Jesus had said, "for they shall inherit the earth." But Trump had inherited the earth, or at least an impressive corner of it, and he was the *opposite* of meek. He was loud. He was shameless. He lived not according to the Ten Commandments, but to a single one: *Give it to me.*

At first, many white evangelicals recognized Trump's boastful impiety for what it was: a mockery of the values they'd spent their lives supporting. *Character matters*, they insisted during the Clinton administration. And yet here was a man whose every utterance suggested precisely the opposite. It was hardly a question, then, that they would support Republican candidates who at least pretended to value biblical principles.

Jerry Falwell, Jr., however, heir to the evangelical throne his father had built in the eighties, came out early in favor of Trump. Falwell Jr. recognized something important in Trump, something crude and bombastic and real that appealed to people less interested in turning the other cheek than in punching back—and punching back hard.

Then, as the months passed, evangelicals began migrating to Trump's camp in droves. Even if Trump was spiritually illiterate, even if he referred, ridiculously, to his communion wafer as "my little cracker," he promised to give evangelicals what they wanted, most significantly, Supreme Court justices who would overturn *Roe v. Wade*. Other GOP candidates shared these policy goals. But Trump was different. Per journalist Tim Alberta, whose father was an evangelical pastor, "By the time Trump declared his candidacy in the summer of 2015 . . . the twin narratives of *America at the abyss* and *Christianity in the crosshairs* were ubiquitous within evangelicalism. Trump instinctually understood this"—and exploited it to his advantage.

And so, as the primary progressed, white evangelicals continued to drift into his column. They liked Trump because he promised to deliver policy wins. But they were also thrilled to see him fighting on their behalf, even if it meant ignoring Jesus's command to "love thy neighbor as thyself." Some prominent conservative Christians remained skeptical, and tried to keep evangelicals from aligning themselves with Trump. But for many, the pull of the man's charisma was simply too great. The sense of meaning and belonging, of *chosenness*, he gave them was impossible to resist.

"On January 1, 2017," Jim wrote on the ACMTC website, "God's Spirit declared (to us) that it was time for 'Holy War' against the nations of the world. The Spirit also told us that God put Donald Trump into the office of President of the United States. He said that Trump was 'His choice.' That is all He said."

The newly elected president intoxicated the Greens in much the same way he intoxicated many on the evangelical right. Trump was an outsider. He maligned political correctness. He'd slain "queen Jezebel HELLary

Clinton." Given her miraculous defeat, it was distinctly possible Trump had been sent by God.

The Greens said bureaucrats had been "spying, blackmailing, assassinating, creating wars and igniting revolutions worldwide for decades . . . at the taxpayers' cost!" It was time to "Drain the Stinking Swamp," they insisted, parroting a popular new bit of Trump-speak. "YES! YES! It can be done! It must be done! Before righteousness can prevail, the necrophilous filth must be dealt with. *Making America great again must entail the draining of the swamp.*"

A rush of ludicrous conspiracy theories had accompanied Trump's rise to power. "PIZZAGATE IS REAL!!!" ACMTC insisted, in reference to a conspiracy theory about an alleged child sex ring in the basement of the Comet Ping Pong pizzeria in Washington, D.C. "Changing the subject?!" Jim raged. "Don't like to talk about it? What about them . . . the children? *Are you going to forget about them so quickly?*" Leftists were "CANNIBALS" who would "eventually EAT each other to stay alive." They were planning an "insurrection," too, though it was unlikely that "self-appointed Emperor, Obama, will lead the charge—seeing [as] he is wanted by the officials for various crimes."

The Greens conceded that Trump had flaws. But "it is not a new thing for God to use 'evil' men / nations to punish other 'evil' men / nations," as Jim put it. This was exactly the same argument, almost to the word, that some prominent evangelical leaders had used to justify their support of Trump. The Greens were extremists—that was nothing new. What was different, however, was the extent to which mainstream culture had embraced conspiracy-crazed ideologies like those that Deborah and Jim had long promoted. The tragic irony was that by fanning the flames of conspiracy theories, far-right Christians were injecting their own destructive mania into the culture. It was a phenomenon long true at ACMTC. The group had been founded to fight the sins of the world, and yet the Greens had so far overshot the mark that the group had become its own horrific furnace of evil. Jim and Deborah were obsessed with child trafficking and pedophilia. But Deborah was an alleged perpetrator of precisely these crimes. She'd become the very conspiracy she believed herself to be fighting.

CHAPTER 32

By January 2016, Lieutenant Harry Hall had worked at the Cibola County Sheriff's Office for sixteen years. He regularly conducted check-in visits with the region's more far-flung residents—ranchers, mostly, or California carpetbaggers who *fancied* themselves ranchers. He'd spoken with Jim and Deborah on several occasions, never with any incident, and was familiar with the 2000 investigation. He'd heard rumors about alleged criminal activity on the compound over the years, but the Greens had always been courteous with him. Deborah made him a fresh vegetable juice whenever he came to visit. She said it could help him lose weight.

Hall was at the Sheriff's Office on the afternoon of January 15 when he received a strange, whispered phone call. A woman with a Caribbean accent was asking for help escaping a cult outside Fence Lake—could someone from the Sheriff's Office come pick her up at seven o'clock that evening? The woman's name was Jamie Bridgewater. She wanted to flee with her eleven-month-old son and a disabled friend from the group.

Several hours later, Lieutenant Hall and a deputy, Officer Anthony Nunez, got in their cars and set out for Fence Lake. The sun dropped from view as they drove down the lonely state highway and through the quiet thousand-acre vistas. By the time they arrived outside the compound, the stars were out. Hall and Nunez flicked off their headlights and waited.

After about fifteen minutes, Jamie Bridgewater emerged from the darkness. She was thirty-one years old, short, Black, with brown eyes and a tall forehead. She opened the door to Hall's white Tahoe and thrust a baby into his arms. She said she'd be back soon with her luggage. Jamie's friend Ahn Khu, who walked with a cane, appeared shortly thereafter. Nunez helped her into his truck.

The baby wailed as Hall waited for Jamie to come back. When, finally, she returned with the luggage, Hall sped away from the compound, ignoring the speed limit. The furtive nature of the pickup made him nervous. He barely slowed down when he hit a coyote.

Hall had only just pulled onto the main road when Jamie launched into an alarming stream-of-consciousness account of the two and a half years she'd spent at ACMTC. She was originally from Saint Kitts in the Caribbean, she said, and had learned about the group from the internet. She'd moved to Fence Lake to become a missionary, but had never received any training at the compound, just a barrage of hardship and mistreatment.

Group members didn't eat enough food, she said. They bought firearms and ammunition. One man was "a child molester based on how he interacts with the youngest children." Jamie had been married to Josh Green (whose earlier wife, Johanna's daughter, had left the group several years earlier). But the marriage had left Jamie "painfully disappointed and absolutely miserable." Josh didn't love her, she said. He had terrible body odor. He showered once every four days, and "only if I complained a lot about it."

It was another allegation, however, that most disturbed Hall. Jamie Bridgewater said that in 2014 a twelve-year-old group member named Enoch had died of the flu. It had been a horrific, entirely preventable death. No one had reported it to the authorities.

At around 8:30, the two cars arrived at a women's shelter in Grants, the county seat. Sheriff Tony Mace came to greet them. Sixteen years earlier, Undersheriff Johnny Valdez had effectively shrugged off former ACMTC member Ja'el Phalen's allegations against the group. Sheriff Mace, however, didn't seem inclined to let Jamie Bridgewater's claims die so easily. He and Hall asked the two women to sit for interviews the next morning.

* * *

ACMTC had been back on law enforcement's radar for some time now.

A year earlier, in March 2015, a former member named Brian Miller had asked the Sheriff's Office for help getting custody of his five children, who still lived on the compound with their mother, Stacey. Brian had spoken with Lieutenant Hall and Undersheriff Mike Munk, who told Brian he could pursue custody through the courts. Brian insisted that would never work. "They're just going to flee and hide the kids," he said. "They're going to say they're not here."

Perhaps so. But Munk's interest was piqued, and he and Hall began looking into the group's history.

Hall soon discovered that ACMTC didn't have the required licensing for the peddling business. People around the Sheriff's Office also confirmed Brian Miller's allegation that the group sent children off the compound at the slightest whiff of trouble.

Over the next several months, Hall and Munk had continued to gather information about the group. Then, in September, three months before Jamie Bridgewater's phone call, Hall issued the Greens a citation and summons for the business licensing violations. Jim and Deborah subsequently visited Munk and Hall at the Sheriff's Office to discuss the matter. The Greens wore dove-white military jackets and berets and identified themselves as Generals. Deborah told Munk the group had been investigated many times before—no one had ever found any evidence of wrongdoing. She spoke in an authoritarian, arrogant tone of voice, as if Munk were an underling.

Munk, himself known to have a sharp temper, responded to the Greens calmly. He had no interest in persecuting Jim and Deborah, he said. They were free to practice their faith as they wished. But they had to follow the law. If, as Brian Miller claimed, the kids on the compound weren't getting immunizations or receiving proper healthcare—or weren't even being registered at birth—the Sheriff's Office had to take action.

In a highly uncharacteristic display of deference to state authority, Jim and Deborah pleaded no contest to the citation and paid the $353 fine. If questions about the treatment of ACMTC children remained open, this particular matter appeared to be settled (though not for Brian Miller, whose children remained at the compound).

Why had the Greens acquiesced so easily? Likely they hadn't wanted to trigger a more comprehensive investigation. Whatever the reason, something about Deborah's initial conversation with Mike Munk had clearly left her spooked. As Jamie Bridgewater later reported to law enforcement, Deborah had returned from the meeting with Munk and Hall on a rampage, convinced the new undersheriff was out to get them. She'd ordered all family photos and memorabilia "placed in large plastic trunks and buried." She and Jim told the members they needed to be "ready for a police raid."

Stacey Miller, Brian Miller's wife, relocated with her children to a town called, ominously enough, Truth or Consequences, likely because Deborah wanted to disassociate the group from the brewing custody battle. ("They were hated," Jamie Bridgewater later recalled, citing the custody issues. "Deborah wanted them all dead or gone.") All Stacey's belongings back at the compound were burned.

Panicked about what an inquiry might reveal, Deborah stopped eating. She stopped sleeping. She railed against Mike Munk, who she said might well be the Antichrist.

Deborah wasn't wrong to be concerned. ACMTC *did* have reason to fear a new investigation. New developments *had* made the group more vulnerable than ever before. The boy who'd died back in 2014 was Enoch Miller, Brian Miller's oldest son—one of the very children he was now working so diligently to find.

The morning after her escape, Jamie Bridgewater sat for an interview at the Sheriff's Office in Grants. Present for the interview were Lieutenant Hall, Undersheriff Mike Munk, and Detective Steve Chavez, among other officials. Jamie Bridgewater repeated and expanded on many of the same allegations she'd made to Lieutenant Hall the evening prior. Deborah forced the children to eat food that adults "would never eat because it is spoiled or rotting," she later wrote. "The children are treated worst [*sic*] than animals." Little girls behaved in a bizarrely provocative manner, too, showing off their bodies and "acting like lesbians." Twenty-one-year-old Josiah, Sarah's oldest son, "loves and owns guns," now buried on the compound. "He buys and sells bullets online. He always downloads and watches videos of different guns and shooting tutorials." (Isaiah, for his part, preferred knives.) Things had clearly changed at ACMTC since Sarah's departure more than sixteen years earlier. The alleged presence of firearms amounted to a major escalation, to say nothing of the fact that Josiah played, let alone *owned*, video games.

Serious health issues were present among members, especially Josh. Jamie wrote:

> His stomach swells sometimes like a large balloon. I believe that he has cancer of the stomach in addition to ulcers. He has debilitating stomach pain all day and night. His pain is chronic. . . . If he lives past five years, I will be surprised. His mother Deborah claims to specialize in "Divine Healing" and can do nothing for him. No medical help is ever arranged for [him]. . . . Joshua looks like he is older than his seventy-year-old father.

And then there was Enoch.

In her interview with Chavez and in a subsequent written statement, Jamie laid out a tale as tragic as it was unsurprising. In December 2013, a terrible flu had spread through the compound. "This particular round of the flu was especially hard on both the children and the adults," Jamie wrote. "The children complained of extreme pain in their joints and body. They had a lot of vomiting, and had to lay in bed upstairs around the clock for over a week. They hardly ate anything besides cantaloupe and oranges."

Enoch Miller, a blond, dimpled twelve-year-old, had fared especially poorly. When he didn't improve, Deborah claimed he was only pretending to be sick. "Don't carry any food upstairs to that rebel," she said, according to Jamie. Days passed and Enoch didn't get any better.

Eventually Deborah said Enoch needed to eat—but only because Deborah "got very afraid that she would be later accused of starving Enoch,"

Jamie believed. Stacey tried to feed him soup (noodle and vegetable, an extreme luxury), but he only got down half a bowlful. "By this point his speech was becoming very minimal and slightly slurred."

Then came the boil, "a small, raised bump" that appeared above his right eyebrow. Days passed and the bump continued to spread, colonizing the right side of the boy's face. Soon the swelling had gotten so bad it had sealed the eye shut.

The boil was still growing when Enoch made a surprise appearance at a prayer meeting early one morning. Deborah gave a prophecy ("Words of the Spirit"), and announced Enoch had something to say. Crying, Enoch stood up and spoke.

"I would like to say sorry to everyone for all the trouble I caused everyone, and for my bad attitude. I'm sorry for causing problems."

Then, according to Jamie, "he sat back down and he continued to sob quietly."

In the days that followed, Enoch's condition worsened dramatically. He had seizures, evidence that he was "slipping back into rebellion," Deborah said. When Stacey asked Deborah what to do, she recommended putting an herb poultice on the boil, but it had little effect. The boy was fast approaching sepsis.

He was also in tremendous pain, enough that "Deborah offered painkillers of some kind," Jamie said. But the pills came with a warning. Deborah told Stacey that if Enoch took them, he risked further seizures. Stacey—once a scientist, a *chemist*—declined the offer, according to Jamie.

Within a few days the boil had popped. Stacey stayed with Enoch night and day, dabbing away the pus until the floor of the bedroom was littered with used toilet paper. Eventually someone wrapped Enoch's head with gauze and a bandage. He looked better now, but his overall condition was much worse. He couldn't move his right hand. "His speech was so incoherent and choppy that he sounded as if he was a deaf person trying to speak."

Deborah ordered Enoch moved down to the kitchen, where he lay, frail and deteriorating, having seizures on a mattress. According to Jamie, "the option for Stacey to get a doctor was discussed briefly," but Deborah told Jamie, "If [Stacey] wants to take him to a doctor it's up to her; but I told her, 'Fourteen years ago, you gave this child up to God, but if you want to take him back [to the outside world] then it's up to you. . . . God told me that he is going to heal Enoch."

On the morning of January 5, Jamie overheard Deborah talking about Enoch. "That boy would not change no matter how we tried to help him," Deborah said. "He was a rebel. He would not repent. Well, if the boy repents, he will live, and if he doesn't . . . well . . . he belongs to God."

Several hours later Jamie went to visit Enoch in the room where he'd been moved. "I knocked on the door, and when no one answered . . . I opened it slowly and let out a very audible gasp at the sight I saw: Enoch was sprawled out on the lower bunk of a red, metal bunk bed." Deborah and Stacey were there, too, along with two members named Ruth and Sabbath. "As soon as Deborah saw me, she said, 'You shouldn't be in here,'" Jamie recalled:

> But I ignored her and pushed my way passed [sic] her into the room, and made my way over to Enoch. I sat on the bed, took a hold of his left hand and did what I saw Sabbath and Ruth doing: they were each rubbing one of his legs. So I began rubbing Enoch's left arm and hand. His right arm lay by his side motionless. He looked extremely emaciated. His legs and arms looked like tooth picks. His breathing was shallow; I saw his slender stomach rising and falling faintly. He looked pale, and his body felt cool.

Jim and Josh entered the room. Jamie picked up Enoch's hand and inspected the skin; it looked pale and greenish. Minutes passed. "His fingers were slightly bent forward at the tips," Jamie observed. "His iris was glazed."

Jamie looked up at Josh. "He's dead," she mouthed. "Hush," Josh mouthed back.

Stacey performed CPR for the next fifteen minutes. Deborah offered to leave the room so that Stacey could determine for herself whether or not the boy had died. ("Only a mother can say for certain if her son is really dead.") Stacey said nothing in reply, remaining crouched on the floor, arms limp at her sides.

Two minutes passed in silence. Then Stacey spoke.

"You told me God would heal him," she said, rocking gently. "You told me God would heal him."

Over the course of his career, Steve Chavez had worked on all sorts of horrific cases—child abuse, child death, child rape. But Deborah's alleged crimes were so grisly and barbarous as to have virtually no comparison. There was no way to explain what she had allegedly done, no framework of understanding that could help it make sense.

Jim was equally culpable, as far as Chavez was concerned, a "fucking cunt" for failing to stand up to his wife.

Following his initial interview with Jamie Bridgewater, Chavez set out to conduct the kind of sprawling, connect-the-dots investigation ACMTC had never received. The group had always benefited from its itinerancy, from the fact that officials in different counties, states, and regions were siloed from each other, not just across geography but also across time. The people who knew about Maura Schmierer's abuse generally didn't know about the mistreatment members had experienced in Klamath Falls, Berino, or Fence Lake; the people who'd investigated the group in 2000 weren't, in large part, the people who'd dealt with Trinity in 2006. What might have looked like isolated incidents of misconduct were not, in fact, isolated; were, rather, points in a many-starred constellation of criminality.

Chavez began reaching out to relevant law enforcement officials and former group members, Brian Miller among them. In 2013, Brian had been "judged" by the Greens and banished from the group. He still didn't know his son Enoch was dead.

On January 28, 2016, two weeks after Jamie Bridgewater's escape from the compound, Detective Chavez met Brian in the parking lot of a Mexican restaurant in Albuquerque. Brian, who delivered seafood to high-end restaurants, got in Chavez's truck, where Chavez gave him the news. Weeping, Brian asked how it had all happened.

Several days later, on February 2, Chavez and Lieutenant Harry Hall visited the compound themselves. Chavez told the Greens he knew about Enoch's death. Jim and Deborah insisted it had been Stacey's decision not to seek medical help. "People think we don't believe in doctors, but we do," Deborah said repeatedly.

A week later, Chavez and Munk went to Truth or Consequences to speak with Stacey. Chavez knew Deborah had played a pivotal role in Enoch's death and pleaded with Stacey to concede as much. But Stacey refused, claiming full and exclusive responsibility for what had happened.

"You need to understand something," Chavez said in an interview he conducted in his car. "What my investigation has [uncovered] is that Enoch died as a result of child neglect resulting in death. That's a capital offense, okay? That's a first-degree felony. And you're just going to sit here and tell me that that was all your decision [not to take him to the hospital], when I know, I know—look at me for a second—it wasn't just your decision."

But Stacey held firm. "[Deborah] just came right [out] and told me; she said, 'If you want to take him to the hospital I stand by you.' And I said, 'No.'"

Now it was time to confirm the cause of Enoch's death. It was time to exhume the body.

February 9 came in sunny and cold, the ground still muddy from a recent rain. About twenty law enforcement officials and state agency representatives arrived at the compound at a time prearranged with the Greens. Jim and several other ACMTC members led everyone on a sopping dirt road all the way to the back of the property; the road was so wet one of the vehicles got stuck in the mud. Eventually the caravan arrived at a shaded grove surrounded by scrub trees. Enoch's grave, one of three, was marked by a perimeter of rocks and wood. The boy's name had been carved into a small headstone.

Members of the Crime Scene Team began digging and scooping at the ground with five-gallon buckets as anthropologists from the University of New Mexico sifted through the dirt with mesh screens. ACMTC members stood by watching and filming the officials as they worked.

Chavez, meanwhile, interviewed Josiah, Isaiah, Steve Schmierer, Peter Green, Jim, and Deborah in his truck and in the house.

An hour passed. Then another. Every so often it rained a little bit.

Later in the afternoon, when the hole was about six feet deep, police discovered Enoch's body wrapped in a striped blanket that had been fastened with exactly twelve brass safety pins. Robert Hays, Field Deputy Medical Investigator, placed the corpse in a white body bag. He zipped the bag shut, secured it with a tamper-proof evidentiary seal, and pronounced the child dead.

In the weeks and months following Enoch's exhumation and autopsy (the cause of death was listed as "probable infectious disease"), Steve Chavez continued to build out the investigation. Mike Munk, meanwhile, coordinated with officials at the Department of Homeland Security to discuss the situation. ACMTC had been the subject of previous investigations, of course. But this was different. It wasn't just the volume of evidence or the credibility of Jamie Bridgewater's and Brian Miller's allegations. This was different because the *staffing* was different. Chavez believed that a sheriff like Johnny Valdez, who'd previously run the agency, would have let the case "die on the vine." Thanks to Munk's advocacy, however, Sheriff Tony Mace was all-in.

"Mike Munk had a hard-on for the Greens," Chavez later said. "He wanted this to happen."

As did Chavez. He traveled around the country, interviewing former ACMTC members including Maura and Nathaniel Schmierer; Julie Gudino and her son Zechariah; Brian Miller; and even Trinity, now eighteen. Trinity's claims of abuse seemed highly credible to Chavez. "She didn't come off as fanatically hateful," he said. "She was very, very articulate. And she was happy she was moving on."

She was also understandably reluctant to get involved. She told Chavez she "didn't really want to testify" if Deborah's case went to trial.

As the investigation progressed, Chavez discovered that the group had allegedly created an alarm system that went off whenever law enforcement came on the compound, alerting the kids to gather at a designated location so they could be driven off the property. He also learned that Jamie Bridgewater suspected Deborah had been drugging her with jimsonweed, the same hallucinogenic plant Ja'el Phalen had mentioned to law enforcement back in 1999. ("I believe [Deborah] would have poisoned me to get rid of me," Jamie recalled.) The group's financial dealings were highly suspicious, too—there appeared to be ACMTC trusts in India and New Zealand, among other strange arrangements.

In March, Brian Miller won an emergency custody order to remove his kids from Stacey's care. He and Julie Gudino also told Chavez about a boarding school Deborah had allegedly opened on a Native American reservation in southwestern Colorado. The school had catered to Native American children, five to ten of whom had come back to live at the Fence Lake compound for up to two years. The children's parents had apparently consented to this arrangement, though Deborah had eventually told them to come take back their kids.

Chavez also learned that Sarah's oldest son, Josiah, now twenty-one, had taken a leadership position in the group. He preached for thirty minutes on Sundays, and was, according to Jamie Bridgewater, "basically the brains behind the overall functioning of the community."

In an almost implausibly bizarre twist, at one point Chavez received a call from his brother Daniel, who worked in a peach orchard six hours north of Fence Lake. Daniel told Steve he'd met a group of children and adults who were renting a house from his boss. The adults in the group had said they were trying to protect the children from the Cibola County Sheriff's Office. One of the moms had even flirted with Daniel. It was ACMTC, clearly—but Chavez didn't yet have enough probable cause to get the kids. He asked his brother to keep an eye on things and to keep feeding him information.

An especially important witness turned out to be one of the hardest to locate: Sarah. But eventually Chavez found her, and on a hot summer day in 2016 he and Mike Munk met with her on a bench in Central Park in New York City. Sarah, now forty-three, was cagey and skittish. She appeared to be worried about incriminating herself, even though Chavez already knew about the scheme to bring Trinity to America. He assured her the District Attorney's office wasn't necessarily interested in pursuing charges against her. Deborah and the group were the focus of the investigation. He and Munk simply wanted to know what had happened.

For Sarah, the interview was excruciating. She'd spent the seventeen years since her escape doing everything she could to build a life apart from the group. And yet here were these uniformed officials, pressuring her to revisit memories she'd worked so hard to suppress. Despite Chavez's assurances, she remained worried about her legal exposure. She wondered if she was about to go to prison, if she was going to lose yet another set of kids, Ellexis and Jeremiyah, now fifteen and twelve. It was unlikely—but it was possible.

Not long before the start of the new investigation into the Greens, a judge had ruled that Maura Schmierer's 1989 judgment was time barred, and thus unenforceable. After almost three decades of legal wrangling, Jim and Deborah appeared to have won—yet another Houdini-like escape in a long history of them. Chavez and Munk's investigation, however, was going to be much harder to shut down, given the investment of the Cibola County Sheriff's Office and the gravity of the alleged crimes Chavez was investigating—child abuse, child sex abuse, kidnapping.

How, though, to prosecute? Mike Munk and Steve Chavez had buy-in from Sheriff Tony Mace. But there were other people they needed to convince, officials who worried that going after the Greens might trigger "another Waco," that dependable old shibboleth. Some officials were skeptical of Jamie Bridgewater's allegations and reluctant to prosecute. According to Chavez, a Deputy District Attorney told him, "You got nothing but stories."

Cibola County officials met with the New Mexico Attorney General's Office, which expressed strong interest in the case and provided state lawyers to assist the local team. Mike Munk wanted to conduct a major raid on the compound, but there were several high-risk factors. The compound was isolated. Minors were involved. The privacy rights of everyone at ACMTC had to be respected.

Eventually Detective Chavez, Undersheriff Munk, and other Cibola County officials went to the Attorney General's office in Albuquerque to lay out a proposal for a mission. According to Munk, Attorney General Hector Balderas asked if Munk could guarantee the operation wouldn't turn into another Waco or Ruby Ridge. Munk said he couldn't make any guarantees. But he assured Balderas that the plan had been thoroughly vetted.

Months passed and the investigation continued. Notwithstanding Chavez's assurances to Sarah back in New York, officials considered pressing federal charges against her for bringing Trinity to America. "There was some talk," Munk later revealed. "I won't lie to you; there was some talk of initially—if we would, through the United States attorney and the federal side."

Eventually Chavez succeeded in distilling many months of investigation into specific criminal charges against four individuals: Deborah, Peter, Josh, and Stacey Miller. The court documents read like something out of a pulp crime novel: "First degree kidnapping," "abuse of a child resulting in death," "criminal sexual penetration of a minor under thirteen years old." Even though she hadn't literally picked up Trinity, Deborah faced a kidnapping charge for her role in the girl's transport to America, and for Trinity's alleged physical mistreatment and sexual abuse. Peter was charged with first-degree criminal sexual penetration of a child under thirteen, while Stacey was charged with abandonment of a child resulting in death, among others. (Deborah faced charges related to Enoch's death, too.) Josh was charged with failure to file a certificate of birth of a child—by far the least significant of the alleged crimes, but a felony nonetheless. Other parents on the compound hadn't reported the births of their children, either, but they would be charged at a later date.

In the end, officials decided not to bring charges against Sarah. She was cooperating with the investigation and had been out of the group for two decades. Prosecuting her seemed pointless.

A raid was planned for August 2016, but it fell through, in part because of disagreements between state and local officials about how best to proceed. The District Attorney, too, expressed uneasiness about the live-wire religious element, according to Mike Munk. This was to say nothing of the tremendous logistical and evidentiary complexity—there was, after all, no physical evidence that the alleged sexual abuse had actually happened.

Eventually the raid was rescheduled. Aircraft surveilled the compound from 30,000 feet as police and SWAT team operators tracked group members from the surrounding fields, assessing when the dogs were let out, when the guards were on duty, which vehicles people used around the property. The idea was to get a comprehensive sense of the essential players, how their days unfolded. Officials prepared for various first-aid contingencies, too, including those that might involve children. Thanks to Jamie Bridgewater and the surveillance footage, they determined the best time for a search-and-arrest raid was on Sunday morning, when everyone would be in the main warehouse worshiping. It was the only time of the week when the whole group was together, the dogs were put away, and no one was on patrol.

Putting everything together took months—so many, in fact, that a full year and a half had passed since Jamie Bridgwater's escape by the time everyone was ready to go. Mike Munk called the investigation and raid Operation Archangel.

It was sunny and warm on the morning of August 20, 2017, when the raid caravan headed out to Fence Lake. All told about thirty people would be present, not just the two tactical teams but also command and administrative staff, emergency medical services, a jail transport team, a backup Quick Reactionary Force, and representatives from the New Mexico Children, Youth, & Families Department.

The tactical teams moved quickly on arrival, hurrying through the low trees, M4 rifles in hand. ACMTC had always conceived of itself as a military operation, but this was the real thing, a highly trained SWAT team in olive-green body armor ready for actual flesh-and-blood conflict. The secondary tactical teams took their positions as Mike Munk and the primary team entered the main area of the compound, where the buildings, trailers, gardens, and farming equipment were located. There were no ACMTC members in sight.

The first tactical team approached the hulking white warehouse. If their intel was correct, everyone was worshiping at Jim's and Lila's feet.

Boom. The sound of an explosion echoed out across the compound. This was a "flash bang," a diversionary device detonated outside the warehouse. The intent was to startle and confuse everyone inside.

The main tactical team rushed into the low-ceilinged, fluorescent-lit sanctuary where everyone was assembled for worship.

"Sheriff's Office!" someone shouted. "Show us your hands! Get on the ground, get on the ground, get on the ground!"

It was a surreal scene, worshipers in their red berets, tactical team members with their huge, intimidating rifles. ACMTC members did as instructed and fell to the floor.

"Is this Deborah?" one officer asked, indicating an elderly woman in a white beret, a white military jacket, and a long white skirt.

It was.

"Deborah," the officer said, "go ahead and stand up for me."

From the floor Deborah turned and looked up at the officer. "Could we ask what this is about?" she said.

Deborah was escorted out of the warehouse as other officers found and arrested Peter and Josh. The tactical teams searched group members for weapons and secured everyone in a so-called hostage corridor they set up in the warehouse. The children were questioned and then reunited with their parents.

Outside, next to a white police vehicle, Officer Maxine Monte zip-tied Deborah's wrists behind her back. Monte had expected someone more obviously monstrous, a woman whose physicality matched the malevolence of her alleged crimes. But Deborah was so small, so frail—so *old*. Surely this couldn't be the figure at the center of the years-long investigation, a woman who'd required a thirty-person operation to be subdued.

General Deborah Green, a little old lady in white military drag: the mastermind, perhaps, of a vast criminal enterprise that, after three decades of operation, was finally facing justice.

CHAPTER 33

It was a scam—it had to be a scam.

That was what Sarah told herself when the 505 number appeared on her phone in the summer of 2016. It had been years since she'd spoken with her parents or anyone else at Fence Lake. She ignored the voicemail and returned to work.

She ignored the next 505 voicemail, too, though by the third message she'd started to grow nervous. On a break at work she listened to the voicemail. It was Steve Chavez. He didn't say much, just that he needed to speak with Sarah urgently.

Anxious, Sarah called him back.

Seventeen years had passed since her escape from the group. She'd built a whole life around the idea that her past basically didn't exist. Ellexis and Jeremiyah, fifteen and twelve, knew about Josiah, Isaiah, Trinity, and their grandparents. Sarah's husband, Xavier, too, was generally aware of what she'd been through, but there was much he and the kids didn't know. Sarah liked it that way.

Chavez's call threatened to upend that equilibrium. When Sarah called him back, he said he needed to speak with her in person about an ongoing investigation. Sarah hung up feeling sick.

When Steve Chavez and Mike Munk met Sarah in Central Park, she gave terse, watchful answers to their questions, uncertain whether or not she could trust them.

Never look back: That was Sarah's guiding catechism. And yet here were Chavez and Munk, telling her that a trial could be on the horizon, that she might have to testify. Chavez said they weren't looking to prosecute her for bringing Trinity to America. But Sarah knew this was far from a guarantee.

Months passed. Donald Trump won the presidential election in November and was inaugurated in January. In August, more than a year after Sarah had spoken with Chavez and Munk in Central Park, white supremacists marched around Charlottesville—and, that same month, officials raided the Fence Lake compound. When Sarah learned her parents had been arrested, she felt a flurry of complicated, contradictory emotions. On the one hand she was pleased: Her parents were finally facing meaningful consequences for their actions. But she also felt ill at the prospect of testifying. Jim and Deborah were still her family, and speaking out against them felt like an almost biological betrayal of their bond. Telling a jury they deserved to be punished meant spurning the part of *her* that was made from *them*. It meant forever marking herself as a daughter who'd failed to be the woman her parents had wanted her to be, even if that failure had been the price of her own survival.

By now Sarah had learned more about Jim, Deborah, and Peter's alleged crimes. It was hard to accept the alleged abuses Trinity had suffered. Sarah had known as well as anyone that her mother was cruel, unforgiving, quick to anger. But this was on another level entirely.

As for Peter, Sarah wanted to kill him. There was nothing further to it.

Intertwined with Sarah's horror and disgust, however, was a quiet sense of relief: At least she hadn't gotten wrapped up in her parents' most appalling crimes. Still, Sarah's guilt for her role in bringing Trinity to New Mexico, and her abandonment of her children, remained oceanic, even debilitating when considered in full. So she didn't consider it.

She wasn't surprised when she received a subpoena to testify at Deborah's trial, scheduled for September 2018, a full year after the raid. Jim's and Peter's alleged crimes would be addressed at some point in the future.

Sarah became increasingly agitated as the trial grew closer. She had dreams of being trapped in a faraway desert. *We have you*, her parents taunted her. *You can't go back.* She tried to tell Xavier the extent of her anguish. "I just want to go to the side of a mountain and scream and scream until I collapse," she said. Xavier was sympathetic, but he clearly didn't fully understand. Then again, how could he? How could anyone?

She sat down with Ellexis and Jeremiyah to talk shortly before flying to New Mexico; it was the most up-front she'd ever been with them about her past. She said she wasn't sure if she was going to face legal scrutiny. Either way, she loved them.

The woman was short, with a deep tan and a jellyfish tattoo on the back of her neck. At first Maura didn't recognize her. Then the woman turned around.

"Oh my god," Maura said. "Sarah."

They were gathered in the lobby of a nondescript hotel in Grants, New Mexico, where Deborah's trial would soon take place. At Maura's side were her son Nathaniel, now forty-three, and Julie Gudino, fifty-one. They'd all been subpoenaed to testify. Now they were waiting for a car to drive them to the courthouse to fill out some paperwork.

Sarah had been a teenager the last time Maura had seen her. Now she was forty-five, the spitting image of her mother when she'd been the same age—bright eyes, sharp jawline. Ever since learning Sarah had run away from the group, Maura had tried to find her online, never with any luck. But here was Sarah, approaching Maura, hugging her, and falling into easy conversation. It was a relief, realizing that Sarah didn't resent her for the lawsuit—which, Maura well knew, had upended not just Jim and Deborah's lives, but also Sarah's.

For a moment they and the others stood chatting in the hotel lobby. Soon a car arrived to pick them up. "Okay," Sarah said, as if leading everyone into battle. "Let's do this."

Only a few months earlier, Maura had made significant progress on her still-active effort to collect on the old judgment. In July, the New Mexico Court of Appeals had reversed a lower court ruling that had found the case time-barred. Not long thereafter, the New Mexico Supreme Court had denied the Greens' appeal. Jim and Deborah were, in fact, still obligated to pay Maura everything they'd owed her since 1989.

At the courthouse, Maura and Nathaniel were told they probably wouldn't have to testify, given the recent developments in Maura's case: Their involvement could muddy the waters of the trial. They would have to remain in Grants for the duration of the trial, however, in case the situation changed. Maura was disappointed. She'd wanted to confront Deborah face-to-face.

Later, when they all went out for pizza, Maura was struck by her and Sarah's shared interest in birth and delivery. Neither woman had exactly followed the path she'd imagined for herself—Maura's nursing career hadn't focused on obstetrics, and Sarah worked as an executive assistant to a wealthy family (though she did some freelance doula work on the side). But it was still something.

Maura also noticed Sarah was missing a tooth along the upper right-hand side of her mouth—the same tooth Maura herself was missing.

Things had remained volatile at the compound in the year since Deborah's arrest.

Back in August 2017, immediately following the raid, officials from the Sheriff's Office had negotiated a time for ACMTC to bring the children to Grants for questioning. When the children didn't appear at the appointed time, however, Chavez immediately suspected they were trying to run. He quickly secured an emergency court order to take the children into state custody. By evening, officials were racing back to Fence Lake to execute the order. Then, at around 6:00 p.m., they passed a pair of vans along State Road 117. The vans belonged to ACMTC—and they were full of children.

When the officials executed a traffic stop and opened the doors to the van, the eleven children inside spoke in eerie unison, announcing they were headed to Albuquerque to see their lawyer. But the vehicles were full of food and luggage; a search revealed an envelope containing $1,000 in cash. The group was clearly on the run. The adults were arrested and the children were delivered to the relevant authorities.

Back on the compound, too, ACMTC members were doing everything they could to thwart the ongoing investigation. On the day of the raid, when officials made a cursory search of the compound, two firearm silencers were found, neither of them registered, as was required by law.

Detective Chavez wanted to do a comprehensive search, but the District Attorney "wanted me to go back a week later," Chavez claimed. By then, however, the compound had been scrubbed of all useful evidence. ("God bless them," Chavez recalled, speaking of the DA lawyers, "but they blew that one.")

The department did have success, however, when it came to Jim, who, in the month following the raid, was indicted on eighteen charges for Trinity's alleged kidnapping and abuse (physical, not sexual), and for the alleged abuse-by-neglect that had resulted in Enoch Miller's death. Jim was also indicted for evidence tampering and failure to file a birth certificate.

Still, Deborah was clearly the main event. Her trial would allow prosecutors the opportunity to paint a comprehensive portrait of the Aggressive Christianity Missions Training Corps in all its alleged horror.

September 18, 2018. A Tuesday.

At the courthouse, jury selection had just entered its second day of proceedings. The trial was being overseen by Judge James Lawrence Sanchez, a handsome figure with thick salt-and-pepper hair. Sanchez had allowed extra time for the process, "more than most cases," he said, "even capital murder cases, double murder cases, because it's a significant case, and it's complicated." Deborah faced a total of thirteen felony counts, but the trial was concerned only with the eight charges related to Trinity. (The five others associated with Enoch Miller's death would be addressed later.)

The jury was set by lunchtime. Just after 1:00 p.m. the jurors filed into the courtroom. Deborah sat at a table with her lawyers. She wore a white, flower-patterned dress. Her hair had turned loose, stringy, and gray.

Assistant District Attorney Brandon Vigil, one of the two leading prosecutors on the case, gave the first opening statement. "As you know," he told the jury, "the defendant, Deborah Green, also known as Lila Green, is charged with crimes that include kidnapping, child abuse, and criminal sexual penetration of a child under the age of thirteen."

Vigil laid out the broad contours of the state's case. He talked about Trinity, and the plot to bring her to America. He talked about Sarah, how she'd executed that plot. And he talked about Trinity's alleged abuse—physical, emotional, sexual.

In defense attorney Robert Lohbeck's opening remarks, he described ACMTC in favorable, even idyllic terms. "This group stood for something, stood for something meaningful" he said. "They stood for biblical living, the idea that they wanted to live as Jesus Christ and his disciples lived and as people lived back around the time of Christ, a very simple life. . . . They believed in holiness."

There was no evidence, he said—none—that Trinity had suffered while under Deborah's care. Lohbeck said he had videotapes proving as much. "You're going to see a smiling child," he said. "You're going to see a child doing funny and goofy things just like kids do." Trinity's claims, he insisted, were "full of holes and contradictions."

Julie Gudino was the first to testify. She explained how she'd come to join ACMTC in 1984, when she was seventeen. She said Deborah had told her followers that God was "raising up an army"; that regular Christians were "pew warmers" and "devil worshipers" who idolized television ("the one-eyed devil"). The Catholic Church was "the whore of all churches," Deborah had raged, "the Queen of Babylon" who sat at "the seat of Jezebel."

Prosecutors asked Julie about the Greens' alleged racism. "Many times I was put down for being Hispanic," Julie said. "I was never allowed to talk about my culture or my family, where I came from, because it was all demonic." When Jim and Deborah returned from mission trips, Julie said, "they would say that Africans were lazy and stupid and ignorant, and they would talk about Filipinos as if they were lazy and stupid and uneducated, and of course those people had no knowledge of the true spirit of God, and this is why we needed to keep sending all of their literature overseas to educate these people."

Julie was also questioned about the failed plot for her to kidnap a child from along the Mexico border. She described some of Trinity's alleged physical abuse, and confirmed the girl's surgery in Mexico: "[The doctors] broke her legs in eight places, restructured her muscles, and put them back together with screws or pins."

But Julie appeared guilty of abuse, too. During cross-examination, Lohbeck read aloud from a statement Julie's son, Zechariah, had written. He said his mother had "tied a belt around my wrists and hung me by my arms to a tree. She proceeded to beat me with a four-foot paddle crafted by hand. . . . This went on every day for about a week."

Julie didn't deny the allegation. "I was told by Lila Green that my son was sexually promiscuous, and him and the children were out in the desert, and they were sexually touching each other, and that I was to beat him to a bloody pulp until he learned his lesson."

Lohbeck continued his cross-examination of Julie the next morning.

"You weren't forced to join the group?" he said.

"No."

"And you were never forced to stay in the group?"

"No."

"You were always free to leave the group if you wanted to?"

"Yes."

Lohbeck also asked, "If Deborah Green had ordered you to jump off a cliff, would you have done that?" he asked.

"I'm unsure, sir."

"If she had ordered you to kill somebody, would you have done that?"

Again, Julie said she wasn't sure.

It was almost time for Sarah to testify. Three days had passed since her arrival in Grants. That morning she'd anxiously gotten dressed at the hotel, slipping on a pair of capris, a white button-down, and a blue three-quarter-sleeve blazer. She'd been told to cover up as many of her tattoos as possible: not just the jellyfish but also the birdcage, the key, the exploding grenade, and the Japanese characters down her left arm. At the courthouse, she paced and breathed in a windowless holding room, trying to calm herself as she did whenever she ran a marathon. She felt like she was going to throw up.

This was it, the moment of confrontation. Sarah firmly believed her mother deserved to be locked up. She felt an obligation, to Trinity and herself, to tell the jury all that had happened at ACMTC. Still, none of that made the prospect of testifying any easier.

As Deborah's daughter, Sarah had experienced better treatment than others at ACMTC. But for Sarah, Deborah's cruelty had been charged with a particular valence. Deborah wasn't just a General. She was Sarah's mother. The gap between how Deborah should have treated Sarah and how she'd *actually* treated her was extraordinarily vast; and it was this gap, this chasm, even more than the physical deprivations and spiritual abuses, that hurt most deeply. Sarah had needed protection and support; she'd gotten punishment, neglect, and restriction. Surely Deborah had loved Sarah, and perhaps even loved her still. But Deborah's love had curdled into a kind of poison.

What did Sarah owe that poison? She owed it exposure. And yet the memory of who her mother had been still pressed at her. To betray Deborah *now* was to betray Deborah *then*: "To know that these people who nurtured you as a child, who were good to you a few years in your life, even though they put you through hell; to know that you have to stand up and tell the whole world that they're absolute fucking monsters, and they should be put away forever, is really hard. It really is."

A representative from the court entered the holding room. It was time.

Deborah. Lila. *Mom.*

The old woman sat hunched at a small table at the front of the room, the wattage of her once-blazing eyes all but extinguished. Sarah's heart beat quickly. Fear flooded her stomach. Deborah didn't look at her but past her, as if Sarah weren't even there, as if she didn't even know who Sarah was.

She's gone, Sarah thought

"Good morning, Ms. Green," said Mandana Shoushtari, another Assistant District Attorney working on the case.

"Good morning."

Shoushtari asked where Sarah lived, and if she had any family.

"I do," Sarah said. "I have two children and a husband."

Shoushtari asked if Deborah was her mother.

"She is."

"And is that person currently in this courtroom?"

"She is."

"Would you please point her out and describe an article of clothing she's wearing."

"She's in the pink shirt over there."

Before Shoushtari could proceed, Lohbeck interrupted to request a conference at the bench. Lohbeck and the two prosecuting attorneys, Vigil and Shoushtari, assembled before Sanchez, their voices muffled from the courtroom.

Lohbeck told the judge he expected that "there is going to be testimony by this witness where she will acknowledge that she may have violated the law, engaged in kidnapping, perhaps violating various federal laws having to do with illegally bringing someone into the country." As such, Sarah needed "to be advised by the Court about her right to consult with an attorney." Lohbeck was perhaps trying to delay or stymie whatever testimony Sarah might have against her mother.

Judge Sanchez asked for the prosecution's response.

"There is no crime this witness can be charged with under the law," Shoushtari said. "There is no proof whatsoever that this witness intended to do anything wrong other than what she was ordered to do."

Sanchez said it was a "great argument. . . . But in the end, [Sarah is] the person with the boots on the ground doing it, so a Nuremberg defense doesn't necessarily work in a court of law."

Vigil was insistent about the spottiness of a potential case against Sarah. "Your Honor, we've gone over this. There is not enough to get to a jury."

Lohbeck disagreed. "There is certainly enough for an indictment on probable cause." He also noted that Sarah might "expose herself to new things that may not have arisen yet in the interviews."

"And, Your Honor," Shoushtari said, "that's the risk she has taken by taking the stand."

In the end, Judge Sanchez sided with Vigil and Shoushtari. "I don't see the exposure," he said, "and if there is exposure, she has already done that by giving statements to the police and to you."

Direct examination continued.

Shoushtari asked Sarah about her early life before turning to Trinity.

"When the time came for you to get [her]," Shoushtari asked, "what was the plan?"

"That I would show up and be there around the time of the birth," Sarah said. "The mom would put my name on the birth certificate. I would therefore be the mom, and I would bring the baby home, and she would be a part of our tribal nation."

Occasionally Sarah employed ACMTC vernacular like this, *our tribal nation*, every usage a reminder of how the group remained, in some ways, alive within her.

"When you went to the consulate, what did you tell them to get the passport for [Trinity]?"

"I told them it was my child."

"And did you begin to breastfeed [Trinity]?"

"Of course. I was lactating."

"And was that the plan all along?"

"Well, you have to kind of make it look like it's your child."

"Who created that plan?"

"Well, my mother did, because it's the only way you can really make it look like it's your child."

At this point Sarah seems to have had some sort of emotional reaction. Shoushtari said, "Ms. Green, I understand this may be hard for you, taking the stand and testifying against your mother. But the jury needs to know."

"Sorry."

Shoushtari continued.

"So your mother was the one who created this plan?"

"Correct."

Deborah betrayed no reaction, and continued to stare vacantly forward.

Shoushtari asked Sarah to explain why she'd brought the baby back to the United States.

"We were building a tribal nation," Sarah said, again using in-group phrasing. "[Trinity] was a sign of things to come." Here it was again, "we."

"Can you please expand on that?" Shoushtari asked.

"At the time, our group wasn't growing, and so we felt we needed to start from scratch, and so we were looking for means and ways to grow our community. And we weren't getting new recruits, so we weren't having children, and blah, blah, blah, so this was like a sign from God. We were getting something beautiful brought to us." As with her previous use of ACMTC phraseology, Sarah's use of "us" and "we" was illuminating. Even now she saw herself as not entirely disconnected from the group.

"And why were you not growing as a group?"

"Religious persecution."

"Was that the only reason?"

"Well, it's really hard to get people to come join you when you have media on your back all the time."

The examination continued.

"Ms. Green, I'm going to show you what has been previously marked as State's Exhibit 1," Shoushtari said, presenting Sarah with a photograph. "Do you recognize the child in that picture?"

For a moment Sarah couldn't speak. Then she started to shake.

"Oh, my god," she said. "I'm so sorry. I'm so sorry."

It was Trinity. The photograph had been taken before the surgery in Mexico, at around the time the girl's legs were at their most contorted.

"Judge, I think it's appropriate to take a break," Lohbeck said.

"Ma'am," Sanchez said, "do you need a few minutes to compose yourself?"

"Just give me a second," Sarah said.

And he did.

When it was Lohbeck's turn to question Sarah, he wasted little time before bringing up Trinity. "Wasn't [it] actually your idea to go to Africa to pick up the child because you already had two boys," he said, "and you wanted a girl, and you had previously made statements that you wanted to adopt an African child; isn't that the truth?"

"I would love to adopt a child. I would love to have more children, sure."

Lohbeck noted that Sarah had "stated previously that Deborah, your mother, was not involved in bringing the child, and she did not inflict any kind of physical injury or sexual offense or abuse on this child during the course of you going and picking her up and bringing her to the United States, correct?"

"Correct."

Lohbeck also asked Sarah why she'd left the group. "You were bored, and you didn't want to be a housewife and just raise kids, correct?" he said.

"I wanted an education," Sarah said.

"You didn't want to just be somebody who raised kids and just stayed at home, and you wanted to get out there in the world, and you wanted to become a midwife, correct?"

"I did."

"Because you thought that living down there at Fence Lake, you weren't doing anything with your life?"

"Correct."

"And so you leave in the middle of the night?"

"Uh-huh."

Lohbeck brought up Anthony, the young man who'd escaped with Sarah. "He had a really cool accent, and you really liked the accent?"

"He made me laugh."

The prosecution objected when Lohbeck asked if Sarah and Anthony had had an affair. Lohbeck justified his questioning at the bench. "It goes to the real motive why she left," Lohbeck told Judge Sanchez. "She didn't leave . . . because she was unhappy at the property. She left because she had an affair with this guy. That's why she left. She left her husband. She left her kids with this guy because she had an affair with him; that's the real reason why she left."

Judge Sanchez concurred that this was a legitimate line of inquiry. Cross-examination resumed.

"So the fact is you had an affair with this gentleman from New Zealand, who was visiting the commune," Lohbeck said, "you kissed and hugged and went on long walks and all that sort of thing, and that's why you left?"

"We held hands and we went on long walks. We did not have an affair until after we left."

Lohbeck pressed harder. "Isn't it actually the case, Ms. Green, the reason that you didn't take your kids with you when you left is because you wanted to go on an adventure with this fellow from New Zealand; you wanted to get out of there, you wanted to go explore the world, and you didn't want to be tied down by having to take care of those kids? That's really why you left them behind, right?"

"Absolutely not."

But Lohbeck wasn't wrong. Sarah *had* wanted to go on an adventure. She *had* wanted to get out of there, to explore the world. Lohbeck's implicit argument was that these were shameful desires for a mother, at least if they came at the expense of her children; that Sarah had lost her right to these freedoms the moment her firstborn son had fallen into Deborah's outstretched hands, his body encased in the strange, mystical caul. Sarah's actions had violated the most fundamental idea about what it meant to be a mother and a woman: *children before all*. (Peter, surely, never would have faced a similar line of questioning had he done the same thing.) The question, then—the ultimate, unanswerable question—was whether or not Sarah's legitimate desire for a life of her own, a life with space for curiosity, hope, excitement, romance, humor, heartbreak, disappointment, the whole tangled tapestry of the human experience: The question was whether or not that desire outweighed, or was deemed irrelevant by, the three little children she'd left almost two decades earlier.

Lohbeck's subsequent line of inquiry, however, underscored that there had been a third way, that grabbing hold of her own freedom hadn't necessarily meant sacrificing theirs, even if Sarah had felt otherwise. "You could have, if you wanted to take [the kids], you could have filed, for example, a custody case or something like that to try to get custody of them?" Lohbeck said. "You chose not to do that, correct?"

"I chose not to. I was fearful."

Lohbeck picked a different tack of inquiry. "Now, you stated before that you were very frustrated with your mother, Deborah, because you didn't like all the religious jargon and her always talking about God and praying three times a day and that sort of thing, correct?"

"Correct."

"And you've stated when I talked to you that you're very happy now;

that you no longer believe in God, believe in Jesus Christ, and that you no longer want any kind of religion or rigid structure in your life, correct?"

"I'm taking a break."

"You're taking a break from?"

"Just everything. I don't believe in anything."

"Do you believe in truth?"

"I do."

"You believe in that one. You acknowledge that you were extremely selfish and only thinking of yourself when you abandoned your kids, correct?"

"At that time, I did what I thought was right."

"At that time, you did what you thought was right for you?"

"Correct."

"Not for your kids."

"I thought—what I thought was right at the time."

Here it was again, the two-sidedness of Sarah's situation made explicit. In leaving her children, was she being bold or selfish? Courageous or harmful? Was she honoring her duty to herself or dishonoring her duty to her children? At the time of Sarah's escape, it hadn't felt like a choice between the two, not fully. She was going to come back and get the kids out of there. She was going to *have it all.*

But things hadn't turned out that way. They'd turned out *this* way, Sarah forever separated from Josiah, Isaiah, and Trinity, seated in a New Mexico courtroom, testifying against the mother who in her own way had abandoned Sarah.

"Ms. Green, have you ever told anybody you hate your mother?" Lohbeck asked near the end of his cross-examination.

"I feel sorry for my mother," Sarah said, deflecting.

Lohbeck tried again. "To this day, do you love your mother?"

An impossible question, a question with as many different answers as there were stars in the New Mexico sky. But today, under oath, in this flyspeck of a town, Sarah gave just one.

"I do."

* * *

All through Sarah's testimony, Deborah had remained a sphinx, unmoving and inscrutable. Gone was the vainglorious prophet of yore, the Brigadier General who'd led her forces through the thick of spiritual warfare. In the wreckage of Deborah's former self sat a skinny, stooped old woman.

When Sarah finished testifying, she gave Deborah a final look and exited the courtroom. She felt drained, exhausted, like the horrible woman and mother Lohbeck had made her out to be. The photo of Trinity, too, had been profoundly upsetting. It was one thing to hear about the alleged abuse, another to actually see it.

Sarah ruminated over her testimony as she made her way back to the hotel. She felt certain she'd said all the wrong things, that her mother was going to walk free. There had been a moment, though, when she'd managed to articulate exactly what she felt; a moment that in many ways summed up her entire post-ACMTC transformation. At the end of Sarah's testimony, Shoushtari had asked about the self-excoriating letters and emails Sarah had sent Peter and her parents in the months and years following her escape.

"When you first come out of a cult," Sarah had explained, "you blame yourself for everything. It's like when you're in a really bad relationship, you blame yourself for everything that went wrong. . . . And as you finally distance yourself, and you grow and you mature and you get away from it, you realize it wasn't always your fault. And you realize, yeah, you could have made mistakes, you could have done things that were wrong, but it wasn't always you. And sometimes you're the victim of the situation, and you grow up, and that's what happened to me. I grew up. I realized. And that's why I'm here. I've grown up."

That night at the hotel, Maura visited Sarah in her room. She told Sarah she was sorry, not just for the difficulties Sarah had faced at ACMTC, but also for the role Maura's lawsuit had played in Sarah's early life instability. She handed Sarah a card with a cactus on the front. The caption said, "I'm sorry I'm such a prick."

But Maura wasn't a prick, not to Sarah. If anything, Sarah was grateful to Maura for starting the long and ongoing process of bringing down ACMTC.

Sarah reached over to Maura and hugged her. She thanked Maura for paving the way.

Maura spoke to the burden she knew Sarah still carried. "Those memories will never go away," Maura said, "but the shame, the blame, the guilt: Those don't belong to you. They belong to Deborah."

There was no way to erase the past, no chance of escaping its consequences. But Sarah and Maura had both forged new paths forward. And now, having confronted Deborah, Sarah had found her way back to Maura. They were different now; but they were also themselves. Would *always* be themselves. Only now, in their own partial, complicated ways, they were free.

The next day, a pair of cars arrived at the hotel to drive Sarah, Maura, Nathaniel, and Julie back to the airport in Albuquerque. Neither Maura nor Nathaniel had testified. Trinity had taken the stand after Sarah, but Sarah hadn't seen her or heard anything about her testimony. The trial was still in progress, and would continue for another four days, a parade of expert witnesses, law enforcement officers, and active ACMTC members. Deborah herself would decline to testify.

Sarah and the others, however, were done. It was time for them to leave Deborah and the group for good.

They were in cars on their way to the airport when Sarah received a text from a victim's advocate at the courthouse. Trinity had finished her testimony—and she wanted to see Sarah.

Yes yes yes yes yes yes yes yes yes yes, Sarah texted back. *Give her my number.* She was thrilled and surprised. She'd thought she was prohibited from seeing or speaking to Trinity.

Sarah received a text from Trinity a moment later. *Please wait for me at the airport*, it said. *I really want to see you.*

When Sarah and the others arrived at the airport, they took an escalator up to the mezzanine level, where they got a table at a Mexican restaurant. They ordered food, drank their iced tea, and waited. Sarah kept her eyes on the clock.

We're like twenty minutes away, Trinity texted. *Please don't leave.*

Sarah's anxiety rose as the minutes ticked by. She wasn't in a position to ask for yet another day off work, but she badly wanted to see Trinity, to know how she was doing.

Then, just ten minutes before Sarah absolutely had to enter security, a young woman arose from the escalator.

It was her. It was Trinity.

Sixteen years had passed since Sarah had last hugged her at the compound. That bubbly four-year-old was now a poised and beautiful twenty-year-old.

Sarah jumped up and ran over. A woman was with Trinity: Trinity's adoptive mother. Heart racing, Sarah asked the woman if she could hug Trinity. The woman said yes.

Sarah and Trinity expressed mutual astonishment that they were here, both of them, after all this time. Sarah had long ago accepted that she would never again see the girl, now a woman, whom she'd always thought of as her daughter. Yet here she was, alive and as well as could be expected, given the circumstances.

Trinity and her adoptive mother joined everyone at the restaurant. Sarah promised to explain everything to Trinity—what had happened in Uganda; her decision to leave the group—when she got back to New York.

"I'm so sorry," she said as she got up to leave. "I love you so much."

On the face of it, this was a beautiful, heartwarming reunion. But it was beauty with an asterisk, beauty that didn't wipe away what Sarah had set in motion when she'd taken Trinity to America two decades earlier. Still, did that history mean the two women could never come to a kind of peace with each other? Did it mean the love between them was any less real than it so clearly was? This was not an unambiguous resolution; this was the real thing. Which is to say, it was resolution that coexisted with rupture. Sarah and Trinity were not avatars in a morality tale where ongoing difficulties did not exist. Because those difficulties *did* exist, and always would. Sarah and Trinity were, instead, inhabitants of the world as it really was, in all its messy, even intolerable complexity. The hard things between them would always be there. But there were good things, too—and in this goodness, this grace, there could be something like peace. Not at the exclusion of everything else, but within and alongside it.

The jury announced its verdict five days later.

Deborah was found guilty on seven of the eight charges the state brought against her. The weight of the evidence had clearly been in the prosecution's favor. And yet the reality of the verdict—guilty—still came with a kind of bewildering shock.

That justice had finally arrived, however, made it no less outrageous that it had taken so long to hold Deborah to account. Why hadn't she been stopped in 1989, when Maura had won her lawsuit against the group? Why hadn't she been stopped in 1999, when Ja'el Phalen had alerted the authorities and the media to the evil unfolding at the compound? And why hadn't she been stopped in 2006, when Trinity had been taken into state custody; or in 2007 or 2008, when Trinity had made allegations of sexual abuse?

Deborah's sentencing hearing was held the day after the jury announced the verdict. Before handing down a sentence, Judge Sanchez gave several people the opportunity to make statements about how much prison time they felt Deborah deserved. When Steve Chavez got up to speak, he said it was "imperative" that Sanchez not think of Deborah "as a lowly, poor seventy-one-year-old grandmother that we need to have mercy on." Mike Munk, too, said that even the maximum sentence would never be enough. "In over thirty years of law enforcement, this was one of the most egregious and impactful cases, and disturbing cases, that I've ever worked," he said.

Trinity, too, got up to speak.

In a slow but deliberate voice, she laid out the devastating and long-standing effects of Deborah's abuse. "Emotionally, she broke me as a child, to the point where I still today struggle with my own self-confidence, my self-esteem, my sense of worth, feeling that I'm deserving of people that care about me.

> She took all of that from me at a very young age, and I've worked really, really hard to reencourage those feelings to where I can have

healthy relationships in my life now. I still struggle a lot from day to day, but I've gotten to a point where I'm better. But physically, I've endured countless surgeries, eleven exactly, to fix my bones, to make them somewhat look normal again. . . . Even though I can hide the emotional part, I can't hide [the scars]. And because of that, I'm constantly reminded every day of the torture that she put me through, and I'm reminded of how much I have to fight myself every day mentally to not be sunken down into that low place that I was as a girl. . . . I would ask you to give her the most [prison time] that you could give her for the eight years of everything she took from me, from my health, to my emotional stability, my well-being, my self-esteem, everything about my being I feel she took from me. That's all.

Trinity's adoptive mother addressed the judge, too. Trinity "struggles still, but she's amazing. She's articulate. She's intelligent, and she's loving, and she's kind. Everybody wants to be around her. And she's in school right now, and ever since I can remember her goal was to become a doctor, a pediatrician, so she could take care of children, because there was no one there to take care of her. And she's on that track right now."

Trinity's adoptive mother also said she hoped Deborah spent the rest of her life "in misery and in pain. . . . I want her to suffer."

For the sexual and child abuse convictions, Judge Sanchez gave Deborah four separate eighteen-year sentences, the maximum, to be served consecutively, for a total of seventy-two years in prison.

There were two convictions to be addressed, those for kidnapping. These convictions involved serious legal questions, Sanchez said. He noted there was a "legitimate argument" as to whether or not it was even possible to kidnap a child whose parents had "consented to the transfer of custody," as Trinity's biological mother had apparently done. The "real deception," according to Sanchez, "was for emigration and immigration," but "those offenses don't necessarily rise to the first-degree crime of kidnapping." Sanchez didn't address Sarah's role in the trafficking scheme. But the jury's conclusion suggested that it was Deborah, not Sarah, they held responsible. Then again, Sarah hadn't been on trial. Perhaps if she had been, the jury would've found her guilty, too. In the absence of any charges, however, it was impossible to say.

In the end, Judge Sanchez gave Deborah two additional eighteen-year sentences for the kidnapping convictions but allowed them to run concurrently to part of the existing sentence, which remained capped at seventy-two years.

Not that it mattered in any practical sense. Absent a successful appeal, Deborah Green was going to spend the rest of her mortal life behind bars.

The charges related to Enoch Miller's illness and death still remained unaddressed. At the sentencing hearing, prosecutor Brandon Vigil indicated the state's intention to proceed with another trial. Soon thereafter, however, Deborah agreed to plead no contest to the abuse charges, and to the evidence tampering charges associated with the 2017 raid; she received one eighteen-year sentence and two eighteen-month sentences, to be served concurrently to the seventy-two-year sentence.

"You'll all be surprised if I live to be 160," Deborah said.

Other ACMTC members would sign similar plea deals in the months to come. Josh and a handful of others avoided prison sentences, but received probation for their failure to file birth certificates for their children, and, in several cases, conspiracy to commit evidence tampering, among other related charges. Stacey Miller took a plea deal for her role in her son Enoch's death, and was sentenced to twelve years in prison, with nine years of "actual incarceration." Jim pleaded no contest to two counts of nonsexual child abuse (for his role in Trinity's mistreatment and Enoch Miller's death); three counts of evidence tampering or conspiracy to commit evidence tampering; and two counts of failure to report a birth or death, and was sentenced to thirteen and a half years in prison, with ten years of "actual incarceration." Only Peter's case remained unresolved as the years passed, delayed by the Covid-19 pandemic and other complications.

Sarah was back at work in New York, at the apartment where she worked for a wealthy family, when she got a text from the District Attorney's office. Deborah's trial was over—and the jury had reached a verdict. Before reading any further, Sarah stepped out onto the patio. The streets of Lower Manhattan rumbled below. It was raining. Heart racing, Sarah opened her phone and read the text in full.

Guilty.

Her immediate reaction was one of relief. It didn't matter that Deborah believed herself to be an oracle, a persecuted martyr for the cause: She was still subject to the laws of the land. Sarah took a screenshot of the text message and sent it to Xavier, Jeremiyah, and Ellexis. She felt a flutter in her stomach, a giddy if still quiet pleasure that this part of the story was over.

At the end of the workday, she took the subway back home to Brooklyn. She hopped in the shower and had a glass of wine. When Ellexis and Jeremiyah got home from school, they expressed relief at the verdict, but Sarah knew they could never appreciate the full extent of it. This was as it should be—she'd never wanted to burden them with the weight of her own history. Xavier wouldn't get home until later, so it was just Sarah and the kids for dinner, as it was most evenings. Sometimes they ordered takeout, but usually Sarah cooked whatever they wanted: pizza, loaded nachos, broccoli mac-n-cheese. As they ate, they talked not about the verdict, but about school, friends, the usual. This wasn't a celebration, not in any obvious sense. But it *was* a celebration, in that it embodied precisely the kind of life Sarah had left the group to create. There would be no deliverance ceremonies tonight, no hellion screeds about the sins of the world. Just a mom and her kids, talking, eating, complaining, laughing. It had taken so long, and so much, to get here. And yet here she was.

Sarah gets in bed at eight o'clock. In a few hours, Xavier will slip in beside her. Until then, she will sleep—better than she has in months, better than she has since the first 505 phone call two years earlier. She will head back to work early in the morning, riding her bike over the bridge to Manhattan, swerving between taxis and coffee carts, racing forward, flying, as the orange skyline announces the beginning of a new, as-yet-unwritten day.

EPILOGUE

The handwriting was girlish, neat, almost cute. But the message was dead serious.

"I, Deborah Green, am currently incarcerated in WNMCF where I am serving a 72 yr. sentence . . . for sexual molestation and penetration of a minor child. However there's now medical evidence proving I did not molest or 'penetrate' the child in any way whatsoever." It was July 22, 2019, not a year after the trial. Deborah was seventy-two years old, in poor health—and determined to get her conviction overturned.

An unlikely, even shocking series of events had led to the request. Four months earlier, Peter's lawyer, Kari Morrissey, had discovered what she described in a court filing as "exculpatory material that had been intentionally withheld by the state." Many of the records concerned inquiries conducted following Trinity's 2006 hospitalization, when Trinity was removed from Jim and Deborah's custody. Trinity had "failed to disclose abuse, and in fact denied abuse, at the time she was removed from Ms. Green's [care]," acknowledged Judge James Sanchez, who'd presided over Deborah's trial in September 2018. This wasn't a new revelation; Robert Lohbeck, Deborah's attorney, had been aware that Trinity had initially denied abuse (even though these denials hardly proved Trinity hadn't been sexually abused by Deborah, or, for that matter, by Peter). The documents in question also suggested Trinity's "foster father was coaching [her] into reporting abuse," among other related evidence that was "clearly favorable to the defense," according to Judge Sanchez.

Motions filed in the wake of Deborah's initial petition suggested that some combination of prosecutorial error and incompetence was to blame rather than intentional unlawfulness. In a criminal case, prosecuting attorneys are required to turn over all potentially exonerating evidence to the defense. It was certainly possible the jury would've found Deborah guilty, if it had heard the evidence from the newly uncovered documents. That it might have made a different call, however, was enough to throw the whole conviction into question. Judge Sanchez said Trinity was "one of the best witnesses I have ever seen." And yet there were still "too many [documents] here that [were] not produced."

As the months went by and opposing motions began to pile up, the situation grew even messier. Assistant District Attorney Mandana Shoushtari, who, together with Brandon Vigil, was prosecuting Peter's case, posted about the case on Facebook. Vigil, meanwhile, was found to have "engaged in prosecutorial misconduct by agreeing to prosecute a case [against Peter Green] that, by his own admission, he lacked the experience to prosecute properly," according to a judge evaluating the situation. For these and other issues, both attorneys, along with all other lawyers at the Cibola County District Attorney's office, were disqualified from continuing to work on Peter's still-active case. (Steve Chavez disputes the suggestion that the Assistant DAs were incompetent, describing Vigil as "very impressive" and Shoushtari as "very intelligent.") Even another judge working on Peter's case, by now intertwined with Deborah's petition for a new trial, was forced to recuse herself after the judge's husband posted disparaging comments about the prosecuting attorneys on Facebook.

It was a mess—a disaster, really. Shoushtari and Vigil had presented a staggering amount of evidence against Deborah; there could be no doubt that she had spent decades walking up to the edge of the law, if not soaring right over it. Even if Trinity had fabricated her allegations of sexual abuse (which the new evidence hardly proved), there was voluminous evidence to suggest Deborah was "one of the most vile and wicked criminals of our time," as Deborah said she'd been falsely portrayed.

In the end, however, none of that mattered. In November 2020, Judge James Sanchez ruled in Deborah's favor, vacating Deborah's convictions and seventy-two-year sentence and ordering a new trial. Because Deborah had pleaded no contest to separate charges related to Enoch Miller's abuse and death, she would remain in prison. But her new lawyers were working on that, too. It was distinctly possible she was going to walk free.

Underlying all the legal technicalities was a simple question: Had Trinity told the truth about what she'd experienced at ACMTC?

It was a question only she, Deborah, and Peter could answer with total certainty. Still, even a cursory examination of Trinity's early life would suggest she'd experienced profound physical and emotional mistreatment in the group. Multiple witnesses had corroborated important elements of her testimony. Photographs showed she'd almost certainly been denied adequate medical treatment. At the trial, she'd shown the jury scars that ran up and down her legs, evidence of the surgery she'd received in Mexico. "These holes are where the metal would stick out of my leg," she said. "These ones are stitch marks from where they were drilled into me."

Had she experienced sexual abuse, too? It wasn't just Trinity's word. Julie Gudino said she'd seen Deborah go with Trinity into the bathroom, where some of the alleged abuse was said to have taken place (though it was also possible Deborah had simply been giving her a bath).

It was also true that an examiner had been unable to "confirm or deny sexual abuse" on Trinity's evaluation in 2006, as Judge Sanchez noted in his 2020 ruling. Trinity had initially denied being abused, but in 2007 and 2008 her story had changed when she'd alleged that both Deborah and Peter had abused her sexually. There were also discrepancies in Trinity's story, particularly related to the timing of her alleged abuse. At one point, she said she'd been abused when she was four; on other occasions, she said it had happened when she was slightly older. There were inconsistencies, too, in Trinity's description of the actual alleged abuse, and whether it was Deborah or Peter who'd committed some of the particularly heinous alleged sex crimes. Child sexual assault experts would have pointed out that it can take years for victims to come forward, and that alterations in a person's memories hardly means they are false. But neither are they necessarily true.

Members of the jury at Deborah's trial had known almost all of this, and yet they'd still found her guilty on almost all counts. But the evidence in the previously unseen reports was enough to "undermine confidence in the verdict," Judge Sanchez wrote in the November 2020 ruling.

Former ACMTC members were angry and frustrated but also resigned to the once-unthinkable development. *There's the New Mexico legal system for you*, thought Maura, who'd spent decades toiling in the courts.

Sarah's response was more rageful. "Serve your fucking sentence and shut up," she said shortly after receiving a subpoena to testify at the new trial.

After the first trial, Sarah and Deborah exchanged limited written correspondence. Deborah appeared to have mellowed in prison. "I'm writing to again ask you to forgive me for whatever hurts I have caused you," she wrote in July 2019 with uncharacteristic contrition. "I am sorry, if you feel I changed—well we all do, it is a fact of life."

But the old severity was there, too. "My daughter do not neglect <u>your father</u> whose seed brought you into my womb," she wrote in a birthday card later that year:

> Your father is 74 ½ yrs. Blind in one eye, has had cancer surgery—cannot support himself. Your brother works 7 days a week and has had hernia surgery—he cannot keep going to support attorneys and your dad. Come back to reality, the liars who framed us are being exposed because of your brother's sacrifice. . . . Sarah please realize that you did your share to put us here in prison can't you do your part to help your own father? We raised your children and never demanded 10¢ from you. Your husband loved you & refused to speak evil against you.

Deborah ended on a startlingly warm and sincere note. "I will always love you & know you will return to God."

Sarah and Deborah's correspondence diminished through the pandemic. Sarah prepared herself to testify again as Deborah's new trial, scheduled for June 2021, grew closer. Shortly before Sarah headed to Grants, however, she received word of yet another stunning development.

The trial had been canceled.

Court documents cited the "unavailability of essential witnesses," "namely [Trinity]," as the reason for the cancellation—in other words, the state couldn't pursue an appeal without Trinity's participation. As a result, the charges related to Trinity's alleged kidnapping and abuse were dismissed. The case was now categorically, definitively over. Because Deborah had pleaded no contest to the Enoch Miller charges, she would remain in prison. But in early 2022, Judge Sanchez vacated the relevant child abuse charge in that case, too, finding that Deborah's actions leading up to the boy's death in 2014 didn't meet the high bar of criminal child abuse.

And so—shockingly, unbelievably—on January 28, 2022, Deborah was ordered released from prison.

There would be an appeal, of course. As the months and then years went by, lawyers argued over the complicated legal issues involved, even as Deborah remained free. ACMTC appeared to have dissolved, or diminished to a vanishingly small faction, though the group continued to publish fanatical online articles about witchcraft, D.E.I., abortion, and "the woke stroke." "The WOKE PIMPLE is about to be popped," Jim raged. "Stinking pustule will flow like a river as the woke-ites become more enraged, even MURDEROUS!" Several former group members took jobs in Albuquerque. But there was no indication that Deborah, rumored to have moved to Arizona, was building another Fence Lake–style compound.

Eventually the appeal worked its way up to the New Mexico Supreme Court, and on April 21, 2025, the five justices issued a unanimous decision reversing the lower court ruling. After three years of freedom, Deborah was headed back to prison. And yet by this point, no one knew where she was, not law enforcement, and not her lawyers, who'd been unable to reach her for several years. As of this writing, in July 2025, Deborah has effectively disappeared, free, yet again, from a legal system that has for decades proven itself institutionally incapable of bringing her to decisive justice.

One lawyer familiar with the cases suspects Deborah is hiding in Alburquerque—though who, really, is to say? Only Deborah and her god can know for certain.

It is not a little bit ironic that even as ACMTC appears (mostly) to have fallen apart, a version of what can be described as "Aggressive Christianity" has found extraordinary new prominence in American culture more broadly. Hundreds, perhaps thousands, of white evangelical churches now spout a version of the vengeful, militaristic, conspiracy-addled ideology that long defined ACMTC. In a 2025 *Atlantic* piece titled "The Army of God Comes out of the Shadows," journalist Stephanie McCrummen reports on the New Apostolic Reformation, a radical "Christian" movement working to overthrow the forces of secularism. The language of war and demonic possession is foundational to NAR; disciples believe "the Church is not so much a place as an active 'army of God,'" writes McCrummen. "Anything short of absolute power is persecution."

"Regular" evangelicals might dismiss the more obviously extremist figures on the Christian right as a fringe minority, hardly representative of the church writ large. "These self-respecting Christians are in denial," writes journalist Tim Alberta, himself a practicing evangelical. At Global Vision Bible Church, an influential evangelical congregation in Wilson County, Tennessee, Head Pastor Greg Locke addresses his followers as "soldiers rising up in God's army"; congregants are guarded by men "dressed in paramilitary gear, firearms strapped to their sides." Locke "has suggested that autistic children are subjugated by demons," writes Alberta, and holds "book burning events to destroy *Harry Potter* novels and other books and games." He says Joe Biden is a "sex trafficking, demon-possessed mongrel."

"Just as with our politics, there is no longer a clear line of demarcation between the fringe and the mainstream," Alberta writes. "Ten years ago, Global Vision would have been considered a cult. Today, Locke preaches to 2.2 million Facebook followers and poses alongside Franklin Graham at the White House."

Jim and Deborah Green had always embodied the most extreme version of important sociopolitical trends and movements in America. By the mid-2020s, however, whole swaths of the culture had caught up to them. In March 2023, Donald Trump held his first major reelection rally in Waco, Texas, as if to suggest that he, like David Koresh and the Branch Davidians, was standing strong against the authoritarian forces of the federal government.

A year and a half before becoming Speaker of the House, Mike Johnson told an interviewer, "The kingdom of God allows aggression. . . . There's a time for every purpose under heaven; there's a time for war." Jesus might have told his followers to turn the other cheek, but not so Johnson. "You have to defend."

In August 2019, a year after Deborah's trial, a judge ordered the sale of the Fence Lake compound, with the proceeds going to satisfy the remainder of Maura's 1989 judgment. Despite three decades of back-and-forth, this was it, Maura's final victory. At this point Deborah was still in prison; the judgment, insofar as Maura had meant to use it to bring down the group, was largely moot. There was nothing moot, however, about the actual cash itself, which, with interest, totaled about $4.7 million, according to Maura's lawyers. When the compound sold, it went for $2.8 million, but the taxes and legal fees were hefty, and in the end, Maura pocketed only a fraction of that amount. Maura's lawyers have continued to search for ACMTC assets that can be seized and sold to satisfy what still remains a substantial portion of the judgment. "I know we'll be able to uncover where they are," says one of them, speaking of Deborah and Jim.

Now in her seventies, Maura lives on a quiet, tree-lined street in Sacramento, just a few miles away from what was once Fort Freedom. She still has bangs, though her hair has faded to a striking silvery gray. She regrets participating in the various ACMTC television programs produced in the 2010s, and wonders if she should have trained her focus on the future rather than on the past. Would she have met a romantic partner if she'd more decisively moved on from the group? Perhaps, perhaps not.

Rebekah is now in her fifties, as is Nathaniel, who has a house close to Maura. Lilly, also known as Lillian Ruth, lives in Arizona; Sarah Chelew in San Francisco. Sarah has made a concerted effort to heal her relationship with her mother, who sent her to live with her father, a musician, when she was ten years old. It has been a long process, Sarah writes, "layered and often painful—but ultimately marked by resilience and shared love and desire to move forward."

Maura continues to struggle with her youngest, Steven, who is in his early forties and still lives with her today. Of all Maura's children, he has been most negatively affected by his years spent in the group. "My relationship with Steven has been the biggest challenge of my life," Maura says, "bigger than anything the Greens ever did to me"—though of course that challenge is surely a product of Steven's formative experiences at ACMTC.

Still, Maura's life has a nice, mellow rhythm to it. She gets dinner with friends. She visits her grandchildren. She paints, draws, and tumbles rocks, smoothing their edges until they are bright, colorful, shiny. Time and again, she went out searching for truth, purpose, and community. Did she ever find them? In fits and starts, yes. But not permanently. There is satisfaction, though, in the knowledge that all her efforts did help lead to ACMTC's collapse, albeit much later than Maura would've liked.

As for her own spiritual beliefs, Maura has settled into an easygoing agnosticism. "I don't know what happens to the soul or the spirit," she says. "I don't know any of that. Nobody does. I used to think I knew, but the older I get, the less I know."

In January 2020, after more than two years in prison, Peter was placed on house arrest; the sex abuse charges were dismissed because of lack of evidence. In August 2022, he pleaded guilty to two counts of nonsexual child abuse for his role in Trinity's mistreatment (physical, not sexual), and was subsequently released from house arrest. Stacey Miller, too, was released early, though Jim remained in prison, his health declining as the years went by. At one point he contracted Covid-19; at another he fell from his upper bunk bed while he was asleep.

As a father, Jim had usually been less severe than Deborah, but in prison he became positively sentimental. There was regret in letters he sent Sarah, a kind of pleading, needy love. "Thank you for your (little) note," he wrote in one letter. "23 words in all! I was hoping for a letter.

For a daughter I've always loved, raised, traveled the world with, been through several nasty wars with, I expected a bit more. I just can't figure out what I did to you that things have become so morbid, morose?"

In another letter he asked about Ellexis: "How old is your daughter and what does she do? Do you ever write Josiah and Isaiah? Isaiah, the last time I saw him, was over 200 lbs and 6'2. I really miss them and the [ACMTC] family." He asked for Sarah's forgiveness, even acknowledging she'd been "a victim in this long drawn out war." He said he'd seen a program about restaurant renovations on his cellmate's television, and that the program had reminded him of Shaker Square, the old ACMTC restaurant in Klamath Falls. "I never did thank you for all the love and hard work you put into that project," he wrote. Jim ended the letter on a wistful note. "Well, I just wanted to write you since this T.V. show made me feel love-sick for you. You may not know it but I still love you. I still see you and Josh putting your faded suitcases in our old 1966 panel truck—going here and there in His service. I miss the good ole days before we started ACMTC. Please write back, ok? Dad."

In May 2023, Jim was released from prison several years early. "Jim is still adjusting to being back with his people," the ACMTC website announced, "for many things have changed during the five years he was locked up. Thank God that we are still marching together as militant soldiers determined to take Jesus to all the world!"—almost certainly a gross exaggeration. What was once an authoritarian, self-sustaining spiritual unit—a cult—is likely flung to the dry New Mexico wind.

Beyond what Jim has told her, Sarah knows almost nothing about Josiah and Isaiah, now in their early thirties and late twenties. Does she still think of them? "It's kind of like a faded memory at this point," she says. Her sorrow at losing them has atrophied, gone brittle. The boys have been "lost in translation," she says. "It's just one of those things that you have to live with."

There remains, in Sarah's observations about her two oldest sons, a curious passivity, an apparent absence of the roaring love she so vehemently expresses for Trinity, Ellexis, and Jeremiyah. In a way, this has been the deepest price of the life she created away from the group—a price paid not just by Josiah and Isaiah, but by Sarah, too. Because surely Sarah does feel that love; feels it but cannot let herself give in to its insistent, umbilical tug.

"She had to choose between her kids and herself," says her old co-worker and friend Abi. "And I don't think she's ever forgiven herself for that."

That Trinity is, conversely, in touch with Sarah may help explain how easily, how radiantly, Sarah speaks of her. Trinity is "a long-lost love," Sarah says, "a star in the sky that doesn't fade, no matter how much they try to destroy it. It's just there."

Shortly after the trial, Sarah called Trinity to explain the circumstances of her transport to America. The two women have remained in contact ever since. In 2021, when Sarah went public with her story for the first time, Trinity texted Sarah: "I am proud of you for your strength and the sharing of your truth. . . . I love you and you will always be my first mom."

Months later, Trinity texted Sarah to wish her a happy Mother's Day: "You were the first mother I really knew, and the only one that I ever truly had a connection with when I called you mom. . . . You are a rare being that I have the honor of knowing in this life."

Trinity's generosity is remarkable, given Sarah's role in all Trinity experienced at ACMTC ("It's all love between us," Trinity said in a 2025 interview). Sarah well understands this. "She's great now," Sarah says, "but she suffered tremendously, and that's the guilt I have to live with. . . . I was a part of that puzzle." She begins to cry with the weight of that fact. "All I wanted to do was be a midwife and deliver babies."

In the months following the trial, a Ugandan woman connected to Ruth reached out to Maura through Maura's blog. As a result of that outreach, Trinity and Ruth were able to reconnect. Ruth is now attempting to reassume a role with Trinity, "mother," she gave up so many years ago.

But every parent, too, is also a child, a truth Sarah knows as well as anyone. She is as much a daughter as she is a mother, even now, years after she left Deborah that cool September night in 1999. Sarah carries both roles within her, like an actor with two sets of costumes, two sets of lines. That she has effectively excised Jim and Deborah from her current life does not actually mean they are not *part of her life*. Because they are; because they always will be, just as Ellexis and Jeremiyah and Trinity—and, yes, Josiah and Isaiah—will always be a part of Sarah's. They are bound and bonded to each other, even if they would prefer not to be, even if Sarah has upended everything to separate herself from her complicated lineage.

"She's the beginning," Jeremiyah says of Sarah. "She is the beginning of my family." Now in his twenties, he has never met Jim and Deborah and doesn't particularly want to. Beyond his mother is a vast nothing, as far as he's concerned.

In a certain sense, he is right. Sarah's past has little obvious bearing on her and her kids' lives today. Jim and Deborah and the churning welter of their god-haunted lives have no valence here, no power over what happens to Sarah and her new family.

And yet.

When Sarah was little, no more than five or six, she would run to Deborah whenever she felt angry, sick, or upset. Deborah would lay Sarah belly down in her lap and trace her fingers from the nape of Sarah's neck, down her back, and back up again.

When Jeremiyah and Ellexis—and Josiah, Isaiah, and Trinity—were children, Sarah would do the same thing with them, summoning them to her lap, gently dragging her fingers up and down their backs.

"Shhh," she would say, their soft bodies heavy against her thighs. "It's going to be okay."

In almost all the most important ways, Deborah has failed as a mother. But there are small things she has passed along, good things. Deborah taught Sarah how to work hard. She taught her how to sew, how to cook. She taught her how to make homemade cards. And she taught her this: how to calm her children, how to communicate the force of her love with the lightest, most intimate brush of a finger.

It's a small inheritance—barely anything, really. But it's something.

ACKNOWLEDGMENTS

In 2018, my brother Edward and his wife Margaret moved into a ground-level apartment in Brooklyn, New York. When their basement flooded one day, a neighbor across the hallway came by to help clean up. This was Sarah Green—forty-five, married, with two teenage children. In the weeks and months that followed, Edward and Margaret became friendly with Sarah, who eventually began to open up about her past. Edward and Margaret said they knew someone who might want to write about her. Which, of course, I did.

First thanks, then, to Edward and Margaret, for making that initial introduction, and to Sarah, whose trust, vulnerability, and commitment (five years!) have been remarkable. My gratitude is profound. Maura Schmierer, too, has been unfailingly generous, thoughtful, and helpful. There is no book without her—without Sarah, without Edward, without Margaret. Thank you.

Heartfelt thanks to my editor, Sally Howe, for steering the ship with such intelligence, care, and good humor. Sally's belief in this book, her vision for all it could be, have been tremendous. Thanks to my agent, Alex Kane, for his creative and strategic expertise, for being a true partner. To everyone at Scribner and Simon & Schuster, my deepest gratitude for your talent and publishing acumen: Marysue Rucci, Joie Asuquo, Mark LaFlaur, Kassandra Engel, Lauren Dooley, Jaya Miceli, Sydney Newman, Rachel Podmajersky, Victor Hendrickson, Jaime Putorti, Barbara Wild, Elliot Linzer, Jessie McNiel, Lisa Nicholas, and so many others. What an honor to be published by a house as storied as Scribner. Many thanks to the team at WME for supporting this project in its journey out into the world; I am particularly grateful to Fiona Baird, my brilliant English emissary; and to Sara Mostafa, Alicia Everett, Nicole Weinroth, Charlotte Simms, Sabrina Taitz, and Claudia Ballard. Thank you to my UK publisher and editor, Sameer Rahim; to Matilda Singer, Georgina Moore, Tom Neilson, Amy Richardson, Meryl Evans, and to everyone at The Bridge Street Press and Little, Brown. Finding a UK home for this book has been one of my highest hopes from the very beginning.

Thanks to Jack Smyth, for designing a cover that so artfully captures the essence of this book. Thanks to my intrepid publicist, Beth Parker, and to Julie Tate for her meticulous fact-checking. (Any errors, of course, are mine.) Thanks to Virginia Butler for her legal know-how, and to Greg Chatterley for his religious review. Thank you to Sebastian Kim for taking my author photo, and to Brandon Butler and Peter Jaszi for legal support. Thanks to Angelina Torre for such helpful research assistance.

The Oracle's Daughter began as an article in *The Cut*. Thanks to Genevieve Smith for fielding a pitch from an unknown freelancer; and to Jordan Larson, who, with Genevieve, edited the piece with such care and rigor. Thanks also to everyone at *The Cut* and *New York* magazine who touched the article in some way, particularly Lindsay Peoples and Jessica Suriano.

Thank you, thank you—and thank you again—to Waverly Herbert, not just for being a peerless writing partner, but for a friendship that means more to me than I can possibly say. Waverly is in every page of this book; my gratitude runs deeper than deep.

Thanks to Makana Eyre and Heather Radke, fellow travelers in the world of publishing, whose support and feedback made the writing of this book so much more rewarding, more doable, more *fun* than it would have been otherwise.

Thanks to my brilliant friends who read drafts of this book and offered such useful and energizing feedback—Elena Glass, Suzannah Herbert, Phoebe Holtzman, and Kate Lucky. Friends in life, friends in art.

Thanks to my many sources, especially Lew Fratis, who provided an essential window into Deborah Green's early life; to Johanna Edwards and Julie Gudino; to Mike Munk and Steve Chavez; and to Brian Miller, whose thoughtfulness about his late son, Enoch Miller, moved me so deeply.

ACKNOWLEDGMENTS

Thanks to the writers, historians, and journalists whose work I consulted while writing this book. I am particularly indebted to Frances FitzGerald (*The Evangelicals: The Struggle to Shape America*), Philip Jenkins (*Mystics and Messiahs: Cults and New Religions in American History*), Chris Jennings (*Paradise Now: The Story of American Utopianism*), Mark A. Noll (*A History of Christianity in the United States and Canada*), Michael D. Langone (*Recovery from Cults: Help for Victims of Psychological and Spiritual Abuse*), and the journalists of the *Sacramento Bee*, *Albuquerque Journal*, *Cibola County Beacon*, and *Gallup Independent*. For former cult members and their families seeking practical guidance with the issues raised in this book, *Recovery from Cults* is a particularly useful resource, as is Steven Hassan's *Freedom of Mind: Helping Loved Ones Leave Controlling People, Cults, and Beliefs*.

Closer to home, thank you to my siblings, Matthew Hill, Edward Hill, and Virginia Butler, champions from the beginning. Thank you to my in-laws, Karen Hill, Margaret Hill, and Dan Butler. Thank you to my beautiful nieces, who bring me so much joy: Lucy, Zoe, Stella, Dabney, Annie, Tilly, and Annabel; and to my wonderful, grinning godson, James Riely.

Thank you Susan Widdicombe, Toni Cruthirds, Ali Accarino, Suzannah Herbert, Waverly Herbert, Nick Vissat: the home team. Thank you Andrew Riely, steady pal and brother. Thank you Elena Glass, for whom the word "friend" is hardly sufficient. Thank you Sara Hanson, Kinsley Suer, Matt dePaola, Kate Lucky, and Sash Bischoff for asking how the book was going, for encouraging me, for delighting in my progress. Thank you Charlotte Hornsby, for being there through all the years, for knowing this was possible.

Thank you Emily Hornsby, Fernanda Riely, Jesse Ruuttila, Shannon Kingett, Santosh Danda, Josiah Urban, Greg Louis, Juliet Fox, Leah Bhabha, Phoebe Holtzman, Massimo Young, Sarah Packford, Eric Hvolboll, Sara Atalay, Katy Hershberger, Alex Kent, Christian Griffin, Dave Hanson, Danit Kleinman, Jessie Evans, Synne Borgen, Rachel Lerner-Ley, Laura Hankin, Charlotte Erb, Sam Terris, Dunja Kay, Caraline Sogliuzzo, Tim Falotico, Weronika Pleban, Elizabeth O'Connell, Kenneth Saathoff, Caroline Brautigan, Hannah Novak, Melanie Bunn, Catherine Assink,

Peter Martin, Rob Weatherley, Steve Perring, Rebecca LaChance, Adam Waller, Mayra Padilla, Karyn Kendall-Edens, Virginia Watkins, Ben Lerude, Sean Powell, Gina Ryder, Virginia Hine, Maria Tridas, Alanna Duncan, Chelsea Newson, Jack Raisch, Brianne Sperber, and so many others.

Thank you to my grandparents, Ruth Hill, the late Billy Hill, the late Honey Passano, and Bill Passano—for life, for everything. Thank you Melinda Hamilton, for all the dinners, all the conversation, all the support.

Thanks to Christie, Paul, Hilary, Glen, and Rob Walker; Paige, Jonathan, Jane, and Nathan Hornsby; Katie Gilbert; Janice and Pinkney Herbert; Birgit Winther, Nella Hendley, and Low Hendley; Carol Manning and Eric Turkheimer; Preston and Esther Terry; Mars Child and Jay Zimmerman; Pat and Mark Vissat; Darlene and Mark Cruthirds; Marilu Thomas; Janet and Harvey Higgs; George and Barbara Beal; Suzanne and Meridith Glass; and Amy Hatfield, "Amy Doodle," editor of what was, in fact, my *real* first book, *Fancy the Hiker*.

Thanks to all my teachers at Venable, Covenant, NYU, and Columbia, especially Liz DeGaynor, Mark Traphagen, Dave Breslin, Spencer Burton, Carolyn Polson McGee, the late Anne Caughey, Christina von Koehler, Chris Stahl, Paul Speiser, and Steve Drukman. Thanks to Leslie Jamison, for her brilliance and her kindness, her belief in books. Thanks to Brenda Wineapple, for opening up a whole new genre of writing to me. Thanks to Sam Freedman, for the best instruction a writer could ask for, and for so graciously ushering me into the world of publishing: It is impossible for me to imagine my career without Sam's advocacy and mentorship, his belief in my capacity to do this work.

Thank you to my broader family in all its wild abundance: Leslie Ford, Thom Ford, Molly Ford, Terry Passano, Will Passano, Caroline Cagney, Will Cagney, Alex Fairbank, Brian Fairbank, Cannon Passano, Joanne Bartlett, Chris Bartlett, Elizabeth Brown, Grason Brown, Bea Bartlett, Nicholas Bartlett, Ruthie Klinck, Jessie Klinck, Philip Klinck, Mason Klinck, Nancy Goodall, Ches Goodall, Aubrey Ford, Rachel Pizatella-Haswell, Billy Ford, Ches Goodall IV, Margie Long, Kate Long,

ACKNOWLEDGMENTS

Graham Long, Melinda Page Hamilton, duVergne Gaines, Mary Frances Bannard, Gussie Bannard, Page Cassin, Alice Cassin, Ellen Langford, Betsey Locke, and all the rest.

Thanks to the Pasquaney community, in particular Vinnie Broderick, Mike Hanrahan, Aimee Wadeson, Jennifer Larochelle, Doug Camp, Camille Bharucha, Parker Griffin, Kirk Phelps, Dave Ryder, Jack Reigeluth, and my godfather Howie Baetjer—*until it be thoroughly finished.*

Thanks to my SpotCo family: Callie Goff, Stacey Lieberman Prince, Tom Greenwald, Jimmy McNicholas, Lisa Lewis, Nicky Lindeman, and Kiki Rathbun.

Thanks to Andrew Chiodo, for seeing me through. Thanks to Matt Zimmerman and Tim Hunt. Thanks to David Turner, for insisting I was a writer. Thank you Chris Calhoun, Lenore Loveman, Jordan Rodman, and the magazine and literary journal editors who have given me a career, in particular Jim O'Quinn, Nicole Estvanik Taylor, Katherine LaGrave, and to Wendy Lesser, who first said yes. Thank you to Joy Parisi at the late, great Paragraph Writers' Studio in New York and to Lydah DeBin, Sebastian Mazza, and the staff of the Center for Fiction in Brooklyn, where much of this book was written. Thank you to booksellers everywhere, and to all the people who helped turn a Word document into *this*, a physical book. Thanks to you, reader, for spending your time in these pages—and if you know of a story you think needs telling, please get in touch (I mean it).

Thanks to Dan Siegel, Jenny Yancey, and Weezie Yancey-Siegel, who in 2015 held a writing workshop in Patmos, Greece, that led me to graduate school and, eventually, this book. Thank you to the extraordinary instructors I met there: Cheryl Strayed, Brian Lindstrom, Zayd Dohrn, and to Rachel DeWoskin, who so generously wrote me a letter of recommendation when I applied to MFA programs.

This book is dedicated to my parents, Kemp and Tommy Hill, and to my godmother, Joanne Bartlett. Thank you, Joanne, for your steadfast love, for always wanting the best for me. Thank you, Mom and Dad, for guiding me through *Hooked on Phonics*; for covering the kitchen table with Roald Dahl paperbacks; for all the time I spent writing this book in Madison. You are so deeply a part of these pages, so deeply a part of who I am. What a gift.

Harrison Hill
July 2025
Brooklyn, New York

A NOTE ON SOURCES

In the years I spent reporting and writing this book, I reached out repeatedly to Deborah Green, Jim Green, and their representatives. Deborah's lawyers did not reply to several requests for an interview; neither did they respond when contacted by an independent fact-checker with an extensive list of questions and allegations raised by this book. Jim Green, too, declined to speak with me, explaining in a 2025 email, "We find [interviews] to be a waste. People who are biased won't print (fairly) what we say anyhow. I'm sure you've made up your mind what you will print. Sarah didn't tell you (?) that she left 3 children & a faithful husband behind when she ran off with another man at Fence Lake. We were left with them to take care of." When the fact-checker reached out to Jim, he directed her to the ACMTC website, and to a fourteen-DVD series where the group attempts to debunk the allegations it has faced since its earliest days in Sacramento. Jim also told the fact-checker, "We are currently doing some fact checking of our own, examining details, serious contradictions, lies and libel. We are also looking into publishing our own book. Additionally, we may have an official documentary in the works."

In the weeks and months following that exchange, I received multiple anonymous or obviously pseudonymous emails calling my reporting into question, and asking if I plan to "give the generals of this outfit some of the money from the sale of this 'non fiction,' where you profit at their expense." The group also appears to have created an email address with a handle that contains the words "I am Harrison Hill," presumably in an effort to impersonate me. In response to an article I wrote about Sarah Green for *The Cut* in 2021, and in anticipation of this book's release, ACMTC First Sergeant Amos River wrote on one of the group's several websites that I have published "conjectures, lies and bitter falsehoods against the Generals." River dismisses my work as "fancy wording that makes you sit tensely at the edge of your seat. *SUSPENSE!*" ("Nonfiction, Hill? Better make sure!") River also says the group is currently investigating me, and that my work is not just "scandalous" but also "a bit misogynistic." River also writes, "As for Harrison's soul, I really do pray he repents and comes to Jesus."

In June 2025, when the fact-checker emailed Peter Green's attorney, Kari Morrissey, with a list of questions and allegations, Ms. Morrissey wrote that Peter "denies the charges, was never convicted of them and all sex offense charges against him were dismissed. Mr. Green pled guilty to two counts of third-degree child abuse that were not related to sex offenses. Mr. Green is not and will not be a registered sex offender and at the conclusion of his probation he will not have a felony conviction on his record." When asked who was paying Peter's attorney's fees (he appears to have come from a wealthy family), Ms. Morrissey declined to comment directly, adding, "I can tell you that it was not his mother (his father was deceased before the charges against him were ever filed.)" Regarding other allegations raised by this book, Ms. Morrissey said Peter had no comment.

Josh Green, Mandana Shoushtari, Brandon Vigil, Johnny Valdez, Lemuel Martinez, Jamie Bridgewater, and Stacey Miller's lawyer did not respond to requests for an interview or for comment. Hector Balderas spoke with me while I was still working on this book, but a fact-checker was subsequently unable to connect with him. Attempts to contact Steve Schmierer, John Green, Anthony, Ja'el Phalen, "Omondi" (a pseudonym), and "Trinity's" birth father were unsuccessful. Though I communicated with "Ruth" for over two years via WhatsApp, she couldn't ultimately decide whether or not she wanted to speak with me on the record. Neither the FBI nor the American consulate in Uganda responded to requests for comment.

NOTES

Epigraph

ix   *"The sanest and best . . ."*: William James, *The Varieties of Religious Experience* (New York: Penguin Classics, 1985; originally published 1902), 47.

Prologue

1   *Sarah is already awake:* Author interviews with Sarah Green; see also *New Mexico v. Deborah Green*, 9/19/18, trial transcript. Geographic descriptions are partially based on my own in-person reporting around Fence Lake, New Mexico, 9/22/22–9/24/22.

2   *"True Spirit-led Christianity,"* etc.: ACMTC tracts; Jim and Deborah Green sermons; aggressivechristianity.net.

PART ONE

Chapter 1

7   *chained to a gurney* and following: Author interviews with Maura Aluzas/Schmierer, and Maura's own personal writings. There is disagreement among sources about how to spell Carlo's name. In his obituary he is identified as "Carl Carter," though it is highly likely "Carlo" was used as a nickname, as is Maura Aluzas/Schmierer's recollection. It is also possible his name was spelled "Carlos"; his brother Calvin provided both spellings as possibilities.

11   *Her parents divorced when*, and other details of Lila's childhood: Author interviews with Lew Fratis and LaVonne Fratis Crumm, who grew up down the street from the Carters; also author interviews with Sarah Green and Maura Schmierer. Lila/Deborah's younger brother, Calvin Carter, confirmed elements of this account to Sarah Green.

12   *a stellar academic record*: Author interviews with Gary Younglove, Spencer

Stout, and Randy Smedley. See also *Argonaut*, James Marshall High School yearbook, 1961, 1962, 1963, and 1964 eds.

13 *"It's now or never . . .":* Aaron Schroeder and Wally Gold, "It's Now or Never," recorded by Elvis Presley, released 1960.

13 *so-called hippies:* W. J. Rorabaugh, *American Hippies* (New York: Cambridge University Press, 2015); Timothy Miller, *The 60s Communes: Hippies and Beyond* (Syracuse, NY: Syracuse University Press, 1999); also "Man of the Year: The Inheritor," *Time*, 1/6/67, and "Youth: The Hippies," *Time*, 7/7/67.

14 *"Is God Dead?":* *Time*, cover, 4/8/66.

14 *Fourth Great Awakening:* William G. McLoughlin, *Revivals, Awakenings and Reform* (Chicago: University of Chicago Press, 1978); Amanda Montell, *Cultish: The Language of Fanaticism* (New York: Harper Wave, 2021), 27.

14 *smoking a pipe*, etc.: Author interviews with Sarah Green; also Jim Green essays, "Flower Power: How the 60's Revolution Changed the World" and "Changed Gods, Changed Directions."

Chapter 2

16 *something had changed:* Author interviews with Maura Schmierer.

16 *a Chippewa medicine chief:* Many Indigenous people use the term "Ojibwe" rather than "Chippewa"; I have used "Chippewa" because it is how Sun Bear chose to describe himself. Similarly, I have referred to Sun Bear as a medicine chief because that is the term Sun Bear used.

16 *filled with vultures:* Sun Bear, Wabun, and Nimimosha, *The Bear Tribe's Self Reliance Book* (New York: Prentice Hall Press, 1988), 4.

16 *described herself as Native American:* It is debatable whether or not Deborah Green has Indigenous ancestry. Lila's paternal grandfather, John Vance Carter, contacted the Department of the Interior to inquire about his own alleged Choctaw/Native American ancestry in 1900; in response, representatives from the DOI wrote: "No one of the said applicants has ever been enrolled by the Choctaw tribal authorities as a member of the Choctaw Tribe, or admitted to Choctaw citizenship by a duly constituted court or committee of the Choctaw nation, or by the Commission to the Five Civilized Tribes, or by a decree of the United States court in Indian Territory, under the provisions of the act of Congress approved June 10, 1896." That said, according to the 1900 census, Carter lived at Township 6, Choctaw Nation, Indian Territory, USA. Lila/Deborah Green herself wrote about her own family history in *The Care Free Tribe and the Legend of the Once Knews*, an ACMTC tract likely from the mid-1990s, 5–6: "I am a mixed blood, born of a Native American father (Sioux) and an American (English) descent mother." It appears unlikely that Lila has any Sioux heritage, and that if she is of Native American descent (which, again, is debatable), she is Choctaw, not Sioux.

NOTES

17   *"go to the mountains..."*: Lila Carter/Deborah Green, "X Street Files to the Present," aggressivechristianity.net.

17   *The Bear Tribe and events at Medicine Rock:* Author interviews with Morning Star, Maura Schmierer, Rebekah/Iantha Schmierer, Sarah Green, and Julie Gudino; also Maura Schmierer writings. Lila Green's younger brother, Calvin Carter, confirmed elements of this account to Sarah Green. See also Sun Bear et al., *The Bear Tribe's Self-Reliance Book*; Morning Star, *Medicine Rock: A Journey of Vision and Healing* (Bloomington, IN: IUniverse, 2009); Sun Bear, Wabun, and Barry Weinstock, *The Path of Power* (New York: Prentice Hall Press, 1983); "All-peoples Indian tribe to inhabit foothills; Sun Bear stresses responsibility to the Earth," *Pony Express*, 1/14/71; Margaret Koch, "Indian with a Mission," *Santa Cruz Sentinel*, 1/17/71; "Squatters Pose a Knotty Problem," *Sacramento Bee*, 4/8/71; and Ursula Smith, "Honest, There Are Injuns on Shoo Fly Ridge," *Mountain Democrat and Placerville Times*, 4/8/71. I myself hiked around the area where Medicine Rock was located, 6/24/22.

18   *"tens of thousands"*: Timothy Miller, *The 60s Communes: Hippies and Beyond* (Syracuse, NY: Syracuse University Press, 1999), xx. Estimates of the number of rural communes in the 1960s and seventies vary widely; see ibid., xix–xx.

18   *"We have it in our power..."*: Thomas Paine, qtd. by Chris Jennings, *Paradise Now: The Story of American Utopianism* (New York: Random House, 2016), 5.

18   *"Drop City brought together..."*: Miller, *The 60s Communes*, 31–32.

19   *"overwhelmingly white"*: Ibid., 154.

19   *a political usefulness*: Sherry L. Smith, *Hippies, Indians, and the Fight for Red Power* (Oxford: Oxford University Press, 2012), 7.

19   *"The way of the hippie..."*: Rupert Costo, "Hippies Are NOT American Indians," *San Francisco Examiner & Chronicle*, 6/25/67, qtd., in part, in Rorabaugh, *American Hippies*, 82.

19   *"More power to them"*: Sun Bear, qtd. in Smith, *Hippies, Indians, and the Fight for Red Power*, 80.

19   *"Sun Bear hasn't started..."*: Rick Williams, qtd. in Ward Churchill, "Spiritual Hucksterism: The Rise of the Plastic Medicine Men," Cultural Survival, 5/7/10.

21   *Then Jim Green arrived:* Jim Green's experiences in the Bear Tribe are drawn, in part, from his autobiographical tract, *Where in Hell Is God?*, early 1980s.

21   *"God told her..."*: Jamie Bridgewater, recounting a 2013 conversation with Lila/Deborah Green, "Written Testimony of Enoch Blessed River's Death and Illness," 4/13/16, 12. Sources have offered conflicting accounts of when Jim and Deborah became a couple. The sequence outlined in this chapter strikes me as the most likely scenario.

22   *"A knife was placed..."*: Green, *Where in Hell Is God?*

22 *"wanted to play Indian . . .":* Sun Bear, Wabun, and Weinstock, *The Path of Power*, 136.
22 *"Tom-toms were still heard . . .":* "Indians Vanish," *Mountain Democrat and Placerville Times*, 4/15/71.

Chapter 3

24 *Spiritual expression was everywhere:* Rorabaugh, *American Hippies*; Miller, *The 60s Communes*; Camille Paglia, "Cults and Cosmic Consciousness: Religious Vision in the American 1960s," *Arion*, Winter 2003; "Youth: The Hippies."
24 *"performed a mock-exorcism . . .":* Paglia, "Cults and Cosmic Consciousness," 58.
24 *"the dawning of the Age of Aquarius," etc.:* Gerome Ragni and James Rando, "Aquarius / Let the Sunshine In," *Hair: The American Tribal Love-Rock Musical*, premiered 1967.
25 *the Jesus Movement:* Ronald M. Enroth, Edward E. Ericson, Jr., and C. Breckinridge Peters, *The Jesus People: Old-Time Religion in the Age of Aquarius* (Grand Rapids, MI: William B. Eerdmans, 1972); "The Jesus Revolution," *Time*, 6/21/71; Rorabaugh, *American Hippies*.
25 *"brick and pews . . .":* "Can Woodstock Survive?," *Hollywood Free Paper*, 5/4/71.
25 *"high on the Lord":* Qtd in Enroth, Ericson, and Peters, *The Jesus People*, 69.
25 *"Let the earth . . .":* Qtd. in "Youth: The Hippies."
25 *"HELL? NO! . . .":* Enroth, Ericson, and Peters, *The Jesus People*, cover.
25 *"in the name of the Father":* Qtd. in "The Jesus Revolution."
26 *"It's so beautiful . . .":* Ibid.
26 *cults have proliferated:* Margaret Thaler Singer, *Cults in Our Midst: The Continuing Fight against Their Hidden Menace* (San Francisco: Jossey-Bass, 2003), 30.
26 *"meteoric rise":* Ronald M. Enroth, *The Lure of the Cults* (Chappaqua, NY: Christian Herald Books, 1979), 42.
26 *the original Latin:* Ibid., 20.
26 *"cult plus time . . .":* Reza Aslan, qtd. in Montell, *Cultish*, 37.
26 *"It is all but impossible . . .":* Philip Jenkins, *Mystics and Messiahs: Cults and New Religions in American History* (Oxford: Oxford University Press, 2000), 13.
27 *fully a third:* Rodney Stark, William Sims Bainbridge, and Daniel P. Doyle, "Cults of America: A Reconnaissance in Space and Time," *Sociological Analysis* (Winter 1979): 347.
27 *"Cultifornia":* John M. Crewdson, "How California Has Become Home for a Plethora of Cults," *New York Times*, 11/30/78.
28 *Cults of the 1960s and the 1970s:* Ronald M. Enroth, *Youth, Brainwashing, and the Extremist Cults* (Grand Rapids, MI: Zondervan, 1977); Enroth, *The Lure of the Cults*; Max Cutler with Kevin Conley, *Cults: Inside the World's*

Most Notorious Groups and Understanding the People Who Joined Them (New York: Gallery Books, 2022); Camille Paglia, "Cults and Cosmic Consciousness"; Singer, *Cults in Our Midst*; Enroth, Ericson, and Peters, *The Jesus People*.

28 *"were willing to do anything..."*: Lisa Bryant, qtd. in Enroth, *Youth*, 29.
28 *a teenage guru*: Ibid., 142.
28 *"had a certain magnificence..."*: Shelley Liebert, qtd. in ibid., 108.
28 *"If you washed..."*: Ibid., 107.

Chapter 4

30 *a diamondback rattlesnake*: Jim Green sermon, "PX2 Files Ch7, 'Asinine Assassins,'" 6/11/12.
30 *Jim's early adulthood*: Green, *Where in Hell Is God?*; Jim Green essay, "Emotional Reconditioning"; *Holy Tribal Nation*, book 4, 2–8; Green, "Changed Gods, Changed Directions," aggressivechristianity.net; "Flower Power: How the 60's Revolution Changed Society," cultofthelivinggod.net; Jim Green sermon, "Stronger and Stronger"; "Ministry Facts," aggressivechristianity.net. See also *Echoes*, Daviess County High School yearbook, 1961, 1962, 1963, 1964 eds.
30 *"I fornicated every woman..."*: Jim Green sermon, "Great Trumpet Lips."
31 *"taken enough acid..."*: Qtd. in Green, *Where in Hell Is God?*
31 *"Day and night..."* : Jim Green, *Son of Dominion: The Warrior, or Tight Squeeze*, ACMTC tract, an account of Jim's spiritual journey, as told through a superhero figure clearly intended to stand in for Jim.
31 *Jim and Lila hitchhiked*: Green, *Where in Hell Is God?*, "Emotional Reconditioning," and "Great Trumpet Lips." Lila's brother Calvin Carter confirmed elements of this account to Sarah Green.
31 *"Cocaine, cocaine for sale..."*: Qtd. in *The Farragut Report* (Nampa, ID: Gold Quill, 1972), 43.
31 *"by means of balloons..."*: Ibid., 52, citing the *Intermountain Observer*, 7/17/71.
31 *"The Lord is really moving..."*: Ibid., 54.
32 *"a gathering of early Christians"*: *Idaho Statesman*, 7/9/71, qtd. in *The Farragut Report*, 30.
32 *"This is what I think..."* and following: Qtd. in Green, *Where in Hell Is God?*
32 *"The more I read..."*: Lila Carter/Deborah Green, "Jack Chick Dies at 92," aggressivechristianity.net.
32 *Jim announced*: This account of Jim and Lila's conversion, including visual descriptions, dialogue, quotations, and internal thoughts, is drawn from Green, *Where in Hell Is God?*, "Emotional Reconditioning," and Carter/Green, "Jack Chick Dies at 92."
33 *"hippie wanderers..."*: Carter/Green, "Jack Chick Dies at 92."

Chapter 5

35 *"a slimy cesspool . . ."*: Green, *Son of Dominion*.
35 *"fervid lostness"*: Green, "Changed Gods, Changed Directions," aggressive christianity.net.
35 *I don't need this. . . .*: Green, "Great Trumpet Lips."
35 *"If you want to know . . ."*: Lila Carter/Deborah Green, *Wisdom's Cry*, no. 23 (1999): 3–4.
36 *"hungry for God . . ."*: Jim Green sermon, "Demons in Christians."
36 *"vast empire"* and following: Glenn Rutherford and Mike King, "Jeffersonville Church More like a Cult, Some Say," *Courier-Journal* (Louisville), 4/12/79; Glenn Rutherford and Mike King, "One Christ Gospel Service Included Praying, Shaking and a 'Love Offering,'" *Courier-Journal* (Louisville), 4/12/79.
36 *The modern Pentecostal movement*: Frances FitzGerald, *The Evangelicals: The Struggle to Shape America* (New York: Simon & Schuster, 2017), 209.
37 "alabahaya," "akabahaya": "A Resurrection message from our Leader Rev. B. R. Hicks, Christ Gospel Churches, Inc.," 4/12/20. These words are representative of those Hicks uttered over the course of her long career.
37 *"It was as though a spell . . ."*: Qtd. in Rutherford and King, "Jeffersonville Church."
37 *"mind control . . ."*: Qtd. in Ibid.
37 *media coverage and political action*: Jenkins, *Mystics and Messiahs*, 187–207; Jo Thomas, "Practices of Cults Receiving New Scrutiny," *New York Times*, 1/21/79; Jo Thomas, "Some in Congress Seek Inquiries on Cult Activities," *New York Times*, 1/22/79; T. R. Reid, "Public Relations a Factor as Sen. Dole Opens Sessions," *Washington Post*, 2/6/79.
37 *Kansas senator Bob Dole*: "Dole to Sponsor Hearing on Cult Phenomenon," press release, *News from U.S. Senator Bob Dole*, 1/23/79.
37 *"cannot under our laws . . ."*: Qtd. in Thomas, "Some in Congress."
37 *"involved in" cults*: Douglas H. Cook, "Tort Liability for Cult Deprogramming," *Ohio State Law Journal*, Vol. 43, 1982, 466. Cook here is citing Richard Delgado, "Religious Totalism: Gentle and Ungentle Persuasion Under the First Amendment," *Southern California Law Review*, Vol. 51:1, 1977.
38 *"We Shall Overcome"*: Reid, "Public Relations."
38 *"tax, banking . . ."*: Ibid.
38 *"I don't know what a cult is. . . ."*: Griffin B. Bell, qtd. in Thomas, "Practices of Cults."
38 *mission trips*: Jim and Lila Green, "Mission of Mercy to the Miserable," *Tribal Call*, issue #21, 2000, 32; Jim Green, "Cristianismo y Marxismo," *Holy Tribal Nation*, book 4, 10–11; author interviews with Sarah Green; also "Some Quotes," aggressivechristianity.net.

NOTES

39 *"Oh! people say..."*: Catherine Booth, "Aggressive Christianity," *Papers on Aggressive Christianity*, 1891 (speech delivered 1880), 13.
41 *"The battle cry has sounded...."*: Jim Green essay, "Don't Set Up Camp."
42 *Mount St. Helens:* "Mount St. Helens Made It a Gray Day Far, Far Away," *Spokesman-Review*, 5/19/80; Kevin Miller, "The Week the Sky Fell," *Missoulian*, 5/25/80; "Ash Eruption and Fallout," United States Geological Survey; Jeff Weathersby, "Ashed Ranch Going Strong," *News Tribune*, 6/4/80; "St. Helens Campers Had No Time for Fear," Associated Press/*Spokane Chronicle*, 5/20/80.
42 *"in our hair..."*: Miller, "The Week the Sky Fell."
42 *"black as sackcloth..."*: Revelation 6:12 (King James Version).
42 *"a dungeon horrible..."*: John Milton, *Paradise Lost*, book 1, lines 61–63.

Chapter 6

43 *Back in the fifties:* Author interviews with Maura Aluzas/Schmierer.
44 *following their departure:* Author interviews with Maura Schmierer and Rebekah/Iantha Schmierer; Steve Schmierer essay, "The California Cabin"; Steve Schmierer videotape, *PX2 Files, Chapter 10, Bio-Liar-Intro, Trailer, Part 4*, and Maura Schmierer writings.
45 *Christian fundamentalism:* FitzGerald, *The Evangelicals*, 5; Susan Friend Harding, *The Book of Jerry Falwell: Fundamentalist Language and Politics* (Princeton: Princeton University Press, 2000); Tim Alberta, *The Kingdom, the Power, and the Glory* (New York: Harper, 2023).
46 *"Evangelicalism is the religion..."*: Kenneth L. Woodward with John Barnes and Laurie Lisle, "Born Again!," *Newsweek*, 10/25/76, 68.
46 *"The Year of the Evangelical"*: *Newsweek*, 10/25/76.
46 *78 million:* Gary Wills, "'Born Again' Politics," *New York Times Magazine*, 8/1/76.
46 *34 percent:* "Poll Finds 34% Share 'Born Again' Feeling," *New York Times*, 9/26/76.
46 *"for the first time..."*: George Dugan, "Religious Services Gained Attendance in 76, Study Finds," *New York Times*, 12/31/76.
46 *"No other sector..."*: David Kucharsky, "The Year of the Evangelical '76," *Christianity Today*, 10/22/76, 12.
46 *"Many young people..."*: Ibid., 13.
47 *Maura baked pies* and following: Author interviews with Maura Schmierer, Rebekah/Iantha Schmierer, Nathaniel Schmierer, and Sarah Chelew; and Maura Schmierer writings.
47 *"These past fifteen months..."*: Jim Green essay, "Our Vision," 1.
48 *The Schmierers* and following, including all quotes not cited below: Author interviews with Maura Schmierer, Rebekah/Iantha Schmierer, Nathaniel Schmierer, and Sarah Chelew; Maura Schmierer writings.

50 *"tried to live a Christian life..."*: ACMTC video, *The Px2 Files, Ch9, Big Fat Liar, Pt. 9.*
50 *"fornication..."*: Ibid.
51 *"I started leaking..."*: Steve Schmierer letter to Maura Schmierer, mid-1990s.
51 *"told me the truth..."*: ACMTC video, *The Px2 Files, CH9, Big Fat Liar, Pt.10a.*

Chapter 7

53 *a majority of evangelicals:* Chris Lehmann, "How Jimmy Carter Lost Evangelical Christians to the Right," *The Nation*, 12/24.
53 *"Preachers are not called..."*: Jerry Falwell, qtd. in Alberta, *The Kingdom*, 56.
53 *"Render to Caesar..."*: Mark 12:17 (King James Version).
53 *"The school's colors..."*: Alberta, *The Kingdom*, 58.
54 *"We are fighting..."*: Jerry Falwell, qtd. in FitzGerald, *The Evangelicals*, 291.
54 *By 1981* and *life in Sacramento:* Author interviews with Sarah Green, Maura Schmierer, Rebekah/Iantha Schmierer, and Sarah Chelew; also Maura Schmierer writings.
55 Pigs in the Parlor: Frank and Ida Mae Hammond, *Pigs in the Parlor: The Practical Guide to Deliverance* (Kirkwood, MO: Impact Christian Books, 1973).
56 *"It is no coincidence..."*: Ibid., 170.
56 *"In my name..."*: Mark 16:17 (King James Version).
59 *"I'm doing this for Jesus..."*: Rebekah/Iantha Schmierer letter to grandparents.
59 *David Gains:* There is a great deal of inconsistency in how Gains's name is spelled in the public record; other spellings include "Gaines," "Gaine," and "Gain."

Chapter 8

61 *Sarah Green hops on a bike* and following: Author interviews with Sarah Green and Nathaniel Schmierer.

Chapter 9

64 *The three houses* and *life around Fort Freedom:* Author interviews with Maura Schmierer, Sarah Green, Brenda Eutsler/Johanna Edwards, Julie Gudino, Nathaniel Schmierer, Carla Swick, and Conrad Dechant; Maura Schmierer blog. I myself visited the property in June 2022.

NOTES

64 *David Gains almost certainly funded*: undated affidavit by Maura Schmierer and author interview with Maura Schmierer.

65 *"sinless perfection"*: "Aggressive Christianity Missions Training Corps," Apologetics Resource Center, 1987.

65 *"You may not find it"* and other Jim/Deborah quotes: Qtd. in Maura Schmierer writings.

66 *"severe child abuse . . ."*: "Lisa Dye's Story, As Told to Rhonda Moffett (Cont.)," received by Robert Blasier 6/9/87, 3.

67 *"I've got news for you. . . ."*: Deborah Green, "Jesus, as a Man," tape #1176, 5.

67 *"most active [Quaker] preachers"*: Jenkins, *Mystics and Messiahs*, 28.

68 *cults and cult-like groups can provide:* Froma I. Zeitlin, "Cultic Models of the Female: Rites of Dionysus and Demeter," *Arethusa*, Spring and Fall 1982, 133.

68 *"recovered memories"*: Michelle Smith and Lawrence Pazder, *Michelle Remembers* (New York: Pocket Books, 1980).

68 *published a book* and following: Sean Horlor, "This book plunged the world into a terrifying obsession . . . ," Canadian Broadcasting Corporation, 1/5/24; Sarah Hughes, "American Monsters: Tabloid, Media and the Satanic Panic, 1970–2000," *Journal of American Studies* 51, no. 3 (8/2017); Jenkins, *Mystics and Messiahs*, 211–14; Joseph Laycock, "Where Do They Get These Ideas? Changing Ideas of Cults in the Mirror of Popular Culture," *Journal of the American Academy of Religion* 81, no. 1 (3/2013), 90; Alan Yuhas, "It's Time to Revisit the Satanic Panic," *New York Times*, 3/31/2021.

68 *"her teeth had been removed . . ."*: Laycock, "Where Do They Get These Ideas?," 90.

68 *"with drills, masks . . ."*: Hughes, "American Monsters," 698.

69 *"in meat markets, bathrooms . . ."*: Ibid., 701.

69 *"to throw babies . . ."*: Ibid., 705.

69 *"Today we have found . . ."*: Tom Jarriel, qtd. in Yuhas, "It's Time to Revisit."

69 *"singularly ill-equipped"*: John Myers, qtd. in ibid.

69 *"Anytime I would give them . . ."*: Kyle Zirpolo, as told to Debbie Nathan, "I'm Sorry," *Los Angeles Times*, 10/30/05.

69 *"investigators could not substantiate . . ."*: Yuhas, "It's Time to Revisit."

70 *"We didn't want . . ."*: Tom Wallace, qtd. in Diane Divoky, "Sacramento Cult Battles Myriad Demons with Vigor," *Sacramento Bee*, 9/25/84.

70 *Brenda Eutsler:* Author interviews with Brenda Eutsler/Johanna Edwards.

71 *A version of this story:* Author interviews with Julie Gudino and Maura Schmierer; also Rachel Johnson, "Response from Rachel, Former ACMTC Member for >20 Years," Maura Schmierer blog.

71 *booze, gangs, and parties:* author interview with Julie Gudino; Julie would later dispute her own self-characterization.

72 *"Villagers of Israel . . ."*: Judges 5:7 (New International Version).

Chapter 10

73 *It can be comforting:* Eileen Barker, *The Making of a Moonie: Brainwashing or Choice?* (Oxford: Basil Blackwell, 1984); Marc Galanter, *Cults: Faith, Healing, and Coercion*, 2nd ed. (Oxford: Oxford University Press, 1999); Kate Gale, "How—and Why—Americans Became Susceptible to the Toxic Allure of Cults," LitHub, 6/14/2021; Zoë Heller, "What Makes a Cult a Cult?," *New Yorker*, 7/5/2021; Robert J. Lifton, *Losing Reality: On Cults, Cultism, and the Mindset of Political and Religious Zealotry* (New York: New Press, 2019); Montell, *Cultish*; Singer, *Cults in Our Midst*; Alexandra Stein, *Terror, Love & Brainwashing: Attachment in Cults and Totalitarian Systems* (New York: Routledge, 2017).
73 *"normal, functioning families . . .":* Singer, *Cults in Our Midst*, 17.
73 *the "Not Me" myth:* Ibid., 15.
74 *"In fact . . . there was a higher proportion . . .":* Barker, *The Making of a Moonie*, 193; Barker here is citing the work of Wolfgang Kuner.
74 *"happy, secure . . .":* Barker, *The Making of a Moonie*, 214.
74 *idealism:* Amanda Montell, interviewed in Gale, *How—and Why—Americans Became Susceptible*.
74 *disinclined to approach:* Montell, *Cultish*, 97.
74 *"have attracted disproportionate . . .":* Heller, "What Makes a Cult a Cult."
74 *"demographically unremarkable":* Qtd. in Alan Travis, "MI5 Report Challenges Views on Terrorism in Britain," *Guardian*, 4/20/08.
74 *"no more evidence . . .":* Ibid.
74 *"totalist":* Stein, *Terror, Love & Brainwashing*, 7.
75 *"craves to be consoled . . .":* James, *The Varieties of Religious Experience*, 46-47.
76 *confession and reeducation:* Lifton, *Losing Reality*, 19.
76 *reparenting:* Margaret Thaler Singer, qtd. in John M. Crewdson, "How California Has Become Home for a Plethora of Cults," *New York Times*, 11/30/78.
76 *"Our brains release . . .":* Montell, *Cultish*, 21.
76 *"sunk cost":* Ibid., 103.
77 *disorganized attachments:* Stein, *Terror, Love & Brainwashing*, 32–35.
77 *"fright without solution":* Ibid., 33.
77 *"Simply put, you cannot force . . .":* Montell, *Cultish*, 34–35.
77 *"This moment of submission . . .":* Stein, *Terror, Love & Brainwashing*, 38.
77 *"Ye shall be his servants. . . .":* 1 Samuel 8:10–19 (King James Version).

Chapter 11

79 *The sky, dark*, and following: Author interviews with Maura Schmierer, Rebekah/Iantha Schmierer, Nathaniel Schmierer, Julie Gudino, Brenda

NOTES   297

Eutsler/Johanna Edwards, Sarah Green, Chrissa Chavarria, Conrad Dechant, and Carla Swick; also, ACMTC tracts and "A Typical day in ACMTC (1980's)," Maura Schmierer blog, 3/12/14.

79 *"I say that I . . .": Words of the Spirit* radio message #1829. This prophesy is representative of those Deborah gave throughout her life.

79 *"Ten times as much . . .":* Jim Green, qtd. in Divoky, "Sacramento Cult Battles."

80 *blot out satanic images:* Ibid.

80 *a restraining order:* Nancy Weaver, "Mom Wants Her Son's Remains after Church Camp 'Martyrdom,'" *Sacramento Bee*, 4/22/87.

81 *"You can't make me . . .":* ACMTC video, *The Px2 Files, Ch10 Bio-Liar, Part 5.*

81 *"Although the devil tormented . . .":* Deborah Green, qtd. in Divoky, "Sacramento Cult Battles."

82 *"primitive Negrito tribals . . .":* "The Sun-Worshippers," *Tribal Call*, issue 21 (2000): 16.

82 *"Thank you for saving . . .":* Qtd. in *Battle Cry Sounding*, 2000, 6.

82 *"General Deborah, I have heard . . .":* Qtd. in *Wisdom's Cry*, 1999, 31.

83 *"If any man come to me . . .":* Luke 14:26 (King James Version).

83 *"He wears a mask . . .":* George Orwell, "Shooting an Elephant," in *A Collection of Essays* (Orlando, FL: Harcourt), 152.

Chapter 12

84 *It was 1986* and following: Author interviews with Sarah Green. "Gabriel" is a pseudonym; Sarah does not remember the boy's real name.

85 *Rather than taking the young man to a doctor:* Author interview with Maura Schmierer and Maura Schmierer writings. Deborah writes that Brad "was hospitalized" and given "the best medical aid available" while ill in Malawi (Deborah Green, "X Street Files to the Present").

85 *"just because they don't feel good":* Jim and Deborah Green, qtd. in Maura Schmierer writings.

Chapter 13

87 *Scattered snowflakes* and following: Author interviews with Maura Schmierer, Sarah Green, Rebekah/Iantha Schmierer, Nathaniel Schmierer, Julie Gudino, and Brenda Eutsler/Johanna Edwards; Maura Schmierer writings; Maura Schmierer affidavit; "Lisa Dye's Story."

87 *"Grow up"* and other quotations related to Maura's judgment: Qtd. in Maura Schmierer writings.

90 *a white sack dress:* Deborah claims that she and Jim "had no knowledge as to

[Maura's] clothing situation," and that Maura was "thankful to receive . . . accommodation" in the chop shop (Deborah Green, "X Street Files to the Present").

90 *a Grand Guignol of suffering:* Jim writes, "NO PHYSICAL ABUSE EVER TOOK PLACE, MS. NO ABUSE OF ANY KIND TOOK PLACE. ALL TALES OF ABUSE *ONLY TOOK PLACE IN YOUR MIND*—IN A LIE. Where, dear MS, is your HARD EVIDENCE? Surely you've got some, don't ya?" (Jim Green, "PSYCHO TERRORISM," aggressivechristianity.net). Deborah says Maura and Jacque Rankin "were given some 'menial tasks,' at their request, to occupy their time," and that Maura was expected to work only "two to four hours" a day (Deborah Green, "X Street Files to the Present"). In another ACMTC essay, a person claiming to be Jacque Rankin writes, "I was personally with MS through this whole episode that has been depicted bizarrely as imprisonment, torture, abuse, etc. That's not how it was . . . We were free to come and go." The essay continues, "We were adequately provided for. We had privacy and lots of free time. All our needs were supplied so that we had plenty of time to read our Bibles reflectively." It is very possible, however, that these are Jim or Deborah's words, not Jacque's; on at least one occasion the couple instructed a member to sign to a notarized letter that had, in fact, been written by the Greens. (Jacque Rankin, "Setting The Record Straight," aggressivechristianity.net). Lisa Dye's written testimony, however, generally corroborates Maura's account. Maura documented her experiences under the judgment extensively in the years immediately following her excommunication from the group. There is some dispute as to whether or not Maura was ever locked inside the chop shop or the clubhouse; the Greens insist she was not, and Maura agrees, but a Complaint for Damages signed by Maura in March 1988 states, "Defendants restrained plaintiff against her will by force or threats of force in that defendants [sic] compound was locked every evening . . ." For years the Greens have pointed to this discrepancy as evidence that Maura is not to be trusted, though at multiple other points in the progression of the lawsuit, Maura said she was always free to leave, just that she was afraid to do so.

90 *"I have taken God too lightly . . .":* Letters from Maura Schmierer to Deborah and Jim Green.

91 *divorce papers:* Deborah claims Maura "willingly signed the [divorce] papers" (Deborah Green, "X Street Files to the Present").

92 *six peanut butter sandwiches:* Deborah says Maura "requested that her food portion be cut" and that Maura "said she would like peanutbutter [sic] sandwiches . . . Several times I asked [Maura and Jacque] if they wanted something else. They replied, no, they loved their peanutbutter." (Deborah Green, "X Street Files to the Present").

92 *"I have to get something off my heart" and following quotes:* Qtd. by Sarah Green, author interviews with Sarah Green.

95 *a young woman with a baby:* "Lisa Dye's Story."
95 *"spiritual betterment":* "Lisa Dye's Story," 4.
95 *spiritual adultery:* For decades Deborah and Jim Green have said Maura was guilty of rampant sexual misconduct while a member of the group, a charge Maura denies.
96 *"I've always prayed for a vision of Hell":* Letter from Maura Schmierer to Deborah and Jim Green.
96 *"They seemed to slip in and out . . .":* "Lisa Dye's Story," 2.
96 *"primary complex tuberculosis":* Ibid., 1.
96 *"the ministry had her baby . . .":* Ibid., 3.

PART TWO

Chapter 14

101 *They howl and they screech, and the Shakers generally:* Jennings, *Paradise Now;* Richard Francis, *Ann the Word* (New York: Arcade, 2000); Valentine Rathbun, *A Brief Account of a Religious Scheme Taught and Propagated by a Number of Europeans, Who Lately Lived in a Place Called Nisqueunia, in the State of New-York, but Now Residing in Harvard, Commonwealth of Massachusetts, Commonly Called, Shaking Quakers,* 1724, University of Michigan Library, Digital Collections.
101 *"Indian":* Rathbun, *Brief Account,* 13.
101 *invisible berries:* Jennings, *Paradise Now,* 60.
101 *draw circles in the dirt:* Rathbun, *Brief Account,* 12.
101 *stamp so forcefully:* Francis, *Ann the Word,* 191.
101 *bang their heads:* Jennings, *Paradise Now,* 60.
101 *"[hang] a woman . . .":* Rathbun, *Brief Account,* 15.
101 *"chastised her mother . . .":* Jennings, *Paradise Now,* 24; see also Francis, *Ann the Word,* 7.
102 *"constantly pregnant":* Jennings, *Paradise Now,* 27.
102 *"trembling, shaking . . .":* Virginia Gazette, 1769, recounting the group's early years, qtd. in Francis, *Ann the Word,* 32.
102 *Did not the snake:* Jennings, *Paradise Now,* 29.
102 *"a woman clothed . . .":* Revelation 12:1 (King James Version).
102 *"a large tree . . .":* James Whitaker, qtd. in Jennings, *Paradise Now,* 30.
103 *"marketplace of religion . . .":* FitzGerald, *The Evangelicals,* 3.
103 *"more innovative . . .":* Jenkins, *Mystics and Messiahs,* 16.
103 *George Whitefield and the First Great Awakening:* Harry S. Stout, *The Divine Dramatist: George Whitefield and the Rise of Modern Evangelicalism* (Grand Rapids, MI: Eerdmans, 1991); George M. Marsden, *A Short Life of Jonathan Edwards* (Grand Rapids, MI: Eerdmans, 2009); Mark A. Noll, *A*

History of Christianity in the United States and Canada (Grand Rapids, MI: Eerdmans, 1992).

103 *"Sometimes he exceedingly wept . . .":* Cornelius Winter, qtd. in Stout, *The Divine Dramatist*, 41.
104 *New Light Stir:* Stephen A. Marini, *Radical Sects of Revolutionary New England* (Cambridge, MA: Harvard University Press, 1982), 38.
104 *Dozens of sects* and following*:* Marini, *Radical Sects*; Jenkins, *Mystics and Messiahs*, 55–57.
104 *"the Voice that spake . . .":* Qtd. in Marini, *Radical Sects*, 49.
104 *"new spiritual wife . . .":* Ibid., 51.
104 *"How many sects . . .":* Samuel Elsworth, qtd. in ibid., 58.
104 *"might more properly . . .":* Jennings, *Paradise Now*, 38.
105 *match the novelty:* Marini, *Radical Sects*, 56.
105 *a strange midday darkness:* Jennings, *Paradise Now*, xi and following; Marini, *Radical Sects*, 47.
105 *"It is not recollected . . .":* Ezra Stiles, qtd. in Marini, *Radical Sects*, 47.
105 *Smoke from Canadian wildfires:* Jennings, *Paradise Now*, xv.
105 "Hiero devo . . .": Thomas Brown, qtd. in Francis, *Ann the Word*, 69.
105 "Of all the relations . . .": Qtd. in Jennings, *Paradise Now*, 43.
106 *"their torment appears . . .":* Ann Lee, qtd. in Francis, *Ann the Word*, 90.
106 *"I have seen her slap . . .":* Qtd. in Jennings, *Paradise Now*, 35.
106 *"strip themselves naked . . .":* Peter Cartwright, qtd. in ibid., 75.
106 *"Sectarianism was not aberration . . .":* R. Laurence Moore, *Religious Outsiders and the Making of Americans* (New York: Oxford University Press, 1968), 18. Moore is writing in reference to the work of H. Richard Niebuhr.

Chapter 15

108 *Maura Schmierer went looking for work*, and following*:* Author interviews with Maura Schmierer, Robert Blasier, and Sarah Chelew; transcripts of audio recordings Maura prepared in the late 1980s; transcripts of Maura Schmierer speeches at Sacramento churches and the Sierra Club; Maura Schmierer sworn declaration (1989); Maura Schmierer writings.
108 *"old, feeble-minded . . ."* and subsequent quotes*:* Letters from Maura Schmierer to Jim and Deborah Green, 1987.
110 *"Thou art my battle axe . . .":* Jeremiah 51:20 (King James Version).
110 *"big African witchcraft demon":* Qtd. in Maura Schmierer writings.
110 *"When the fruit is ripe . . .":* James, *The Varieties of Religious Experience*, 181.
110 *"Emotional occasions . . .":* Ibid., 198.
111 *"deprogramming"* and following*:* Michael D. Langone, ed., *Recovery from Cults: Help for Victims of Psychological and Spiritual Abuse* (New York: W. W. Norton, 1993); Steven Hassan, *Freedom of Mind: Helping Loved Ones Leave Controlling People, Cults, and Beliefs* (Newton, MA: Freedom of Mind

Press, 2022); Singer, *Cults in Our Midst*, 275–94; Douglas H. Cook, "Tort Liability for Cult Deprogramming," *Ohio State Law Journal* 43 (1982): 465–89; Laycock, "Where Do They Get These Ideas?," 88–89; Jenkins, *Mystics and Messiahs*.

112 *vetoed a bill:* E. J. Dionne Jr., "Carey Kills Bill Allowing Removal of 'Coerced' Members from Cults," *New York Times*, 7/21/81.
112 *"mini-interactions":* Hassan, *Freedom of Mind*, 127.
112 *"reconnect with the authentic":* Hassan, *Freedom of Mind*, 118.
112 *90 percent:* Singer, *Cults in Our Midst*, 286.
112 *about two years:* Lorna Goldberg, "Guidelines for Therapists," in Langone, *Recovery from Cults*, 234.
113 *weekend visitation:* Maura Schmierer Affidavit, 16.
113 *"opened up [her] legs . . .":* Maura Schmierer writings.
114 *Maura hit him with a switch . . . :* Maura Schmierer behavior log.
114 *"continued contact . . .":* "Mediation Report," Steven D. Schmierer and Maura A. Schmierer, Office of Family Court Services, Superior Court of the State of California, 10/20/87, 7.
114 *"The heresies that men do leave . . .":* William Shakespeare, *A Midsummer Night's Dream*, act 2, scene 2, lines 146–47, qtd. in Jenkins, *Mystics and Messiahs*, 195.
115 *"the Burrito Wars":* Author interview with Julie Gudino.
115 *Child Protective Services:* Unsigned essay, likely by Jim or Deborah Green, "Good Conquers Evil," aggressivechristianity.net; also author interview with Julie Gudino.
115 *"Congress shall make no law . . .":* First Amendment, Constitution of the United States.
115 *"How can I put into words . . .":* Maura Schmierer, "Declaration of Maura A. Schmierer as Offer of Proof for Default Proceeding," *Maura A. Schmierer v. Free Love Ministries et al.*, 22.
115 *causes of action:* Maura Schmierer, "Complaint for Damages," *MAS v. FLM et al.*, filed 3/15/88. In response to Maura's allegations, Deborah wrote, "The lies were so outlandish that we could not even fathom such a thing being accepted in court" (Deborah Green, "X Street Files to the Present").
116 *"The Lord did not want . . .":* Ibid.
116 *buried the paperwork:* Author interview with Robert Blasier.
116 *$1.2 million:* Judge Ronald B. Robie, "Default Judgement by Court," *MAS v. FLM et al.*, 3/10/89, 2.
117 *gutting the four houses:* Author interviews with Sarah Green and Nathaniel Schmierer. See also testimony by Nathaniel Schmierer in *Maura Schmierer v. The Tribal Trust*, 2/1/12, trial transcript, 122; Richard Abrams, "Christian Cult Lost Home, Wealth—Now Members," *Sacramento Bee*, 9/18/89; and Melinda Welsh, "Sacramento's Army of God,"

Sacramento News & Review, 5/4/89. The Greens denied having anything to do with what Jim described as the vandalism of Fort Freedom.

118 *"ICHABOD . . ."*: Author interview with Nathaniel Schmierer.

Chapter 16

119 *The months following:* George Thurlow and Melinda Welsh, "Militaristic Sect Comes to Butte County," *Chico News & Review*, 5/4/89; George Thurlow, "The Corps Moves to the Country," *Sacramento News & Review*, 5/4/89; Don Lattin, "Battling Secularism, Sin and Lawsuits," *San Francisco Chronicle*, 5/18/89; Charles Gallardo, "Christian Cult Sets Up Camp North of Gridley," *Gridley Herald*, 5/3/89; author interviews with Sarah Green, Brenda Eutsler/Johanna Edwards, Julie Gudino, Nathaniel Schmierer, and Rebekah/Iantha Schmierer; see also testimony of Julie Gudino and Nathaniel Schmierer, *MS v. TTT*, 2/1/12, trial transcript. I myself visited the farm property in June 2022.
119 *"judgment terrorism":* Deborah Green, "X Street Files to the Present," aggressivechristianity.net.
119 *"We dismissed her . . .":* ACMTC press conference videorecording.
119 *"We are merely Christians . . .":* Jim Green, qtd. in Thurlow and Welsh, "Militaristic Sect."
119 *the art shops were seized:* Richard Abrams, "Sheriff Hauls Off Some of Sect's Assets," *Sacramento Bee*, 5/17/89.
119 *"roughly 800,000 . . .":* Deborah Green, qtd. in Gallardo, "Christian Cult."
120 *the parents of member Mike Brandon:* Julie Gudino testimony, *MS v. TTT*, 2/1/12, trial transcript, 61.
120 *$55,000:* Property Search Online, Klamath County, Oregon.
120 *"desperate days . . .":* Deborah Green, "X Street Files to the Present," aggressivechristianity.net.
120 *twenty-year-old Iantha:* Author interviews with Rebekah/Iantha Schmierer.
120 *"escape hatch":* Stein, *Terror, Love, & Brainwashing*, 99–100.
120 *just nineteen members:* Richard Abrams, "Militant Christian Cult Lost Home, Wealth—Now Members," *Sacramento Bee*, 9/18/89.
121 *a restaurant they opened,* and *life in Klamath Falls:* Author interviews with Sarah Green, Brenda Eutsler/Johanna Edwards, Julie Gudino, and Nathaniel Schmierer.
121 *$80,000:* Klamath County Assessor's Name Ledger.
121 *"hungry people . . .":* Qtd. in case files for *New Mexico v. Deborah Green*.
121 *She'd read about Ann Lee:* Author interviews with Julie Gudino.
121 *Deborah even suggested:* Ibid.
122 *"There are no slovens . . .":* Ann Lee, qtd. in Jennings, *Paradise Now*, 45.
122 *line up before her:* Author interview with Nathaniel Schmierer.
123 *get rid of his wife:* Author interviews with Julie Gudino and Sarah Green.

Chapter 17

124 *Bhagwan Shree Rajneesh and Rajneeshpuram generally:* Anthony Storr, *Feet of Clay: A Study of Gurus* (New York: Free Press, 1996), 46–63; Carl Abbott, "Revisiting Rajneeshpuram: Oregon's Largest Utopian Community as Western History," *Oregon Historical Quarterly*, Winter 2015, 414–47; Doyle W. Buckwalter and J. Ivan Legler, "Antelope and Rajneeshpuram, Oregon—Clash of Cultures, a Case Study," *Urbanism Past & Present*, Summer/Fall 1983, 1–13; Win McCormack, *The Rajneesh Chronicles*, 2nd ed. (Portland, OR: Tin House Books, 2010); Lawrence K. Grossman, "The Story of a Truly Contaminated Election," *Columbia Journalism Review*, Jan./Feb. 2002.
124 *"so many that his mother sewed . . .":* Storr, *Feet of Clay*, 59.
124 *"psychosynthesis" and "bioenergetics":* *New York Times*, 9/26/81, cited in Buckwalter and Legler, "Antelope and Rajneeshpuram," 2.
124 *"Dynamic Meditation":* Storr, *Feet of Clay*, 54.
124 *bone fractures:* Ibid., 55.
124 *inserted mangoes:* Ibid., 56.
124 *"passage of energy":* Ibid.
124 *"[Rajneesh] used to give out boxes . . .":* Ibid., 54.
124 *"I am the Messiah . . .":* Bhagwan Shree Rajneesh, qtd. in Storr, *Feet of Clay*, 57.
125 *Eighty-three percent:* Ibid., 58.
125 *doctors and lawyers, engineers and professors:* Buckwalter and Legler, "Antelope and Rajneeshpuram," 3.
125 *heiress to the Baskin-Robbins fortune:* Ibid., 4.
125 *"water and sewer . . .":* Abbott, "Revisiting Rajneeshpuram," 419.
125 *"they encouraged chickens . . .":* Ibid., 431.
125 *separation of church and state:* Ibid., 420.
125 *Kermit and Miss Piggy:* Buckwalter and Legler, "Antelope and Rajneeshpuram," 10.
125 *Adolf Hitler:* Abbott, "Revisiting Rajneeshpuram," 434.
125 *three thousand voter registration cards:* Ibid., 441.
126 *dog feces:* Author interview with Brenda Eutsler/Johanna Edwards.
126 *"Look at your brother . . .":* Home video courtesy of Julie Gudino.
126 *a ransom letter* and following: Julie Gudino testimony, *MS v. TTT*, 2/1/12, trial transcript, 52–54; author interview with Julie Gudino.
127 *"the Lord wanted . . .":* Deborah Green, "X Street Files to the Present," aggressivechristianity.net.
127 *painters and writers:* Charles C. Poling, "Flashbacks: Voices from the Epicenter of '60s Communes, Which Flourished like Wildflowers in the Hills of New Mexico," *New Mexico Magazine*, 5/8/13.
128 *more cults per capita:* Stark, Bainbridge, and Doyle, "Cults of America," 349.

128 *"coarseness and strength . . ."*: Frederick Jackson Turner, "The Significance of the Frontier in American History," *The Frontier in American History* (New York: Henry Holt, 1921), 37.
128 *"freshness, and confidence . . . "*: Ibid., 38.
128 *"empty West . . ."*: Abbott, "Revisiting Rajneeshpuram," 423.
128 *"Rajneeshpuram was a western community . . ."*: Ibid., 416.
128 *"We were sure . . ."*: Green, "Cristianismo y Marxismo," 8.
129 *"Let's pray . . ."*: Author interview with Julie Gudino.
129 *$300 a month:* Julie Gudino testimony, *MS v. TTT*, 2/1/12, trial transcript, 55.
129 *In Berino* and following: Author interviews with Sarah Green, Julie Gudino, and Brenda Eutsler/Johanna Edwards. See also Dan Williams, "'Soldiers of God' Have New Mexico Town Abuzz," *El Paso Times*, 6/25/95.
129 *"Consider what I am saying . . ."*: *Words of the Spirit: Our Daily Bread* 1, issue 12 (2000): 37.
131 *She awakes in pain:* Author interviews with Sarah Green.

Chapter 18

134 *"The next opening . . ."*: Ann Lee, qtd. in *Testimonies of the Life, Character, Revelations and Doctrines of Mother Ann Lee, and the Elders with Her, Collected from Living Witnesses, in Union with the Church* (Albany, NY: Weed, Parson, 1888), 174.
134 *an explosive revival* and the Second Great Awakening generally: Noll, *A History of Christianity in the United States and Canada*, 166–90; FitzGerald, *The Evangelicals*, 25-47; Jennings, *Paradise Now*, 67–68, 297–305; Richard M'Nemar, *The Kentucky Revival, or A Short History of the Late Extraordinary Outpouring of the Spirit of God in the Western States of America, Agreeably to Scripture Promises and Prophecies concerning the Latter Day, with a Brief Account of the Entrance and Progress of What the World Call Shakerism among the Subjects of the Late Revival in Ohio and Kentucky* (1808; repr., New York: Edward O. Jenkins, 1846); Patrick N. Allitt, "The Second Great Awakening," *American Religious History*, The Great Courses.
134 *"Thus, O sinner! . . ."*: Qtd. in M'Nemar, *The Kentucky Revival*, 26, and qtd. in Jennings, *Paradise Now*, 68.
134 *"At that moment some fell . . ."*: M'Nemar, *The Kentucky Revival*, 26.
135 *"The deliverance must come . . ."*: James, *The Varieties of Religious Experience*, 162.
135 *"I have seen so many . . ."*: Peter Cartwright, qtd. in Allitt, "The Second Great Awakening."
135 *"Every theological vagabond and peddler . . ."*: Philip Schaff, qtd. in FitzGerald, *The Evangelicals*, 30.
135 *Mormonism:* Noll, *A History of Christianity in the United States and Canada*,

- 195–97; Patrick N. Allitt, "Oneida and the Mormons," *American Religious History*, The Great Courses; Moore, *Religious Outsiders and the Making of Americans*.
- 135 the *American religion*: Moore, *Religious Outsiders and the Making of Americans*, 25, emphasis Moore's; Moore here is citing Klaus J. Hansen, *Quest for Empire: The Political Kingdom of God & the Council of Fifty in Mormon History* (Lansing: Michigan State University Press, 1967); and Thomas J. Yates, "Count Tolstoy and 'The American Religion,'" *The Improvements Era*, February 1939, 94.
- 136 *"Outsiderhood is a characteristic way . . ."*: Moore, *Religious Outsiders and the Making of Americans*, xi.
- 136 *more than a hundred* and following: Catherine A. Brekus, "Female Preaching in Early Nineteenth-Century America," *Women and the Church* (Waco, TX: Center for Christian Ethics at Baylor University, 2009).
- 136 *"in barns, schools . . ."*: Ibid., 20.
- 136 *Phoebe Palmer*: Noll, *A History of Christianity in the United States and Canada*, 181–83.
- 136 *"the holy zeal . . ."*: Phoebe Palmer, *The Promise of the Father* (Boston: Henry V. Degen, 1859), 2.

Chapter 19

- 138 *Sarah struck up a friendship* and following: Author interviews with Sarah Green. "Wally" is a pseudonym. None of my sources could remember the man's real name.
- 140 *"a homosexual"* and *"a lesbian"*: Transcript of Special Agent Pete Baca interview with Ja'el Phalen, 12/7/99.
- 141 *"given use"*: Deborah Green, "X Street Files to the Present," aggresivechristianity.net.
- 141 *a collection of trusts*: Robert Blasier, unpublished memoir.
- 141 *Shim Ra Na*: Jim Green sermon, "Inauguration of a New Age."
- 142 *"If you can hear Jesus"*: Author interviews with Rebecca Melson. Julie Gudino disputes ever saying, "He's telling you . . ."
- 142 *Julie's observation* and kidnapping scheme: Julie Gudino testimony, *NM v. DG*, 9/18/18, trial transcript, 184–85; author interview with Julie Gudino; *People Magazine Investigates: Cults*, episode 5, "Army of God," Jess Cagle, Dan Wakeford, et al., Executive Producers, Investigation Discovery, 7/2/18.
- 143 *money orders*: Author interviews with Sarah Green and Nathaniel Schmierer; also *MS v. TTT*, 2/1/12, trial transcript, Nathaniel Schmierer (p. 130) and Julie Gudino (p. 88).
- 143 *"superior orders"*: Elies van Sliedregt, "Superior Orders," *Individual Criminal Responsibility in International Law* (Oxford: Oxford University Press, 2012).

144 *"make another way"*: Julie Gudino testimony, *NM v. DG*, 9/18/18, trial transcript, 185.
144 *the mission had been a success*, and subsequent quotes: Jim and Deborah Green essay, "Revolution against Religion!"
144 *In Kenya*, and the planned *"adoption"*: See notes for chapter 20. "Ruth" and "Omondi" are pseudonyms ("Omondi"'s real name could not be determined). Julie Gudino corroborated Sarah's account of the plan to pick up the child while under oath, *NM v. DG*, 9/18/19, trial transcript, 179–80: "[Deborah] told me that she was sending Sarah over there [to Uganda] to get the baby, that she had previously asked the woman to give up when she was there in Africa. . . . Sarah had been nursing her own child, so she told Sarah . . . that she would get the baby and begin to nurse the baby with her own breast, go to a local hospital in the village, tell the hospital that the baby was an illegitimate child, a love child she said, and ask for a birth certificate. And when she got that birth certificate, she would go to the embassy to get ["Trinity"] citizenship and a passport to get over here back to the United States."
147 *"a great idea"*: Sarah Green testimony, *NM v. DG*, 9/19/18, trial transcript, 126.

Chapter 20

149 *Sarah's plane lands* and following: Author interviews with Sarah Green, and Sarah Green testimony, *NM v. DG*, 9/19/18, trial transcript, 194–96. Julie Gudino corroborated elements of Sarah's account while under oath (*NM v. DG*, 9/18/18, trial transcript, 179–80), and in interviews with the Cibola County Sheriff's Office. I myself reviewed passport stamps, "Trinity's" birth certificate, a Consular Report of Birth Abroad, and personal photos to verify Sarah Green's account. Though I corresponded with "Ruth" (a pseudonym) via WhatsApp for over two years, she could never decide whether or not she wanted to speak with me on the record. I was unable to reach "Omondi" (a pseudonym) or "Trinity's" birth father.

Chapter 21

156 *The boom arrived* and following: Kathryn Joyce, *The Child Catchers* (New York: PublicAffairs, 2013).
156 *"Adoption is the new pregnant"*: Qtd in ibid., 66.
156 *almost twenty-three thousand children:* Ibid., 215.
156 *manufactured or paper orphans:* Ibid., xiii.
156 *"explicitly to relinquish"*: Ibid., 134.
156 *"understand the concept . . ."*: Ibid., 12.
156 *one out of every hundred:* Ibid., x.

NOTES

157 *burlap robe* and *"nose wall":* Author interview with Sarah Green.
157 *"Jane the Pain"* . . . : Brenda Eutsler/Johanna Edwards text message to author.
157 *a cookie sheet:* Author interview with Brenda Eutsler/Johanna Edwards.
157 *"There are saints . . .":* James, *The Varieties of Religious Experience*, 50.
158 *almost eight thousand acres: MS v. TTT*, 3/12/19, hearing transcript, 80.
158 *$550,000:* Cibola County Sheriff's Office, Supplemental Narrative Report, 8/5/15.
158 *"$305,000 . . .":* Author interview with Mel O'Reilly.
158 *"authorities say it's Peter Green . . .":* Russell Contreras, Associated Press, "Cibola Sheriff Tells Court of Inquiry into Child Abuse," *Albuquerque Journal*, 8/26/17.
159 *more than $1.5 million:* "Application for and Renewal of Judgment," *Maura Schmierer v. Free Love Ministries, et al.*, Sacramento County Superior Court, filed 3/9/99.
159 *"We count it a privilege . . .":* Jim Green, "Cult *Hysteria!*," aggressive christianity.net.
160 *Julie Gudino noticed:* Author interview with Julie Gudino.
160 *His name was Anthony:* Sources disagree about Anthony's name; I have used "Anthony" because this name was cited by more people than any other; I was unable to contact him.
160 *Sarah was immediately attracted* and following: Author interviews with Sarah Green.

PART THREE

Chapter 22

165 *The dew is nearly dry* and following: Author interviews with Sarah Green; Sarah Green photos and ticket stubs.

Chapter 23

169 *Abi Stewart was nineteen* and following: Author interviews with Abi Stewart and Sarah Green.

Chapter 24

172 *Sarah was hardly alone* and following: Langone, *Recovery from Cults*; Cecilia Hadding, Olof Semb, Arja Lehti, Martin Fahlström, Mikael Sandlund, and Valerie DeMarinis, "Being In-between; Exploring Former Cult Members' Experiences of an Acculturation Process Using the Cultural Formulation

Interview (DSM-5)," *Front Psychiatry*, 9/13/23; Kerry Gibson, Mandy Morgan, Cheryl Woolley, and Tracey Powis, "Life after Centrepoint: Accounts of Adult Adjustment after Childhood Spent at an Experimental Community," *New Zealand Journal of Psychology*, vol. 40, no. 3, 2011, reprinted in *International Journal of Cultic Studies* 8 (2017); Singer, *Cults in Our Midst*.

172 *little help:* Michael D. Langone, "Helping Cult Victims," *Recovery from Cults*, 23.

173 *depression, etc.:* Carol Giambalvo, "Post-Cult Problems," in Langone, *Recovery from Cults*, 152.

173 *provide for themselves:* Madeleine Landau Tobias, "Guidelines for Ex-Members," in Langone, *Recovery from Cults*, 317.

173 *wandering around:* Author interview with Brian Miller.

173 *sexually transmitted infections:* Tobias, "Guidelines for Ex-members," 314.

173 *cologne, etc.:* Ibid., 305.

173 *"carry on casual conversations . . .":* Patrick L. Ryan, "A Personal Account," in Langone, *Recovery from Cults*, 138.

173 *Dating:* Tobias, "Guidelines for Ex-members," 317.

174 *unfamiliar with the movies, books, and music:* Ryan, "A Personal Account," 138.

174 *"lack of humor . . .":* Singer, *Cults in Our Midst*, 309.

174 *rage, regret, and sorrow:* Goldberg, "Guidelines for Therapists," 239.

174 *floating:* Paul R. Martin, "Post-cult Recovery," in Langone, *Recovery from Cults*, 208.

174 *"diminished abilities . . .":* Goldberg, "Guidelines for Therapists," 234.

174 *Loneliness:* Tobias, "Guidelines for Ex-members," 317.

174 *"I had always had close friends . . .":* Qtd. in Gibson et al., "Life after Centrepoint," 8.

175 *cult hopping:* Tobias, "Guidelines for Ex-members," 316.

175 *"don't generally return . . .":* Langone, *Recovery from Cults*, 40.

175 *recognizing the good:* Martin, "Post-cult Recovery," 217.

175 *"spiritual abuse":* Langone, *Recovery from Cults*.

175 *"spiritual rape":* Qtd. in Richard L. Dowhower, "Guidelines for Clergy," in Langone, *Recovery from Cults*, 251.

175 *a pinprick of adoration:* Author interview with Rebecca Melson.

Chapter 25

176 *At the end of 1999 and Sarah's life in Seattle:* Author interviews with Sarah Green, Geoff Edwards, and Abi Stewart.

179 *"Praise God, we are all glad . . .":* Deborah Green email to Sarah Green, 6/16/00.

180 *"i can not state it . . .":* Sarah Green email to Deborah Green, 6/17/00.

181 *"one continuing message . . ."*: Deborah Green email to Sarah Green, 6/27/00.
181 *"You are a good man . . ."*: Sarah Green letter to Peter Green, undated.
182 *"bad vibes . . ."*: Sarah Green email to Peter Green, 7/9/00.
182 *"JUST A SHORT NOTE . . ."*: Sarah Green letter to Deborah Green and others, undated.
182 *"If you only knew . . ."*: Sarah Green email to Julie and Bernie Gudino, 12/29/00.
183 *"Maybe I'm coming . . ."*: Sarah Green letter to Deborah Green, 4/22/02.

Chapter 26

184 *Sarah stares* and following: Author interviews with Sarah Green, Julie Gudino, and Johanna Edwards; also Sarah Green testimony, *NM v. DG*, 9/19/18, trial transcript, 114–16; "Trinity" and Julie Gudino also talked about Sarah's visit while under oath at Deborah's trial, 9/19/18, trial transcript, 40 and 214–16.

Chapter 27

189 *nine hundred groups*: John Philip Jenkins and Brian Dunigan, "Militia Movement," *Encyclopedia Britannica*. (Forty thousand is a conservative estimate: Per *Britannica*, "some claims put the number of members at more than 250,000.")
189 *National Rifle Association* and the events described in this chapter: Jeff Guinn, *Waco: David Koresh, the Branch Davidians, and a Legacy of Rage* (New York: Simon & Schuster, 2023); Jenkins, *Mystics and Messiahs*; David Thibodeau, *Waco: A Survivor's Story* (New York: Hachette Books, 2018).
190 *A Baptist minister*, and following: Guinn, *Waco*, 13–14; see also Noll, *A History of Christianity in the United States and Canada*, 193; and Bruce L. Shelley, "American Adventism: The Great Disappointment," *Christian History*, issue 61 (1999).
190 *"quite hysterical"* and teeth anecdote: Qtd. in Clara Endicott Sears, *Days of Delusion: A Strange Bit of History* (Boston: Houghton Mifflin, 1924), 179.
191 *"My lot is to procreate. . . ."*: David Koresh, qtd. in Guinn, *Waco*, 93.
191 *"If [Koresh] was wrong . . ."*: Guinn, *Waco*, 88.
191 *Randy Weaver*: "Ruby Ridge," *Encyclopedia Britannica*; Guinn, *Waco*, 134–35.
192 *golf plans*: Guinn, *Waco*, 189.
192 *"They didn't fear an assault. . . ."*: Ibid., 165.
193 *"while before the siege . . ."*: Jason Wilson, "30 Years Later: Waco and Extremism," Southern Poverty Law Center, 4/19/23.

193 *"constantly referenced"*: Guinn, *Waco*, 319.
193 *"It's because of Waco"*: William McVeigh, qtd. in ibid.
193 *Jones also made . . .*: Justin Ling, "How a Crazy Plan to Rebuild Waco Compound Gave Us Alex Jones," The Daily Beast, 11/26/21.
193 *"persecuted for righteousness's sake"*: Deborah Green, qtd. by Johanna Edwards, author interview.
194 *"You can go to Waco . . ."*: Deborah Green sermon, "The Px2 Files Ch2 Demonizing."

Chapter 28

195 *first person to discover* and following: Author interviews with Johanna Edwards and Julie Gudino.
196 *"bleeding, crying . . ."*: Jim Green letter to Sarah Green, 7/27/19.
196 *Ja'el Phalen had joined*, and following: Transcript of Special Agent Pete Baca interview with Ja'el Phalen, 12/7/99, 38.
199 *authorities had looked into*: Gallardo, "Christian Cult."
199 *"just another religious group"*: Sergeant William Elliot, qtd. in "Ministry Facts," aggressivechristianity.net.
199 *Officials from state and local agencies*, and subsequent investigation, including quotes: Internal state report, 12/99–2/00.
200 *Darren White*: Author interview with Darren White.
200 *"were being forced to kill . . ."*: Internal state report, summarizing Phalen's Channel 13 interview.
200 *"I want to heal. . . ."*: Ja'el Phalen, qtd. in internal state report.
200 *"turned out to be nothing"* and following: Johnny Valdez, qtd. in Mike Taugher, "Attempt to Seize Kids Criticized," *Albuquerque Journal*, 2/16/00.
201 *"agreed readily . . ."*: and following: "Fence Lake Religious Organization Visited," *Cibola County Beacon*, qtd. in internal state report.
201 *"My job is not . . ."*: Ja'el Phalen, qtd. in internal state report.
201 *"We saw a lady . . ."* and following: Internal state report.
202 *"In time of war . . ."*: Ibid.
202 *"Nobody comes back . . ."*: Jim Green, qtd. in internal state report.
202 *"based on statements . . ."*: Taugher, "Attempt to Seize Kids."
202 *"Our department . . ."*: Johnny Valdez, qtd. in ibid.
202 *"I think you have to take . . ."*: Taugher, "Attempt to Seize Kids."
203 *"Hey, this is America. . . ."*: District Attorney Mike Runnels, qtd. in ibid.
203 *the legal case was dismissed*: Deborah Green writes, "The Children's Protective Services kept us under investigation and by September of 2000 they wrote us a letter of clearance stating that the charges had no basis in reality" (Deborah Green, "X Street Files to the Present"), aggressivechristianity.net.

Chapter 29

204 *"France has become..."*: Jon Henley, "France Arms Itself with Legal Weapon to Fight Sects," *Guardian*, 5/31/01.

204 *up to five years and following:* French penal code, Article 223-15-2.

204 *years of study and debate:* "Sects and New Religious Movements," Parliamentary Assembly; Sofia Graziano, "Cults' Criminal Accountability in the EU Legal Framework," *Plot Politics*, 9/17/21; Christopher Beam, "Cult Busters," *Slate*, 10/28/09.

204 *"fully respecting...":* "Report on Cults in the European Union," European Parliament, 12/11/97.

204 *"charred...":* Scott Kraft, "16 Bodies Found in French Alps; Cult Ritual Suspected," *Los Angeles Times*, 12/24/95.

205 *"the right of freedom of thought....":* Universal Declaration of Human Rights, United Nations.

205 *"ignorance or weakness":* French penal code, Article 223-15-2.

205 *"the work of a handful...":* Marc Bromberg, qtd. in Henley, "France Arms Itself."

205 *"has told Mr. Clinton...":* Paul Webster, "France to Crack Down on Sects," *Guardian*, 6/13/00.

206 *freedom of religion:* Rachel Donadio, "Why Is France So Afraid of God?," *Atlantic*, 11/22/21, among others.

206 *Arnaud Mussy:* John Lichfield, "This Europe: Why a Cult Leader Is Suddenly No Laughing Matter," *Independent*, 9/6/02; Susan J. Palmer, "France's About-Picard Law and Neo-Phare: The First Application of 'Abus de Faiblesse,'" paper presented at the Center for Studies on New Religions, 7/06.

206 *"The United States [sic] position...":* Qtd. in Webster, "France to Crack Down."

207 *"I literally watched...":* Author interview with Julie Gudino.

207 *Deborah allegedly forced [Trinity] to work harder and allegations of physical abuse:* "Trinity" testimony, *NM v. DG*, 9/19/18, trial transcript, 203–237; and Julie Gudino testimony, *NM v. DG*, 9/18/18, trial transcript, 188–195; also author interviews with Johanna Edwards and Julie Gudino.

207 *"source of pride":* Deborah Green, qtd. by Johanna Edwards, "I Am an Accuser," Maura Schmierer blog, 8/26/17.

207 *one meal a day:* "Trinity" testimony, *NM v. DG*, 9/19/18, trial transcript, 222.

207 *facing the wall:* Julie Gudino testimony, *NM v. DG*, 9/18/18, trial transcript, 191.

207 *got in her food:* "Trinity" testimony, *NM v. DG*, 9/19/18, trial transcript, 203–4.

207 *"I can remember there being like round welts...":* Ibid., 219.

207 *"It usually left a bruise..."*: Julie Gudino testimony, *NM v. DG*, 9/18/18, trial transcript, 190.
207 *"to shut up..."*: Ibid.
207 *she needed to be tough:* Edwards, "I Am an Accuser."
207 *black because she was cursed:* "Trinity" testimony, *NM v. DG*, 9/19/18, trial transcript, 208.
207 *"yelled at or whipped..."*: Ibid.
208 *"why this was happening to me..."*: "Trinity" testimony, *NM v. DG*, 9/19/18, trial transcript, 210–11.
208 *"I can't believe..."*: Author interview with Johanna Edwards.
208 *didn't tell Sarah:* "Trinity" testimony, *NM v. DG*, 9/20/18, trial transcript, 13.
208 *"like a boomerang":* "Trinity" testimony, *NM v. DG*, 9/19/18, trial transcript, 209.
208 *"because God told her to..."*: Ibid., 223.
208 *Deborah started abusing her sexually:* "Trinity" testimony, *NM v. DG*, 9/19/18, trial transcript, 227–33.
208 *Peter... allegedly started sexually abusing Trinity:* Steve Chavez, Affidavit for Arrest Warrant, *New Mexico v. Peter Green*, 8/14/17.
209 *a cosmetic issue:* Author interview with Julie Gudino.
209 *a surgeon in Mexico:* "Trinity" testimony, *NM v. DG*, 9/19/18, trial transcript, 231–36. "Trinity"'s account is corroborated by Julie Gudino's testimony at the same trial (9/19/18, trial transcript, 193–95), and in an author interview. Deborah, too, told state officials "Trinity" was treated in Mexico.
209 *broke Trinity's legs:* Brandon Vigil, *NM v. DG*, 9/20/18, trial transcript, 245.
209 *Deborah refused:* "Trinity" testimony, *NM v. DG*, 9/19/18, trial transcript, 233.
209 *"You don't need..."*: Author interview with Julie Gudino.
209 *"a really happy kid..."*: Victoria River testimony, *NM v. DG*, 9/21/18, trial transcript, 225.
209 *"little chores..."*: Josh Green testimony, *NM v. DG*, 9/21/18, trial transcript, 113.
209 *Josh said Trinity took painkillers:* Ibid., 138.
209 *"Deborah loves all races..."*: Ibid., 174.
209 *Julie Gudino... began to think, and Julie's departure:* Author interviews with Julie Gudino. See also Julie Gudino testimony, *NM v. DG*, 9/18/18, trial transcript, 198–99, and 9/19/18, trial transcript, 57–61.
210 *they left Zechariah:* Author interview with Steve Chavez.
210 *"a curved blade..." and entire incident:* Jim Maniaci, "General Sense of Well-being," *Gallup Independent*, 11/5/05; Jim Maniaci, "Would-be Victims Beat Religious Leader," *Gallup Independent*, 11/2/05; Jim Maniaci,

"Religious Leader Bonds Out," *Gallup Independent*, 11/4/05; Bruce Daniels, "'Aggressive Christians' Bury the Hatchet in Cibola County," *Albuquerque Journal*, 11/7/05.

210 *"apologized to each other . . .":* Daniels, "'Aggressive Christians,'" citing Maniaci's reporting.
210 *"been trying . . .":* Maniaci, "General Sense."
210 *"It turned into a shouting match . . .":* Jim Green, qtd. in Maniaci, "General Sense."
211 *"the condition of my break . . ."* and following, including "Trinity" and Deborah quotes*:* "Trinity's" testimony, *NM v. DG*, 9/19/18, trial transcript, 235–57. Elements of "Trinity" testimony are corroborated by contemporaneous law enforcement reporting I reviewed.
211 *Trinity said yes* and following*:* "Trinity" testimony, *NM v. DG*, 9/19/18, trial transcript, 252.
212 *"failed to disclose . . .":* James Lawrence Sanchez, "Findings of Fact and Conclusions of Law Granting Deborah Green's Motion for a New Trial," *NM v. DG*, filed 11/23/20.
212 *"I was in fear . . .":* "Trinity" testimony, *NM v. DG*, 9/20/28, trial transcript, 80.
212 *"documented as substantiated . . .":* Internal state report, 8/8/06.
212 *"closed as unsubstantiated . . .":* Internal state report, 9/20/06.
213 *"loving home . . .":* Kristina Faught-Hollar, qtd. in 2019 pretrial transcript cited in "Defendant's Second Addendum to Motion to Dismiss for Preindictment Delay," *NM v. Peter Green*, filed 4/16/20, 2.

Chapter 30

214 *Meanwhile, Maura,* and following*:* Author interviews with Maura Schmierer, Mel O'Reilly, and Brendan O'Reilly.
215 *"Not only do we not have . . .":* Bart Ehrman, *Misquoting Jesus* (San Francisco: Harper San Francisco, 2005), 10.
215 *"a very human book":* Ibid., 11.
215 *Sarah had returned to Seattle,* and following*:* Author interviews with Sarah Green, Johanna Edwards, Geoff Edwards, and Abi Stewart.
218 *"I couldn't shake the drugging":* Author interview with Geoff Edwards.
218 *"showing off her vaginal . . .":* "TWENTY MILLION DOLLAR LIE EXPOSED! PART TWO," ACMTC press release, 4/25/89, 3.
218 *over $1.5 million:* "Application for and Renewal of Judgment," Sacramento County Superior Court, filed 3/9/99.
220 *"IF YOU WERE TO FACE DEATH . . .":* Deborah Green email to Sarah Green, 11/15/12.
220 *"I don't know. . . .":* Sarah Green, qtd. by Abi Stewart, author interview.

PART FOUR

Chapter 31

225 *In 2008, and this chapter broadly:* Alberta, *The Kingdom*; Tim Alberta, *American Carnage: On the Front Lines of the Republican Civil War and the Rise of President Trump* (New York: Harper, 2019); Steven P. Miller, *The Age of Evangelicalism: America's Born-Again Years* (Oxford: Oxford University Press, 2014); Daniel K. Williams, *God's Own Party* (Oxford: Oxford University Press, 2010); FitzGerald, *The Evangelicals*; Barbara Bradley Hagerty, "How McCain Shed Pariah Status among Evangelicals," *All Things Considered*, NPR, 10/23/08.

225 *"Hail Mary":* Alberta, *American Carnage*, 22.

225 *"Bible-believing Christian":* Sarah Palin, qtd. in "Religion and Politics '08: Sarah Palin," Pew Research Center, 11/4/08.

225 *"extremists . . .":* John McCain, "Agents of Intolerance," speech transcript, delivered 2/28/00.

225 *"supposedly erased . . .":* Amy Sullivan, "Are Evangelicals Really Sold on Palin?," *Time*, 9/6/09.

225 *"The Religious Right's Era . . .":* Jim Wallis, "The Religious Right's Era Is Over," *Time*, 2/16/07.

226 *71 percent:* Drew DeSilver, "Clinton's Impeachment Barely Dented His Public Support, and It Turned Off Many Americans," Pew Research Center, 10/3/19.

226 *"I am left to conclude . . .":* James Dobson, qtd. in Williams, *God's Own Party*, 244.

226 *"I believe we have probably lost . . .":* Paul Weyrich, qtd. in FitzGerald, *The Evangelicals*, 434.

226 *$125 million:* Chris Nashawaty, "What 'The Passion's' Success Means for Hollywood," *Entertainment Weekly*, 3/4/04.

226 *80 million:* Tom Gjelten, "Tim LaHaye, Evangelical Legend behind 'Left Behind' Series, Dies at 90," NPR, 7/25/16.

226 *"the fastest-selling . . .":* Publishers Weekly, qtd. in FitzGerald, *The Evangelicals*, 547.

226 *"Unless we act . . .":* James Dobson, qtd. in Williams, *God's Own Party*, 257.

226 *high-water mark:* FitzGerald, *The Evangelicals*, 536.

227 *"the worst defeat . . .":* Ibid., 618.

227 *27 percent:* "Support for Same-Sex Marriage at Record High, but Key Segments Remain Opposed," Pew Research Center, 6/8/15.

227 *"We're prepared . . .":* Wilfredo De Jesús, qtd. in Michael Paulson, "With Same-Sex Decision, Evangelical Churches Address New Reality," *New York Times*, 6/28/15.

227 *"sodomite captain":* Jim Green, "Transmogrifying Times," aggressivechristianity.net.

NOTES

227 *"Pink House"*: Ibid.
227 *"The United Nations is full of demons..."*: Jim Green, "Retire, Not Retire!," aggressivechristianity.net.
227 *"FBI, KGB, CIA..."*: Jim Green, "'If' Clause Continued," aggressivechristianity.net.
227 *"WRITE FOR OUR (free) DVD..."*: Jim Green, "The Global Apparatus," aggressivechristianity.net.
227 *"The abortionists have got to bear some burden..."*: Jerry Falwell, qtd. in Laurie Goodstein, "After the Attacks: Finding Fault; Falwell's Finger-Pointing Inappropriate, Bush Says," *New York Times*, 9/15/01.
228 *"Pink Stink,"* etc.: Jim Green, "Valorizing Gay Marriage," aggressivechristianity.net.
228 *"Blessed are the meek..."*: Matthew 5:5 (King James Version).
229 *"my little cracker"*: Donald Trump, qtd. in Josh Voorhees, "Donald Trump Tried to Tip Jesus," *Slate*, 2/1/16.
229 *"By the time Trump declared..."*: Alberta, *The Kingdom*, 25.
229 *"On January 1, 2017"*: Jim Green, "Trump: Divine or Devil?," 4/7/17, aggressivechristianity.net.
229 *"queen Jezebel HELLary Clinton"*: Jim Green, "The Necrophilous Left," aggressivechristianity.net.
230 *"spying, blackmailing, assassinating"*: "'Deep State' EXPOSED!!!," aggressivechristianity.net.
230 *"Drain the Stinking Swamp"*: Jim Green, "The Necrophilous Left," aggressivechristianity.net.
230 *"PIZZAGATE IS REAL!!!"*: aggressivechristianity.net.
230 *"Changing the subject?"*: "Pedophilia Red Alert!," aggressivechristianity.net.
230 *"CANNIBALS"*: Jim Green, "Transmorgifying Times," aggressivechristianity.net.
230 *"it is not a new thing for God to use"*: Green, "Trump: Divine or Devil?," aggressivechristianity.net.

Chapter 32

231 *Lieutenant Harry Hall* and following: Author interviews with Harry Hall, Mike Munk, and Steve Chavez; also Sheriff's Office "Supplemental Narrative Report," by Hall, 1/15/16.
232 *firearms and ammunition:* Jamie Bridgewater email, 6/29/16.
232 *"a child molester..."*: Jamie Bridgewater email, 6/22/16.
232 *"painfully disappointed..."*: Jamie Bridgewater email, 6/29/16.
233 *A year earlier* and following: Author interviews with Steve Chavez, Mike Munk, Harry Hall, and Brian Miller; also Cibola County Sheriff's Office Incident Narratives and a Supplemental Narrative Report by Chavez, 2/2/16.

233 *"They're just going to flee . . ."*: Brian Miller, qtd. by Munk Munk, author interview.
234 *"They were hated. . . ."*: Jamie Bridgewater email, 6/29/16.
234 *"would never eat . . ."*: Ibid.
235 *"acting like lesbians"*: Ibid.
235 *"loves and owns guns . . ."*: Ibid.
235 *"His stomach swells . . ."*: Ibid.
235 *And then there was Enoch:* This account of Enoch Miller's death, including all quotes, is drawn from testimony provided by Jamie Bridgewater, "Written Testimony of Enoch Blessed River's Death and Illness," 4/13/16. I have used Enoch Miller's real name with the permission of his father, Brian Miller, who told me he wanted his late son's name "proclaimed loud and clear."
237 *January 5:* Sources offer conflicting accounts of when Enoch died. I have used the date that appears on Enoch's gravestone.
238 *"fucking cunt"*: Author interview with Steve Chavez.
238 *Following his initial interview* and investigation broadly: Author interviews with Steve Chavez, Mike Munk, Hector Balderas, and Brian Miller; and Cibola County Sheriff's Office Incident Narratives.
239 *"People think we don't believe . . ."*: Deborah Green, qtd. by Steve Chavez in Cibola County Sheriff's Office Incident Narratives.
239 *"You need to understand something. . . ."* and following: Video footage, Steve Chavez interview with Stacey Miller, excerpted in "The Generals," *Cult Justice*, Law & Crime Productions, 2022.
239 *exhume the body:* Author interviews with Robert Hayes, Steve Chavez, and Mike Munk; Cibola County Sheriff's Office Incident Narratives; and Donald Jaramillo, "Missing Persons Report Filed," *Cibola Beacon*, 3/13/26.
240 *"die on the vine":* Author interview with Steve Chavez. Johnny Valdez did not respond to a request for comment.
240 *"Mike Munk had a hard-on . . ."* and following: Ibid.
241 *"I believe [Deborah] would have poisoned . . ."*: Jamie Bridgewater email, 6/29/16.
241 *ACMTC trusts in India and New Zealand:* Author interview with Mike Munk.
241 *a boarding school:* Author interview with Steve Chavez.
241 *"basically the brains . . ."*: Jamie Bridgewater email, 7/1/16.
242 *excruciating:* Author interview with Sarah Green.
242 *"You got nothing but stories":* Qtd. by Steve Chavez, author interview.
243 *"There was some talk. . . ."*: Author interview with Mike Munk.
244 *raid caravan* and following: Author interviews with Mike Munk, Steve Chavez, and Maxine Monte.
245 *"Sheriff's Office!"* and subsequent quotes: Body camera footage, *People Magazine Investigates: Cults*, episode 5, "Army of God."

Chapter 33

246 *It was a scam* and following: Author interviews with Sarah Green, Maura Schmierer, Ellexis Green, Jeremiyah Green, Nathaniel Schmierer, and Julie Gudino.

249 *Things had remained volatile:* Author interview with Mike Munk and Steve Chavez; and Russell Contreras, Associated Press, "4 More Sect Members Arrested in New Mexico," *Carlsbad Current-Argus*, 8/25/17.

250 *"wanted me to go back . . .":* Author interview with Steve Chavez.

250 *"God bless them . . .":* Ibid. Then-District Attorney Lemuel Martinez did not respond to a request for an interview.

250 *eighteen charges:* Grand Jury Indictment, *New Mexico v. Jim Green*, filed 9/13/17.

250 *At the courthouse* and following: *NM v. DG*, 9/18/18, trial transcript.

250 *"more than most . . .":* James Lawrence Sanchez, ibid., 5.

250 *"As you know . . .":* Brandon Vigil, ibid., 93–94.

251 *"This group stood for something. . . .":* Robert Lohbeck, ibid., 115.

251 *"You're going to see a smiling child. . . .":* Ibid., 134.

251 *"full of holes . . .":* Ibid., 111.

251 *"raising up an army . . .":* Julie Gudino, ibid., 166.

251 *"pew warmers"* and following: Julie Gudino, quoting Deborah Green, ibid., 162–163.

251 *"Many times I was put down . . .":* Julie Gudino, ibid., 164.

251 *"[The doctors] broke her legs . . .":* Ibid., 194.

252 *"tied a belt . . .":* Zechariah Edwards, qtd. by Robert Lohbeck in *NM v. DG*, 9/18/18, trial transcript, 212. (Zechariah's parents, Julie and Bernie Gudino, at one point took the last name Edwards.)

252 *"I was told by Lila Green . . .":* Julie Gudino, *NM v. DG*, 9/18/18, trial transcript, 213.

252 *"You weren't forced . . .":* Robert Lohbeck, *NM v. DG*, 9/19/18, trial transcript, 18.

252 *"If Deborah Green had ordered . . .":* Ibid., 41.

253 *"To know that these people . . .":* Author interview with Sarah Green.

253 *"Good morning, Ms. Green,"* and following: Mandana Shoushtari and Sarah Green, *NM v. DG*, 9/19/18, trial transcript, 74–75.

254 *"there is going to be testimony . . ."* and following: Robert Lohbeck, James Lawrence Sanchez, Mandana Shoushtari, and Brandon Vigil, ibid., 76–80.

255 *"When the time came . . ."* and following: Mandana Shoushtari and Sarah Green, ibid., 97–98.

255 *"We were building . . ."* and following: Sarah Green and Mandana Shoushtari, ibid., 108–10.

256 *"Wasn't [it] actually . . ."* and following: Robert Lohbeck and Sarah Green, ibid., 126.

256 *"stated previously"* and following: Ibid., 147–56.
259 *"Ms. Green, have you ever told"* and following: Ibid., 197.
260 *"When you first . . ."*: Sarah Green, ibid., 197.
260 *"I'm sorry I'm such a prick"*: Maura Schmierer blog.
261 *"Those memories . . ."*: Ibid.
261 Please wait for me . . . : "Trinity," qtd. by Sarah Green, author interview.
262 *a young woman arose* and following: Author interviews with "Trinity," Sarah Green, and Maura Schmierer.
263 *"imperative . . ."*: Steve Chavez, *NM v. DG*, 9/26/18, sentencing hearing transcript, 13.
263 *"In over thirty years . . ."*: Mike Munk, ibid., 14.
263 *"Emotionally, she broke me . . ."*: "Trinity," ibid., 15–16.
264 *"struggles still . . ."*: "Trinity's" adoptive mother, ibid., 17.
264 *the sexual and child abuse convictions*: "Judgment, Sentence and Commitment to NM Corrections Department," *NM v. DG*, filed 10/16/18.
264 *"legitimate argument"* and following: James Lawrence Sanchez, *NM v. DG*, 9/26/18, sentencing hearing transcript, 23–24.
265 *two additional eighteen-year sentences*: "Judgment, Sentence and Commitment to NM Corrections Department," *NM v. DG*, filed 10/16/18.
265 *one eighteen-year,* and following: "Judgment and Sentence on Remaining Severed Counts and Commitment to NM Corrections Department," *NM v. DG*, filed 11/26/18.
265 *"You'll all be surprised . . ."*: Deborah Green, *NM v. DG*, 10/16/18, plea hearing transcript, 8.
265 *nine years of "actual incarceration"*: "Plea and Disposition Agreement," *NM v. Stacey Miller*, filed 12/17/19.
265 *ten years of "actual incarceration"*: "Judgment, Sentence and Commitment to New Mexico Corrections Department," *NM v. James Green*, filed 1/23/19.

Epilogue

267 *"I, Deborah Green . . ."*: Deborah Green, Petition for Writ of Habeas Corpus, *NM v. DG*, 7/22/19, 3.
267 *"exculpatory material . . ."*: Kari Morrissey, "Defendant's Response to Motion to Disqualify Defense Counsel Kari Morrissey," *NM v. PG*, 10/19/20, 2.
267 *"failed to disclose . . ."*: Sanchez, "Findings of Fact," 2.
267 *Lohbeck . . . was aware*: *NM v. DG* appeal, motion hearing, 8/29/22, 112.
267 *"foster father was coaching . . ."*: Sanchez, "Findings of Fact," 10.
267 *"clearly favorable . . ."*: Ibid.
268 *"one of the best witnesses . . ."*: James Lawrence Sanchez, *NM v. DG* appeal, motion hearing, 8/29/22, transcript of proceedings, 199.
268 *"engaged in prosecutorial misconduct . . ."*: Judge George P. Eichwald, "Order

Granting In-Part and Denying In-Part Defendant's Motion to Dismiss for Prosecutorial Misconduct, or in the Alternative, to Disqualify the Thirteenth Judicial District Attorney's Office from Prosecuting the Defendant," *NM v. PG*, filed 8/19/20, 1–2. Mandana Shoushtari and Brandon Vigil did not respond to requests for an interview.

268 *"very impressive"* and *"very intelligent"*: Author interview with Steve Chavez.

268 *forced to recuse:* Mike Gallagher, "Facebook Posts an Issue in Sect Leader's Trial," *Albuquerque Journal*, 6/22/20.

268 *"one of the most vile . . .":* Deborah Green, "Petition for Writ of Habeas Corpus," 3.

268 *Judge James Sanchez ruled in Deborah's favor:* Sanchez, "Findings of Fact," 11.

269 *"These holes . . .":* "Trinity" testimony, *NM v. DG*, 9/19/18, trial transcript, 236.

269 *Julie Gudino said she'd seen:* Julie Gudino testimony, *NM v. DG*, 9/18/18, trial transcript, 192–93.

269 *"confirm or deny . . .":* Sanchez, "Findings of Fact," 4.

270 *"undermine confidence . . .":* Ibid., 13.

270 *There's the New Mexico legal system for you:* Author interview with Maura Schmierer.

270 *"Serve your fucking sentence . . .":* Author interview with Sarah Green.

270 *"I'm writing to again . . .":* Deborah Green letter to Sarah Green, 7/13/19.

270 *"My daughter do not neglect . . .":* Deborah Green letter to Sarah Green, 12/26/19.

271 *"unavailability of essential witnesses":* Assistant District Attorney J. Michael Thomas, "Nolle Prosequi," *NM v. DG*, filed 6/9/21, 1.

271 *"namely [Trinity]":* The State of New Mexico, qtd. by New Mexico Attorney General Raúl Torrez and Assistant Attorney General Lauri Blevins, "Direct Appeal from the Thirteenth Judicial District Court, Cibola County, New Mexico, the Honorable James Sanchez, Presiding," *NM v. DG*, filed 1/6/23, 9.

271 *Sanchez vacated:* James Lawrence Sanchez, "Findings of Fact and Conclusions of Law, Deborah Green Habeas Corpus Petition," *DG v. James Yates, Warden of the Western New Mexico Correctional Facility*, filed 1/28/22.

271 *the complicated legal issues:* Author interview with Sue McLean.

271 *"the woke stroke"* and following: Jim Green, "The WOKE STROKE!," aggressivechristianity.net, 1/29/25.

271 *a unanimous decision:* "Opinion," *NM v. DG* appeal, filed 4/21/25.

272 *"the Church is not so much . . .":* Stephanie McCrummen, "The Army of God Comes out of the Shadows," *Atlantic*, 2/25.

272 *"These self-respecting Christians . . .":* Alberta, *The Kingdom*, 230.

272 *"soldiers rising up . . .":* Greg Locke, qtd. in ibid., 218.

272 *"dressed in paramilitary gear . . .":* Alberta, *The Kingdom*, 219.

272 *"has suggested that autistic children . . ."*: Ibid., 218.
272 *"Just as with our politics . . ."*: Ibid., 230.
273 *ordered the sale:* Brett Barrouquere, "Anti-LGBT Group's Compound Ordered Sold for $2.8 Million," Southern Poverty Law Center, 10/29/19.
273 *"I know we'll be able to uncover":* Author interview with Mel O'Reilly.
273 *Now in her seventies* and following: Author interviews with Maura Schmierer, Sarah Chelew, Nathaniel Schmierer, and Rebekah/Iantha Schmierer.
274 *"layered and often painful":* Email from Sarah Chelew.
274 *"It's the biggest challenge . . ."* and following: Author interview with Maura Schmierer.
274 *Peter was placed on house arrest:* "Order Setting Conditions of Release," *NM v. PG*, filed 1/29/20.
274 *In August 2022, he pleaded guilty:* "Plea and Disposition Agreement," *NM v. PG*, filed 8/17/22.
274 *"Thank you for your (little) note. . . .":* Jim Green letter to Sarah Green, 12/21/19.
275 *"How old is your daughter . . .":* Jim Green letter to Sarah Green, 7/23/19.
275 *"a victim . . .":* Jim Green letter to Sarah Green, 7/16/19.
275 *"I never did thank you . . .":* Jim Green letter to Sarah Green, 7/27/19.
275 *"Jim is still adjusting . . .":* "General Jim Released!," aggressivechristianity.net.
275 *"It's kind of like a faded memory . . ."* and following: Author interviews with Sarah Green.
276 *"She had to choose . . .":* Author interview with Abi Stewart.
276 *"I am proud of you . . .":* "Trinity" text message to Sarah Green, 6/8/21.
276 *"You were the first mother . . .":* "Trinity" text message to Sarah Green, 5/14/23.
276 *"It's all love . . .":* Author interview with "Trinity."
277 *"She's the beginning. . . .":* Author interview with Jeremiyah Green.
277 *god-haunted:* For this term I am indebted to Flannery O'Connor, who in 1960 described the American South as "Christ-haunted" ("Some Aspects of the Grotesque in American Fiction").

INDEX

Abbott, Carl, 125, 128
adoptions, 226
    international, 156
Aggressive Christianity Missions Training Corps (ACMTC), 2–3
    in Africa, 144–46
    Branch Davidians and, 193–94
    Bridgewater escapes from, 231–32
    calls itself a cult, 159
    continuing ideology of, 272
    daily life in, 79–83
    after Deborah's arrest, 249–50
    during Deborah's trial, 250–60
    after Deborah's trial, 271
    destruction of Sacramento headquarters of, 117–18
    FBI investigation of, 213
    Fence Lake property of, 141
    Free Love Ministries becomes, 72
    Ja'el's accounts of abuse within, 197–202, 206
    at Klamath Falls, 126–27
    after loss of Maura's suit, 119–20
    Maura expelled from, 97
    after Maura's expulsion, 109
    Maura's suit against, 115–17
    in New Mexico, 127–33
    in Oregon, 120
    police raid on, 243–45
    Ruth's baby and, 145–48
    Sarah returns to, 184–88
    on September 11 terrorist attacks, 227–28
    Sheriff's Office investigations of, 232–43
    television programs about, 219
    Trump supported by, 230
Alberta, Tim, 53, 225, 229, 272
Alberto, 80
Alcohol, Tobacco, and Firearms, US Bureau of (ATF), 191, 192
Alcott, A. Bronson, 137
Aluzas, Iantha (Rebekah; Maura's daughter), 11, 47, 49, 97
    at Bear Tribe, 17, 18, 23
    becomes Rebekah, 71
    birth of, 9
    in cult schoolhouse, 80
    Greens and, 48
    leaves cult, 120, 214
    lives with grandparents, 58–59
    after Maura's expulsion, 113
    at present, 273
Aluzas, Maura, *see* Schmierer, Maura Aluzas
Antelope (Oregon), 125, 127
Anthony (full name unknown)
    named during Deborah's trial, 257–58
    Sarah leaves cult with, 3, 4, 161, 165–66, 195
    Sarah meets, 160
Aum Shinrikyo cult, 74

Baca, Pete, 197–98
Balderas, Hector, 243
Barker, Eileen, 74

INDEX

Bear Tribe (commune), 16–22, 31
    end of, 22–23
    spirituality in, 24
Beattie, Don (Bear Marks), 45
Bell, Griffin B., 38
Biden, Joe, 272
Blasier, Bob, 113, 115, 116
Blatty, William Peter, 56
Booth, Catherine, 39
brainwashing, 77
Branch Davidians, 189–94, 202, 273
Brandon, Mike, *see* Green, Peter
Brekus, Catherine A., 136
Bridgewater, Jamie, 231–32, 234–38, 241, 242, 244
Bush, George W., 225, 226

California, religious cults in, 27–28
Calvary Christian church, 25–26
Cane Ridge (Kentucky), 134–35
Carey, Hugh, 112
Carlson, Amy, 68
Carter, Bonnie (Lila's sister), 12
Carter, Calvin (Lila's brother), 12
Carter, Carlo (Lila's brother), 66
    death of, 15, 16
    hospitalization of, 7–8
    Maura's visit with, 10–11
Carter, Jimmy, 46, 53
Carter administration, 37
Cartwright, Peter, 135
Chavez, Daniel, 241
Chavez, Steve
    after Deborah's arrest, 249, 250
    at Deborah's sentencing, 263
    Jamie Bridgewater interviewed by, 234, 235
    on Peter's trial, 268
    Sarah interviewed by, 246–47
    in Sheriff's Office investigation of cult, 238–43
Chelew, Rick (Sarah's father), 56–57
Chelew, Sarah (Maura and Rick's daughter), 44, 49
    leaves cult, 214
    after Mauna's expulsion, 113, 114
    at present, 273–74
    Rick Chelew and, 56–57
child abuse
    among Branch Davidians, 191
    Bridgewater's allegations of, 232–38
    false allegations of, 68–69
    Ja'el's accounts of, 198–202
    parents' recognition of, 120
    rape of Sarah, 38–39
    reported by Nathaniel against Maura, 114
    Sheriff's Office investigations of, 238–43
    of Steven Schmierer, 65–66
    of Trinity, by Deborah (alleged), 207–13
Child Protective Services (New Mexico), 202
Child Protective Services (Sacramento, California), 199
Children of Nations, 142, 146
Chirac, Jacques, 205
Christ Gospel Church, 36–39
Christianity
    becomes official religion of Roman Empire, 27
    charismatic renewal in, 36
    evangelical, 46
    Jesus Movement in, 25–26
    New Apostolic Reformation in, 272
Church of Jesus Christ of Latter-day Saints (Mormonism), 135–36
Clinton, Bill, 140, 189, 225–26
Clinton, Hillary, 140, 230
communes, 18–20
    during Second and Fourth Great Awakenings, 137
conservatorships of cult members, 112
conspiracy theories, 230
Costo, Rupert, 19

INDEX

counterculture
    Christianity in, 25, 36
    former cult members in, 172
    during Fourth Great Awakening, 137
    Jim on, 128
    Lila falls into, 13, 15
    Maura in, 47
    Native imagery in, 19
    of 1960s and 1970s, 14, 28–29
    spirituality in, 24
cults
    Aggressive Christianity Missions Training Corps calls itself, 159
    Branch Davidians as, 189–94
    decision making within, 143
    definitions and history of, 26–29
    European, 204–6
    false allegations of child abuse by, 68–69
    former members of, 172–75
    Greens' ministry as, 57–58
    leaders of, 77
    legal actions against, 115
    media interest in, 37
    members of, 73–77
    methods of leaving, 111–12
    in New Mexico, 128
    during Second Great Awakening, 135
    sects distinguished from, 103–5
    women in leadership in, 67–68
Cyrus (biblical), 190–91

David (biblical king), 190
Deborah (biblical), 137
Deborah, *see* Green, Deborah
deliverance, 56
deprogramming of cult members, 111–12
disorganized attachments, 77
Divine Light Mission, 28
divorce, 109
Dobson, James, 226
Dole, Bob, 37, 38
Drop City (commune), 18–19
Dye, Derek, 71, 95

Dye, Lisa, 71, 95–96
    after expulsion, 110, 113

Ehrman, Bart, 215
elections, presidential
    of 1980, 54
    of 1992, 189
    of 2000, 226
    of 2008, 225, 226
Enroth, Ronald M., 26
European Parliament, 204
Eutsler, Brenda (Esther; Johanna), 70–71, 76
    becomes Esther, 126, 127
    becomes Johanna, 129
    discovers Sarah missing, 195
    Geoff and, 219
    leaves cult, 217
    moves to New York, 218
    on Trinity's alleged abuse by Deborah, 207–8
evangelical Protestantism, 45–46
    cultural and political influence of, 226–27
    in election of 2008, 225
    fundamentalism in, 53
    international adoptions encouraged in, 156
    on New Apostolic Reformation, 272
    Trump supported by, 229, 230
evolution, 45
exit counseling, 112
exorcisms, 56
    in Shakers, 105

Falwell, Jerry, 53–54, 225, 227–28
Falwell, Jerry, Jr., 229
Federal Bureau of Investigation (FBI)
    Branch Davidians and, 191, 192, 203
    cult investigated by, 212, 213
    Julie interviewed by, 126
feminism, 67
First Great Awakening (1750s), 103–4
FitzGerald, Frances, 103, 227

INDEX

floating (losing train of thought), 174
Fonda, Jane, 140
Ford, Gerald, 53
Fourth Great Awakening (1960s), 14, 137
Fox, Kate, 136
Fox, Maggie, 136
France, cults in, 204–6
Free Love Ministries, 59, 65
    becomes Aggressive Christianity Missions Training Corps, 72
    Greens in leadership positions in, 67
    growth of, 70–71
    radio program of, 69–70
Frohnmayer, David, 125
fundamentalism, 45–46, 53
    Third Great Awakening leading to, 137

Gabriel (pseudonym), 85–86
Gains, David, 64, 88
    cult activities funded by, 82
    cult houses bought by, 71
    joins cult, 59
    loss of art shops owned by, 119
Geoff (Geoff Edwards), 178, 183
    in New York, 218, 219
    proposes to Sarah, 216
Gibson, Mel, 226
Global Vision Bible Church, 272
Goldberg, Lorna, 174
Graham, Billy, 45
Graham, Franklin, 272
Green, Deborah (Lila Mae Carter)
    adoption of Trinity plotted by, 157–58
    African trip of, 144–46
    on allegations of child abuse, 201–2
    appeal of conviction of, 267–68
    arrest of, 245, 247
    banishes children of ex-cult members, 216
    in Bear Tribe, 16–18, 20–23
    becomes Christian, 35–36
    becomes Deborah, 72
    on Branch Davidians, 193–94
    Brenda Eutsler and, 76
    Carlo's death and, 15, 16
    in Christ Gospel Church, 37–39
    compared with Ann Lee, 121–22
    contacts Sarah, post-cult, 178–81
    conviction and sentencing of, 263–65
    criminal charges against, 243
    daily life of, 80–82
    disappears, 271
    Falwell and, 54
    Free Love Ministries created by, 59
    on God's will for women and men, 67–68
    granted second trial, 268–71
    as hippie, 13–14
    at Idaho concert, 31–32
    Ja'el and, 196–99
    Jesus Movement and, 33–34
    on John's proposal to Sarah, 92–94
    Josiah (grandson) and, 140
    after loss of Maura's suit, 119
    Maura and, 60, 82–83
    Maura ostracized by, 89–91, 97
    Maura's opinion of, after expulsion, 109–11
    Maura's suit against, 116–17
    in Missoula, 40–42
    in New Mexico, 127–33
    prophecies of, 79, 88, 107
    radio program of, 69–70
    Ruth's baby and, 145–48
    in Sacramento, 54–58, 64–67
    Sarah (daughter) and, 84–85, 277
    after Sarah leaves cult, 195–96
    when Sarah returns to Fence Lake, 184–87
    on Sarah's friends, 62
    on Sarah's pregnancy, 138–39
    Schmierers and, 47–52
    Sheriff's Office investigations of, 231, 233–36, 238–43
    threatened by Deborah, 210
    trial of, 248–60
    Trinity allegedly abused by, 207–12

INDEX

Trump supported by, 230
website of, attacking Maura, 218–19
Green, Ellexis (Sarah and Geoff's
    daughter), 242, 248, 275, 277
  birth of, 183
  after Deborah's sentencing, 266
  at Fence Lake, 184–88
Green, Isaiah (Sarah and Peter's son), 140
  Bridgewater's allegations against, 235
  at Fence Lake, 158–61
  at present, 275, 277
  after Sarah leaves cult, 195
  when Sarah returns to Fence Lake, 184, 186, 188
Green, Jeremiyah (Sarah and Geoff's son), 242, 248, 277
  birth of, 217
  in Portland, 218
  after sentencing of Deborah, 248
Green, Jim
  African trip of, 144–45
  on allegations of child abuse, 201, 202
  in Bear Tribe, 21–22, 30–31
  on birth of Sarah and Josh, 35–36
  on Branch Davidians, 193–94
  in Christ Gospel Church, 37, 38
  after Deborah's trial, 271
  on demonization, 81
  Falwell and, 54
  Free Love Ministries created by, 59
  at Idaho concert, 31–32
  indictment and arrest of, 247, 250
  Ja'el's allegations of child abuse against, 200
  Jesus Movement and, 32–34
  on John's proposal to Sarah, 92–94
  after loss of Maura's suit, 119
  Maura ostracized by, 89–91, 95
  Maura's opinion of, after expulsion, 109–11
  Maura's suit against, 116–17
  in Missoula, 40–42
  in New Mexico, 127–30
  Peter Green and Steve Schmierer threatened by, 210
  at present, 274–75
  radio program of, 69–70
  restaurant opened by, 121
  in Sacramento, 54–55, 64–67
  after Sarah leaves cult, 196
  when Sarah returns to Fence Lake, 184, 187
  Schmierers and, 47–51
  sentencing of, 265
  Sheriff's Office investigations of, 233–34, 238–43
  Trinity allegedly abused by, 212
  Trump supported by, 230
  on US politics, 227
  website of, attacking Maura, 218–19
Green, John (ACMTC member), 92–94, 116
Green, Josh (Deborah and Jim's son), 48, 49, 195
  African trip of, 144
  arrest of, 245
  birth of, 36
  criminal charges against, 243
  in cult schoolhouse, 80
  Enoch Miller and, 237
  health of, 235
  Johanna and, 217
  married to Jamie Bridgewater, 232
  in Mexico, 38
  in Missoula, 40–41
  in old schoolhouse, 61–63
  in Sacramento, 64
  when Sarah returns to Fence Lake, 186
  sentencing of, 265
  on Trinity's alleged abuse, 209
Green, Josiah (Sarah and Peter's son), 140
  birth of, 132, 138–39
  Bridgewater's allegations against, 235
  at Fence Lake, 158–61
  at present, 275, 277
  after Sarah leaves cult, 181, 195

Green, Josiah (Sarah and Peter's son) (*cont.*)
   when Sarah returns to Fence Lake, 184, 186, 188
   Sheriff's Office investigation of, 241
Green, Lila Mae Carter, *see* Green, Deborah
Green, Peter (Mike Brandon; Sarah's husband), 179
   arrest of, 245, 247
   contacts Sarah, post-cult, 179
   criminal charges against, 243
   as father of Josiah (Sarah's baby), 131, 132, 139
   marries Sarah, 123
   Mike Brandon becomes Peter Green, 122–23
   at present, 274
   after Sarah leaves cult, 181–82, 195
   when Sarah returns to Fence Lake, 184, 187
   threatened by Jim Green, 210
   trial of, 265, 268
   Trinity allegedly abused by, 208, 269
   wealthy family of, 120, 121, 158–59
Green, Sarah (Deborah and Jim's daughter), 48, 49
   attempts to run away, 84
   becomes pregnant (with Josiah), 130–32
   birth of, 35–36
   childhood rape of, 38–39
   in cult schoolhouse, 80
   on Deborah being granted second trial, 270
   Deborah's sentencing and, 264–66
   at Deborah's trial, 252–60
   in destruction of Sacramento headquarters of cult, 117–18
   at Fence Lake, 158–59
   gives birth to Ellexis, 183
   gives birth to Isaiah, 140
   gives birth to Jeremiyah, 216–17
   gives birth to Josiah, 132–33
   homeschooling of, 116
   Jim's letter to, 274–75
   John Green proposes to, 92–94
   leaves cult, 1–4, 165
   after leaving cult, 166–68, 215
   marries Mike Brandon, 123
   Maura and, 260–61
   meets Abi Stewart, 169–71
   in Missoula, 40–42
   in New Mexico, 127–30
   in New York, 218–21
   in old schoolhouse, 61–63
   in Oregon, 120–22
   in Philippines, 85–86
   plots to leave with Anthony, 160–62
   at present, 275–77
   removed from public school, 71
   returns to Fence Lake, 184–88
   Ruth's baby and, 146–48
   in Sacramento, 54–55, 64, 65
   in Seattle, 176–82
   Sheriff's Office interview of, 245–46
   in Sheriff's Office investigation, 241–43
   Trinity adopted by, 157
   Trinity and, after Deborah's trial, 261–63
   in Uganda, 149–55
   Wally and, 138–39
   Grey Wolf, 18, 20
Guatemala, 156
Gudino, Bernie, 188
   banished from Fence Lake, 196
   leaves cult, 210
   in Philippines, 84–85
   Sarah's email to, 182
   on Sarah's punishment, 143
Gudino, Julie Padilla, 120, 188
   Anthony recruited by, 160
   in attempted kidnapping scheme, 141–44
   banished from Fence Lake, 196

on Deborah's alleged abuse of Trinity, 207, 209
at Deborah's trial, 248, 251–52, 269
interviewed by Child Protective Services, 199
joins cult, 71
leaves cult, 210
in Philippines, 84–85
protests by mother of, 126
in Sheriff's Office investigation, 241
Gudino, Zechariah (Julie and Bernie's son), 196, 209–10, 252
Guinn, Jeff, 191–93

Hall, Harry, 231–34, 239
Hammond, Frank, 56
Hammond, Ida Mae, 56
Hare Krishna movement, 28, 37
Harrison, George, 24
Hassan, Steven, 112
Hays, Robert, 240
Heller, Zoë, 74
Hicks, Berniece, 36, 37, 39, 40
hippies, 13–14
    communes of, 18–19
    during Fourth Great Awakening, 137
    Jesus Movement and, 25–26
    in New Mexico, 128
    spirituality of, 24
Holiness Movement, 136
Holy Spirit Association for the Unification of World Christianity ("Moonies"), 28, 38
Houteff, Victor, 190
Howell, Vernon, *see* Koresh, David

Immigration and Nationality Act (US, 1965), 24
Indigenous American customs, 19
Interministerial Mission for Vigilance and Action against Sectarian Deviances (France), 205
international adoptions, 156

Ireland, Shadrack, 104
Israelites (biblical), 77–78

Jacque (Jacque Rankin), 91, 92, 95–96, 98
James, William, 75, 110, 135, 157
Jenkins, Philip, 26, 67, 103
Jennings, Chris, 101–2, 104
Jesus Christ, 25, 56, 228
    divorce condemned by, 109
    on politics, 53
    predictions of return of, 190
Jesus Movement, 25–26, 31–34
    evangelicalism and, 46
Johanna, *see* Eutsler, Brenda
John (Lila Carter's boyfriend), 9–12
    in Bear Tribe, 17, 22
    Carlo's death and, 15
    meets Lila, 14
John (Johanna's husband), 217
Johnson, Mike, 273
Johnson, Rachel, 71
Jones, Alex, 193
Jones, Jim, 28, 39, 40
Joyce, Kathryn, 156

Kathie, 13
Khu, Ahn, 232
Koresh, David, 189
    death of, 193
    as leader of Branch Davidians, 192
    Trump and, 273
    Vernon Howell becomes, 190–91

Langone, Michael D., 175
Lankford, Sarah, 136
Laycock, Joseph, 68
Leary, Timothy, 24
Lee, Ann (Mother Ann), 67, 101–3, 105–6, 140
    on future of Shakers, 134
    Lila Green compared with, 121–22
Left Behind (book series, LaHaye and Jenkins), 226

Lifton, Robert Jay, 75–76
Locke, Greg, 272
Lohbeck, Robert
    as Deborah's defense attorney, at trial, 251, 252, 254, 256–60
    on Trinity, 267

Mace, Tony, 232, 240, 242
Manson, Charles, 28
Marini, Stephen A., 104
Mary Magdalene, 80
Maura, *see* Schmierer, Maura Aluzas
McCain, John, 225
McCrummen, Stephanie, 272
McLoughlin, William, 137
McVeigh, Timothy, 193
Melson, Rebecca, 141–42
men
    in Branch Davidians, 191
    Lila on God's will for, 67
Michelle Remembers (book, Smith and Padzer), 68
militia groups, 189
    legal crackdowns on, 206
    Ruby Ridge incident and, 191–92
    Southern Poverty Law Center estimate of, 193
    Waco incident and, 203
Miller, Brian, 233–34, 238
    awarded custody of children, 241
Miller, Enoch (Stacey and Brian's son), 232, 234–37
    death of, 237–38, 250
    Deborah and Stacey sentenced for death of, 265
    Deborah granted second trial for death of, 268–69, 271
    exhumation of body of, 239–40
Miller, Stacey, 233, 234, 236–38
    criminal charges against, 243
    loses custody of children, 241
    at present, 274
    sentencing of, 265
Miller, Timothy, 18–19

Miller, William, 190
Monte, Maxine, 245
Montell, Amanda, 76, 77
Moon, Sun Myung, 28
Moonies, *see* Holy Spirit Association for the Unification of World Christianity
Moore, R. Laurence, 106–7, 136
Moral Majority (organization), 54
Mormonism (Church of Jesus Christ of Latter-day Saints), 135–36
Morrissey, Kari, 267
Mother Ann (Ann Lee), *see* Lee, Ann
Mount Carmel (Texas), 191–93, 203
Mount St. Helens (Washington), 42
Munk, Mike
    cult investigated by, 233, 234, 239–44
    at Deborah's sentencing, 263
    Sarah interviewed by, 246–47
Mussy, Arnaud, 206

National Rifle Association (NRA), 189
Native Americans, 19–20, 120
    cult's boarding school for, 241
Nettles, Bonnie, 67
New Apostolic Reformation, 272
New Hope Christian Fellowship, 111, 113, 215
New Light Stir (1770s), 104
Nunez, Anthony, 231, 232
Nuremberg war crime trials, 143

Obama, Barack, 226, 227, 230
Omondi (pseudonym), 145, 147, 149–52
Oneida Commune, 137
Order of the Solar Temple cult (France), 204
Orwell, George, 83

Padilla, Julie, *see* Gudino, Julie Padilla
Padilla, Virginia, 126
Paine, Thomas, 18
Palin, Sarah, 225

Palmer, Phoebe, 136–37
The Passion of the Christ (film), 226
Pentecostalism, 36–37, 46
Peoples Temple of the Disciples of Christ, 28
Phalen, Ja'el, 196–202, 206, 232, 241
Prophet, Elizabeth Clare, 67–68
Protestantism
    fundamentalism in, 45–46, 53
    see also evangelical Protestantism
Puritans, 103
The Purpose Driven Life (book, Warren), 226

racism, 251
Rajneesh, Bhagwan Shree, 124–26, 128
Rajneeshpuram (commune), 125–27, 128
Reagan, Ronald, 54
Rebekah, *see* Aluzas, Iantha
"recovered memories" of abuse, 68–69
Republican Party, 54
River, Victoria, 209
Robertson, Pat, 225
Ruby Ridge (Idaho), 192, 202–3
Runnels, Mike, 202–3
Ruth (ACMTC member), 237
Ruth (pseudonym; Trinity's birth mother)
    at present, 276
    Trinity given to Sarah by, 145–48, 149–54, 157
Ryan, Patrick L., 173

Sabbath (person), 237
Salvation Army, 39, 40
Salzman, Nancy, 68
same-sex marriage, 226–28
Sanchez, James Lawrence
    Deborah sentenced by, 263–65
    grants Deborah second trial, 268–71
    as judge for Deborah's trial, 250, 254, 257, 267
Sandy Hook Elementary School mass shooting, 193
Satanic Panic, 69

Schmierer, Lilly (Lillian Ruth; Maura and Steve's daughter), 48–49
    leaves cult, 214
    Maura gains custody of, 113
    at present, 273
Schmierer, Maura Aluzas, 7–11
    at Bear Tribe, 17–18, 20–23
    Carlo's death and, 15
    childhood religious background of, 43–44
    converts to Christianity, 44–45
    daily life of, 82–83
    Deborah and Jim's website attacking, 218–19
    on Deborah being granted second trial, 270
    at Deborah's trial, 248–49
    expelled from cult, 97, 98
    after expulsion, 108–15
    as former cult member, 174
    gives birth to Steven, 60
    Greens and, 47–52, 58
    ostracized by Greens, 87–91, 94–97
    at present, 274
    in Sacramento, 55–56, 64–66
    sale of Fence Lake compound to benefit, 273
    Sarah Chelew and, 56–57
    Sarah Green and, 260–61
    in Sheriff's Office investigation, 242
    Steve divorces, 91–92
    sues cult, 115–17, 199
    after winning suit against cult, 119–20, 214–15
Schmierer, Nathaniel (Maura and Steve's son), 44, 49
    in cult schoolhouse, 80
    at Deborah's trial, 248–49, 261
    leaves cult, 214
    after Maura's expulsion, 113–14
    in old schoolhouse, 61–63
    at present, 273
Schmierer, Steve (Maura's husband), 44–45

Schmierer, Steve (Maura's husband) (*cont.*)
    on allegations of child abuse, 201, 202
    becomes Philip, 71
    after divorce from Maura, 113
    divorces Maura, 91–92
    in Fence Lake, 141
    furniture made and sold by, 158
    gets custody of Maura's children, 97
    Greens and, 47–52
    after loss of Maura's suit, 119
    Maura and, 83
    Maura's ostracization and, 87–90, 94–95
    Rick Chelew and, 56–57
    in Sacramento, 55, 64–66
    threatened by Jim Green, 210
Schmierer, Steven (Maura and Steve's son), 97–98
    abused by Steve (father), 65–66
    birth of, 60
    Maura gains custody of, 113
    at present, 274
    serious psychological distress of, 214
Scientology, Church of, 38, 205
Scopes "Monkey" Trial (1925), 45, 137
Seattle (Washington), Sarah in, 176–83
Second Great Awakening (1800s), 135–37
sects, 103–5, 205
September 11 terrorist attacks, 183, 227–28
Seventh-day Adventists, 190
sexuality
    in Branch Davidians, 191
    Lila's, at Medicine Rock, 20
    Lila's and Ann Lee's attitudes toward, 121
    Sarah's, after leaving cult, 177
    Shakers' abstinence from, 102, 105
Shakers, 101–3, 105–7
    Deborah's interest in, 140–41
    Lee on future of, 134
    Lila's interest in, 121–22

Shaker Square (restaurant), 121, 122
Shakespeare, William, 114
Sheela, Ma Anand, 125
Shim Ra Na Holy Tribal Nation (Aggressive Christianity Missions Training Corps), 141
Shoushtari, Mandana, 253–56, 260, 268
Singer, Margaret Thaler, 73, 174
Smith, Joseph, 135
Southern Poverty Law Center (SPLC), 193
spiritual adultery, 95–96
Stein, Alexandra, 74, 77, 120
Stewart, Abi
    meets Sarah, 169–71
    in New York, 220
    on Sarah, at present, 276
    in Seattle, 216, 218
Storr, Anthony, 124
Sun Bear, 16–20, 22, 40
Supreme Court (US)
    on abortion rights, 46
    on same-sex marriage, 226–28
    Trump on, 229

terrorist cells, 74
Theodosius I (Roman emperor), 27
Third Great Awakening, 137
Tobias, Madeleine Landau, 174
Tolstoy, Leo, 135–36
Trinity (pseudonym; Sarah's adopted daughter), 151–54, 156
    adoption of, 157–58, 247
    broken leg of, 210–12
    charges against Sarah for kidnapping of, 243
    Deborah's alleged abuse of, 207–9
    Deborah's second trial canceled because of, 271
    at Deborah's sentencing, 263–64
    Deborah's trial on alleged abuse of, 250–61, 267–69

at Fence Lake, 158–61
interviewed in Sheriff's Office investigation, 240
Ja'el on alleged abuse of, 198–200
at present, 276, 277
removed from Deborah and Jim, 212–13
Sarah and, after Deborah's trial, 261–63
after Sarah leaves cult, 181, 195
when Sarah returns to Fence Lake, 184–87
Trump, Donald J., 228–30, 247, 272–73
Turner, Frederick Jackson, 128

Uganda, 149–55
United States
cults protected by Constitution in, 206
on French law on cults, 205
history of religious groups in, 102–4, 106–7
increased immigration into, 24

Universal Declaration on Human Rights, 205

Valdez, Johnny, 202, 232, 240
Vigil, Brandon, 250–51, 254, 265, 268

Waco (Texas), 189–94, 202–3, 273
Wally (pseudonym), 138–39
Warren, Rick, 156, 226
Weaver, Randy, 191–92
White, Darren, 200
Whitefield, George, 103–4
Wilkinson, Jemima, 104
Williams, Rick, 20
Winthrop, John, 103
women
in Branch Davidians, 191
in leadership of cults, 67–68
as religious leaders, during Second Great Awakening, 136–37
World Trade Organization (WTO; 1999), 170

Xavier, 220, 247–48, 266

ABOUT THE AUTHOR

Harrison Hill grew up in Charlottesville, Virginia, and lives in Brooklyn, New York. He received his MFA in nonfiction from Columbia University, where he also taught undergraduate writing. His journalism and essays have appeared in *The Cut, GQ, Vogue, Travel + Leisure, AFAR, The Threepenny Review, The Guardian,* and other outlets. *The Oracle's Daughter* is his first book.